ADVENTURES OF A LIGHTKEEPER

ADVENTURES OF A LIGHTKEEPER

BARRY PORTER

FLANKER PRESS LIMITED
ST. JOHN'S

Library and Archives Canada Cataloguing in Publication

Title: Adventures of a lightkeeper / Barry Porter.
Names: Porter, Barry (Barry M.), author.
Identifiers: Canadiana (print) 20220193622 | Canadiana (ebook) 20220193649 | ISBN 9781774570869 (softcover) | ISBN 9781774570876 (EPUB) | ISBN 9781774570883 (PDF) | ISBN 9781774570869
Subjects: LCSH: Porter, Barry (Barry M.) | LCSH: Lighthouse keepers—Newfoundland and Labrador—Biography. | LCSH: Lighthouses—Newfoundland and Labrador. | LCSH: Newfoundland and Labrador—Biography. | LCGFT: Autobiographies.
Classification: LCC VK1140.P67 A3 2022 | DDC 387.1/55092 — dc23

PRINTED IN CANADA

FSC www.fsc.org MIX Paper from responsible sources FSC® C016245

This paper has been certified to meet the environmental and social standards of the Forest Stewardship Council® (FSC®) and comes from responsibly managed forests, and verified recycled sources.

Cover Design by Graham Blair

FLANKER PRESS LTD.
1243 KENMOUNT ROAD, UNIT 1
PARADISE, NL
CANADA

TELEPHONE: (709) 739-4477 FAX: (709) 739-4420 TOLL-FREE: 1-866-739-4420
WWW.FLANKERPRESS.COM

9 8 7 6 5 4 3 2

Canada | Canada Council for the Arts | Conseil des Arts du Canada | Newfoundland Labrador

We acknowledge the [financial] support of the Government of Canada. *Nous reconnaissons l'appui [financier] du gouvernement du Canada*. We acknowledge the support of the Canada Council for the Arts, which last year invested $153 million to bring the arts to Canadians throughout the country. *Nous remercions le Conseil des arts du Canada de son soutien. L'an dernier, le Conseil a investi 153 millions de dollars pour mettre de l'art dans la vie des Canadiennes et des Canadiens de tout le pays*. We acknowledge the financial support of the Government of Newfoundland and Labrador, Department of Tourism, Culture and Recreation for our publishing activities.

Dedicated to my wife, Alice, and Dylan and Sarah,
plus all the "keepers of the lights" around
Newfoundland and Labrador

"I didn't have time to write a short letter, so I wrote a long one instead." — Mark Twain

Contents

Introduction

This book has been kicking around in the back of my brain for over ten years, so with extra "COVID time" on my hands, I decided to put my lighthouse stories to paper and into this book. Lightkeeper, or lighthouse keeper, is a unique career and lifestyle that few people get to experience and most people know very little about. I hope my stories will enlighten the reader about this little-known way of life that existed around the rugged coast of Newfoundland Labrador.

This book covers the twenty-three years I was in the Canadian Coast Guard "lightkeeper department." These tales are my stories and events told to the best of my ability using my personal photo collection and notes from my diary. The dates, events, and names mentioned are accurate to the best of my knowledge. I apologize if I missed a name or mentioned some minor detail incorrectly.

Throughout this book I use CCG to refer to the Canadian Coast Guard, and instead of always writing the word lightkeeper, lighthouse keeper, or keeper of the light, I sometimes just use "keeper." I use Surgeon's Cove Head instead of Surgeon's Cove Point, because locally that is the name used. Sometimes I also use just the Head or the Light. I use miles and feet, instead of kilometres and metres, because that was the measurement we used at work. I also call the large paper freighters out of the port of Botwood "paper boats," which is what they were locally named.

So, sit back and join me on my recollection of my many adventures as a lightkeeper. I hope my book brings you some enjoyment.

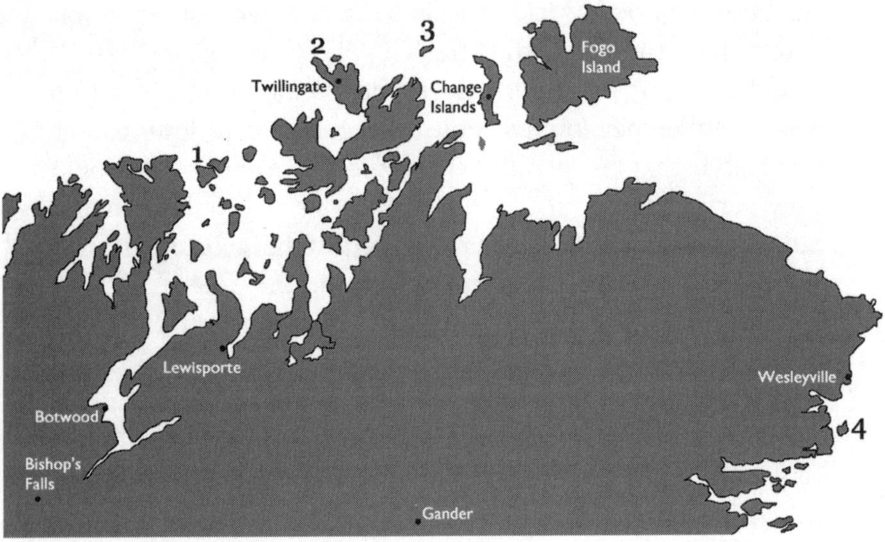

Lighthouse Locations, Notre Dame Bay

(1) Surgeon's Cove Head Lighthouse on Exploits Island
(2) Long Point Lighthouse on Twillingate Island
(3) Bacalhao Island Lighthouse off Herring Neck and Change Islands
(4) Puffin Island Lighthouse off Greenspond

ADVENTURES OF A LIGHTKEEPER

1 Bacalhao Island and the Beginning

It was almost midnight, and I was sitting on the frozen, jagged rocks at the base of the light tower on Bacalhao Island, over 325 feet above sea level. I was spying out through the cold darkness of a November night with a 100-year-old brass telescope in my grasp. I had braced it on my knees to steady it from my shivering body and the freezing wind. There was not a star nor a moon to be seen—it was as black as your boot. The wind was raw and blowing out of the north, cutting right through my bones. I was determined to have a detailed look out into the abyss since I had made the extra effort to get up there. We had gotten word on the VHF radio a few hours earlier that there was a lone speedboat overdue. An elderly man from Fogo Island had been out hunting turrs by himself and had not returned. Not a good situation to be in.

Bacalhao Lighthouse is located on a small island approximately three miles northeast of Herring Neck and four miles west of Change Islands in Notre Dame Bay. I had been working as an official lightkeeper on this secluded island for a couple of years by now and had spent day after day observing the local small speedboats and the large ships cruising past this light station. Over time, I had gotten keen at identifying who was out on these rough Atlantic waters around this island. I knew the colours of the speedboats, their shapes, and even the silhouettes when cruising back home in the failing light of the evening. In some cases, I could recognize the fishermen's stance in the boat, how they wore their cap, the shape and flair of the vessel's bow, and the favoured routes certain local boat operators used. On that particular day, all the local boats from Herring Neck, Pikes Arm, and the Too Good Arm area had returned home safe and sound. But this overdue boat was from a little farther to the east of our lighthouse.

After supper I had walked out on our helicopter pad a couple of times for a look out through the bleak darkness but did not see anything. Our view to the east was somewhat limited from where the lightkeeper's dwelling and engine room were located. The best vantage point was way up on the mountaintop, where the old cast-iron light tower and main light were located. This was the highest land on Bacalhao Island. To get up there would mean a challenging twenty-five-minute hike in the dark up over the snow- and ice-covered hill.

For the next couple of hours, my co-worker and I monitored the Canadian Coast Guard radio and our own CB radio for updates on the missing hunter. From time to time there would be some chatter about this missing boat on the airwaves from the local Twillingate and Change Island CB radio operators. Several people had their opinions on what happened and even where the hunter might be located, considering the tides and the winds. The radio operator at Comfort Cove Coast Guard Radio had informed us a little earlier that a Canadian Coast Guard ship was tasked to the case and was heading to the area to conduct a search for the lost hunter. I must say, that was comforting news to us.

As time passed, I kept thinking how miserable it would be to spend a long, dreary night out in an open boat like this poor bird hunter. I knew I would not want to be broken down out in the middle of the wild, cold Atlantic Ocean in an open speedboat on any night. I discussed it with the other lightkeeper, and after some thought, I decided I would make the trek to the top of Bacalhao Island for a proper spy out over the vast, lonely ocean. My co-worker mumbled and said it was probably a total waste of time. Maybe it was, but deep down I felt I should at least take one more look. I slowly got dressed for the cold I knew I was about to face once I stepped outside the dwelling. I grabbed the flashlight, a set of binoculars, and the trusty old telescope, which was issued to the station way back in 1894, and headed out the door.

The narrow trail was slippery and rough going, with icy patches mixed with four to five inches of snow in places. I took my time—I did not want to break into a sweat and then freeze, or even worse, slip and injure myself while climbing up this greasy hill in the dark. It was pitch black except for the bright beam of light that flashed from the tower every nine and a half seconds—shooting out a bright ray of light, miles and miles into the darkness, like a laser beam. Eventually, I reached the summit and took a couple of minutes to catch my breath. I was pleased the visibility was still good—I could see for miles from up here. I did a quick scan across the horizon, straining my bare eyes to see a light, a flare, a reflection, or maybe even a glow from a burning rag dipped in gasoline. But nothing! I looked over at the glowing lights of the town of old Twillingate, then a little farther along shore, northward to the comforting beam of light shining out from Long Point Lighthouse, my old workplace. I could see all the way out to the east. Behind me, the lights of Change Islands were twinkling in the frosty air, but I could not see Fogo Island. Fogo was roughly eleven miles away, and there was a fog bank or snow flurries occurring over in that area.

I sat down on the most comfortable rock I could find. I pressed my back against the cold, cast-iron light tower and let my eyes adjust to the lack of light and the bleakness. For the next sixty minutes, I spied through the darkness using the old telescope and the binoculars, slowly scanning across the vast ocean inch by inch, looking, searching for anything. Finally, after many unsuccessful sweeps and with the wind biting into my unprotected face, I surrendered. I carefully made the slow journey back down the hill to the comfort of the warm house, located far below me, near the freezing ocean's edge. Once I got inside the house and warmed up with a hot cup of tea, I signed off in the lightkeeper's logbook. My long shift was now complete. I crawled into my cozy bunkbed with a contented feeling that I had at least tried. Slowly I drifted off to sleep, all the time thinking about the poor hunter out there floating around in his speedboat, somewhere. Early next morning, just as I got up, my co-worker informed me he had received word that one of our Coast Guard ships had successfully located the missing bird hunter—cold, wet, but thankfully alive!

Bacalhao Lighthouse aerial winter pic

Let me rewind back a few years and tell you how I ended up working in this unique career as a lightkeeper for the Canadian Coast Guard. On a stormy February 15 back in 1982, the mighty *Ocean Ranger* sank off the Grand Banks of Newfoundland, and that was the day I gave up my desire to work offshore. Just a few months earlier, I was sitting in a huge office on the top floor of Atlantic Place, being questioned by a gentleman with a Texan accent and wearing a genuine stetson hat and cowboy boots. I had driven into St. John's and was being interviewed for the position of welder on a prized drilling rig, the *Ocean Ranger*. It was owned by Ocean Drilling and Exploration Company Inc. (ODECO) of New Orleans, USA. The office overlooked the well-sheltered harbour of St. John's—the view was beautiful. On the wall was a huge mural of the mighty drilling rig. The photo extended from the floor all the way to the ceiling and was approximately fourteen feet wide. It was very impressive.

There were several dozen men there that day hanging about the hallways for interviews on a wide range of positions on this drilling rig. The men had come from all parts of the island hoping for that prized berth. I had over five years welding experience under my belt, having worked in the mines at Labrador City for the Iron Ore Company of Canada (IOC) and for the International Nickel Company of Canada (INCO) in Thompson, Manitoba, and for Sherritt Gordon Mines in Leaf Rapids, Manitoba. I also worked at other welding positions connected with the oil industry in the Wetaskiwin/Camrose area in Alberta. Also, I had worked the last year at Freake's Welding, a local welding shop on Stanhope Road near Lewisporte.

The Texan cowboy asked me several thought-provoking questions during my interview, about isolation, working offshore, and being away from family. The interview was a success, and shortly after that, a small handful of us interviewees had to proceed to the Health Sciences Centre for a thorough medical examination. I passed that as well. Then I was instructed to go home and wait for a phone call from their office. After a month or two of patiently waiting at home in Porterville, I phoned ODECO's office in St. John's inquiring about the job. I was told that day I was on the list to be hired. There were two welders assigned to the rig, and the next time one welder quit, the job would be mine.

But it was not to be. After hearing the terribly tragic news that February morning, I decided I was finished with my welding career once and for all. Since that terrible sinking, I have never worked as a welder.

The time had come for me to change careers. It was time to head in a different direction—major decisions to be made again on my journey through life. The question was thrown at me once again: What am I going to be when I grow up? Maybe I could go back to school, take another trade, or maybe I could go farming with my dear father in Porterville. My little hometown was blessed with acres of rich, level topsoil when the glaciers receded thousands of years ago. This eventually resulted in the small village of Porterville becoming an important farming community for the area. Most of my distant ancestors, and several of my current living relatives, were hard-working farmers. The Porter farmers had been growing crops and supplying the nearby communities of Lewisporte, Twillingate, Fogo, and Change Islands with some of the best locally grown vegetables for about a hundred years.

Being a farmer was a hard physical career working from daylight to dark. I had watched my father, Max, farm all his life, and he had harvested his final crop last fall, a few months short of his ninetieth birthday. Not only was it hard work, but the only paydays were in one short season. You would only receive payment in the fall of the year after all the crops were harvested. I could not see myself working and living that lifestyle. I had spent too many blistering hot summers as a kid dragging my bony knees through endless drills of turnips and potatoes, weeding, thinning, or making hay in the fields. I just did not have a strong enough desire to become a full-fledged farmer for the next thirty or forty years. So, I went to Plan C.

My buddy Ed Loveless, who I had been with in Alberta a couple of years earlier, had just begun working with the Canadian Coast Guard as a relief lighthouse keeper. After some thought, I decided to make a 180-degree turn in my career and check into that line of work. A month or so later, I heard the Canadian Coast Guard was updating its relief lighthouse keepers list for the manned lighthouses on the northeast coast of Newfoundland.

I drove into Gander to visit the manpower/unemployment office to inquire into this possible new career. As it happened, the career counsellor there informed me that personnel from the Canadian Coast Guard were conducting interviews in Lewisporte that very day. I thought I had blown my opportunity because I had not even submitted an application. The lady at Manpower was extremely helpful. She phoned the Brittany Inns in Lewisporte and spoke to Mr. Randy Dawe from the Canadian Coast Guard and informed him I was looking for a job. Luckily, Mr. Dawe told her to send me out for an interview. I quickly filled out a general application page and drove back to Lewisporte.

Nervous, I arrived at the hotel late that afternoon. By now all the interviews had been wrapped up, and I entered one of their hotel rooms and was given a thorough interview there. Mr. Dawe, Mrs. Noftall, and Mr. May fired questions at me non-stop for almost twenty minutes. It was unnerving, but when it was over, they were incredibly positive, and I made it onto their revised lightkeeper relief list. The two men who had previous lightkeeper work experience scored ahead of me on the list, but at least this was a start—a start to a new career for me as a "keeper of the light" with the Canadian Coast Guard.

Taken from the lightkeeper's manual printed by the Ministry of Transport Canada in 1970:

> A lightkeeper is responsible for maintaining a high standard of performance in all light station activities; maintain a watch for fog or other weather phenomena that produce reduced visibility below approximately 2 miles; operate and carry out routine service on navigational light or lights; operate and perform routine running maintenance on fog signal equipment; operate and perform routine running maintenance

> on main generating equipment; upkeep of buildings and grounds; maintain light station logbooks of operation, work performed, plant and equipment.

Expanding on the description of a lightkeeper's job: a lightkeeper had to work on some of the most remote, isolated, and beautiful islands surrounded by the mighty, cold Atlantic Ocean, on windswept points of land perched up on a cliff. There were no neighbours to talk to, no grocery stores next door, or building supply shops down the road. You were stuck on a rock for four and a half weeks or more, away from your loved ones, for better or for worse.

A lightkeeper had to be a handyman, a jack of all trades. We were responsible for the maintenance of the station, including the dwelling, the light tower, the outbuildings (sheds), helicopter drop pads, the many outdoor stairs and steps, handrails and fences. Also the boat and outboard motor, boathouse, spar and boom, and winch. If something required repairs or general upkeep, the lightkeeper would have to perform it. If there was a more serious issue, we would have to contact our supervisors at the Marine Aids Office at the Canadian Coast Guard base on the southside of St. John's harbour. That important office was our main contact for all work-related issues, whether a helicopter request for shift changeover, diesel motor problems, holiday request, supplies, or personal issues. We dealt mainly with Randy Dawe and Debbie Stead. In later years, Gerry Cantwell and Paul Bowering were in the office. They were all good people, and they must have had their hands full dealing with all the lightkeepers and their issues.

Lightkeepers were required to be half-decent carpenters. We had to maintain and repair the dwelling and outbuildings. Occasionally we would have to replace a broken window, a blown-off door, or a handrail on the fence or walkways. Sometimes we would replace a section of rotten or damaged clapboard. It was a never-ending process.

Another thing we did was apply lots of paint. The lighthouses were continually battered by harsh winds and salt spray from the wild Atlantic waters. Everything wooden or metal had to be scraped, chipped, primed, and painted regularly or it would not take long before it looked rundown. We had paint-splattered ladders and dozens of partly worn-out paintbrushes in stock all the time, not to mention the cases of gallons of paint on hand in the stockroom. Matchless oil was the paint of choice, in white, red, and grey colours. These were the main colours used by the Coast Guard, and we did not spare them.

Our mechanical skills were required from time to time. We would perform oil changes on the well-run Lister diesels or repair or adjust the air-cooling systems attached to them. Occasionally we would perform minor maintenance on the outboard motor, chainsaw, or the winch.

We were bookkeepers—we kept a daily log in our lightkeeper logbooks of weather and fog conditions and all duties carried out at the station. Also, we kept an inventory of all supplies required to operate the station, from toilet paper to oil paint to diesel fuel. And there were our own personal groceries inventory. We also kept records of every species of whale we sighted from the lighthouse. These reports were sent into Dr. Jon Lien, the head of the Whale Research Group with Memorial University in St. John's.

Radio operation was another part of our job. Daily weather and ice reports were radioed via VHF radio to Comfort Cove Coast Guard Radio station, which was located on the crest of Loon Bay Hill. It was also our responsibility to report all icebergs visible from our lighthouse, especially any icebergs or growlers located near the main shipping routes. We contacted the Canadian Coast Guard helicopters and ships through the VHF radio when required. All our Coast Guard communications were carried out on channel 19 of the VHF radio or through the mobile telephone. There were four manned lighthouses in this area within radio range with whom we communicated almost daily—Gull Island (Cape St. John, White Bay), Surgeon's Cove Head (Exploits Island), Long Point (Twillingate), and Bacalhao Island. Also, there were the never-ending daily communications to fisher persons, hunters, and recreational boaters with local weather, sea, and ice conditions, plus calls from the many radio buffs on VHF and CB radios in the bay.

Electronic technician was another, unofficial, box we had to tick to be a lightkeeper. A lightkeeper would have to replace the odd fuse, cable, or microphone on the VHF radio or sometimes relocate the external antenna. Lightkeepers used their personal radio equipment to communicate to loved ones back home. This required a radio system at home and an identical system at the lighthouse. During my years working at the lighthouses, I and most other lightkeepers I know spent thousands of dollars on radio systems. If I wanted to talk to my sweet wife, Alice, I had to have a good working radio. Back then, we did not have cellphones or computers with the option to connect by Facetime or Zoom calls. Over the years, my own communication inventory included two regular CB radios, two CB radios with sideband (which had extra power and range), two power converters, two VHF radios that required two more power converters, one portable VHF radio, hundreds of feet of radio coaxial cable, dozens of cable fittings and joiners, C-clamps, and five or six different antennas ranging in sizes for CB and VHF. The high winds and salt spray were brutal on any antenna and cables out on those windswept islands. In addition to this, I had various lengths of pipe, made up for radio towers, to which I could attach the antennas. This also required hundreds of feet of cable used as guy wires to keep the towers and antennas secure during high winds.

Lightkeepers had to be counsellors, shrinks, and mentors. This was not in the job description, but it certainly was part of life out there. The shifts on the "island" stations were a long thirty-two days on and a short thirty-two days off. Later, our department office changed it to twenty-eight days on the lighthouse and twenty-eight days off. The shift on "land" lighthouses (accessible by road) was one eight-hour shift every day, fifty-two weeks of the year.

The scenery and the landscape around us at our office were breathtaking. We had stunning icebergs and whales practically in our backyards. The peacefulness and connection with Mother Nature were almost spiritual, but it was not always a picnic on these remote islands. Being away from home and stuck on an isolated island with another human for long stretches of time can be trying on your personal life and on your mental well-being. Throw in days or weeks of zero visibility in rain, snow, or fog, with gale-force winds and the noisy foghorn blasting non-stop. You look out the window hoping to see the ocean, maybe a passing boat, but day after day after day, everything is a white cloud. This would get under the skin of the strongest-willed lightkeeper. We missed family and friends' weddings, funerals, birthdays, Christmases, and other special events. The worst I found was when I became a father and my dear children came into my life—missing their special birthdays, first Halloween, first day of school, and the list goes on. I found that quite difficult, compounded by the loneliness and isolation on the islands, but I had to suck it up. It was the way of life as a lightkeeper on the northeast coast of Newfoundland.

Working at a remote lighthouse was no place to be during any serious health issue or personal problem in one's family. The issue can play on your mind and eat away your soul. That radio call or mobile telephone call from your loved one or from a friend meant so much during difficult times. I struggled with it occasionally but learned how to cope with it the best I could. Many lightkeepers could not handle the difficult periods. I saw lightkeepers get upset because they could not make radio contact with their loved one back home at their set time schedule. I also saw rookie lightkeepers have difficult times adjusting to the sometimes gloomy life on the islands. The most difficult season was during the long periods of darkness in late fall and winter. A couple of times I had to take a fellow lightkeeper out for a calming walk in the cold, salty air just to talk things over. I would pick out some sheltered hilltop with a scenic view and just chat about life. Breathe, relax, and stay positive. It was all part of the job. You and your co-worker had to be healthy, and you had to get along with each other. This other person was your partner for an entire shift. If you did not get along, you were going to have a miserable time on the island. My general belief was life is too short for that kind of extra stress or pressure. I know of incidents when the CCG had to fly counsellors out to a lighthouse to resolve serious issues between the two lightkeepers on an island. I also heard of cases from years back when the two lightkeepers would not speak to each other during an entire shift—they would pass work instructions under each other's bedroom doors.

During the winter months, with unfavourable weather and reduced marine traffic, there was less work to be carried out on the station—just long stretches of time to kill. Boredom can turn into anxiety and stress. Over the years, I tried to keep busy during these slow periods by trying my hand at various hobbies. I bought a Dremel tool for carving wood, moose antler, soapstone, and more. I carved out miniature speedboats, motorboats, whale tails, lighthouses, and Christmas tree ornaments, which I really enjoyed doing. Also, I tried drawing/sketching and oil paintings, self-taught guitar lessons, woodwork, sewing, writing poetry, and reading—lots of reading. I started writing a diary in 1986.

My outdoor activities included farming vegetables, berry picking, major hiking and exploration, cross-country skiing, skating, and photography. While working on Exploits Island over a four-year period, I built a lovely cabin by myself in the harbour. I must say, that was an extremely satisfying make-work project for me. I also did a lot of video work on both islands. On Bacalhao Island, I once videotaped over 3,000 of my photo slides. I set up my camera on its tripod and filmed every individual slide for six to seven seconds. I pressed the slides against the window for proper lighting and recorded them on the macro lens setting. You name it, I tried it. I used to joke around and say the only thing I did not try was knitting.

One thing I learned over time was that every individual is different, and every person has their own beliefs, ideas, habits, and opinions. When you are placed together with a stranger on an isolated island, this can be challenging. In my case, because I was the new kid in the lightkeeper system, often there was an age gap of ten, twenty, or more years between me and the lightkeepers I worked with. I tried to find common interests and appreciate each person, and things usually balanced out just fine.

Lightkeepers were also cooks. On Long Point Lighthouse I cooked for myself, which was not a problem. When working on the islands, it meant you were responsible for cooking every second day. My regular shift was thirty-two days on, which meant I had to plan for at least sixteen cooked suppers or dinners. On Bacalhao Island we always had cooked dinners, but on Surgeon's Cove Head our main meal was supper. We had to buy our own food, tie it up in boxes, and carry our food supply out to the remote lighthouses. We always made a point of having tasty meals while working on the island. I had heard dreadful stories of rookie keepers showing up on the islands with a month's supply of precooked frozen meals because they did not know how to cook! Another guy used to bring out a month's supply of just turkey legs and necks and only cook for himself, totally ignoring his co-worker and the standard tradition of most lighthouses.

Lightkeepers could be called on to be a medic. We were all first-aiders, trained regularly every three or four years. One was always aware that we were working on remote islands, and you did not want to injure yourself. Much of our daily work was quite physical—carrying ladders or boxes of supplies, turning over the speedboat, painting, moving ladders or forty-five-gallon drums of oil or fuel. If you pulled a back muscle, you would have to rest it for a few days. Minor cuts, splinters, or dirt in one's eyes were also common occurrences. You had to address it, or else it could get infected and become a more serious problem.

My most serious medical procedure was on Surgeon's Cove Head when I had a really bad ingrown toenail. It was infected and very painful. I tried soaking it in hot, salted water and alcohol, but no sir, it would not heal. It was during the winter, and I did not want to have to request a helicopter to fly me in to see a doctor, plus get a relief lightkeeper to replace me, at least not yet. After several pain-filled days, one night I finally got up my nerve and decided to fix this infected toe once and for all. I boiled some water, sterilized one of my super-sharp woodcarving knives, then placed an ice cube against the top of my swollen big toe. A couple of ice cubes and several minutes later, the tip of my toe was fairly numb. I carefully cut a small incision in the tip, releasing a splatter of blood and pus. Beads of sweat broke out on my forehead, but surprisingly, it was not that painful. I cleaned it all up and applied lots of hot water and alcohol for the next few days. It healed up fine, no problem. Dr. Porter, at your service!

Lightkeepers were also tour guides. Many people, from the local folks to visitors from the other side of the world, are attracted to and interested in lighthouses. They love the views the lighthouses provide but also the history and the stories about these unique places. We had a handful of visitors on remote Bacalhao Island Lighthouse the four years I worked there. That would only happen in the summer months. On Surgeon's Cove Head, we would get many visitors to the station. In the winter, when the ice conditions allowed, visitors from Lewisporte and Summerford area would travel out over the ice-packed bays by snowmobile. In the summertime, we would get visitors by speedboat or hikers who would take the adventurous walk out from Exploits Harbour to visit the lighthouse. It was always good to see a new face and have a chat with any visitors. We would always offer them a cup of tea or a glass of ice water, depending on the season.

We were also weathermen—a very important skill to have—trained on the job with experience and by the senior lightkeepers. We recorded in our logbooks the local weather and ice conditions at the beginning and at the end of every shift. The more experience you acquired as a lightkeeper, the more accurate you became with reporting weather conditions. We had no weather equipment, so estimating the wind speed, wind direction, and the visibility ranges were important. I would be a human weather detector—I would stand outdoors, letting the raw wind hit my face and my body, and at the same time look out over the sea—observing the wave height, the whitecaps, the tide rips, studying Mother Nature all around me.

When I first went to Long Point Lighthouse, I would occasionally radio one of our CCG ships, the *Sir Humphrey Gilbert* or the *Sir Wilfred Grenfell*. If I observed them a few miles out in the bay, I would ask them exactly how many miles they were from Long Point. This enabled me to get a guide or a scale of what the ship looked like five miles or fifteen miles offshore. I found this very helpful for calculating the distances over the endless miles of wide-open ocean surrounding me, especially when reporting numerous icebergs miles offshore. Lightkeepers also had to record and report the ever-changing ice conditions around the lighthouse—grey ice, white ice, and the amount of coverage; for example, seven-tenths coverage in rough white ice with strings of open water. These daily ice and weather reports could get complicated, but I tried my best to paint a clear picture of the conditions near my lighthouse.

I observed Mother Nature at her very finest and sometimes at her most wicked. Every day, I would walk out on the helicopter pad nearby or onto the rocks, anchor my two feet, and just breathe, taking it all in, standing on the very edge of the cliff, binoculars gripped in hand, with the wild ocean churning below me. Scanning over the turbulent seas, I let the salt air blow over every inch of my skin and my soul. The endless sky, the clouds, the sea conditions, the wind direction and its strength, the visibility, the colours—my senses were on overload. Most days I could see for endless miles, right to the horizon, where the sky would drop into the sea. It was so beautiful and so peaceful but also wild and dangerous. Many days I could see dozens of icebergs soaking by the station, humpback whales feeding just offshore, or gannets diving into the dark blue ocean at sixty mph, like javelins thrown by Olympic athletes.

During this time, I would take a mental note of any marine traffic, maybe a fuel tanker passing by and resting frighteningly low into the ocean. They would be bursting with full loads of jet fuel, steaming toward the port of Lewisporte, or a fishing longliner would shoot out a seine, hunting for the elusive mackerel near a rugged shoreline. Maybe I would see a sailboat tacking hard to catch a breeze, a recreational speedboat out for a cruise, or a diehard turr hunter punching back home after a successful hunt. It could be a couple of kayaks, out pushing their luck in the oversized swells, or a tide rip tearing across miles of ocean like a hook in a wool sweater, the way the wind blew the whitecaps off the waves, or a wild squall of wind and rain passing by five or ten miles offshore. The longer I looked, the more I realized there was more to observe. It was a never-ending performance, every hour, every day. If it floated or if it moved on the ocean, I have observed it from a lighthouse.

A lightkeeper was on watch.

2 Surgeon's Cove Head Lighthouse, 1983

My first shift working as a lightkeeper was in 1983 on Surgeon's Cove Head, located on beautiful Exploits Island. This light station was built on the far western side of the island overlooking the Ships Run, which led into the port of Botwood. It has been guiding ships and speedboats around the Bay of Exploits and Notre Dame Bay since 1911. The original dwelling was attached to the light tower with a wooden passageway. The main light is 242 feet (73.8 metres) above sea level with a range of sixteen nautical miles. Characteristics: flash three white, and fifteen-second eclipse. The light tower is circular, with red and white stripes and a white dome, built out of cast iron. Fog signal: blast three seconds, and silence for twenty-seven seconds.

Historic Exploits Island consists of two islands located approximately twenty miles north of Lewisporte and seventeen miles west of Twillingate. There is an eastern island and a western island called Burnt Island. Nestled in between the two islands is a well-protected harbour connected at the narrowest location by a beautiful arched concrete bridge built in 1945. Previously, there were at least two wooden bridges built at the same location. Exploits Island was a booming fishing community and a hub for sealing, fishing, and trading with Labrador. First settled around the mid-1700s, the 1836 census recorded 200 inhabitants living there. The last known Beothuk, Shanawdithit, lived and worked there as a servant for the Peyton household from 1823 to 1828. Her English name there was Nancy. (John Peyton Sr. is buried along with his son John Jr. in the same gravesite in the Lower Harbour cemetery.) The 1874 census records 623 residents living in Exploits, and the population peaked around the year 1900. Along with the increased population came three large churches, five cemeteries, a couple of blacksmiths, and a government wharf with coastal boat services. There was a post office with a wireless telegraph service. Exploits Island also had two large merchant businesses operating there. It had two shipyards set up in the harbour, one on each side. Several hundred schooners were constructed in the harbour and in the Bay of Exploits. There was even a doctor stationed in Exploits, some say the first in Notre Dame Bay. (There is a Dr. H. K. Aberton buried on the island.) The last school was built there in 1949, perched on the hill near the bridge, overlooking the picturesque harbour. Previously there were two schools, one on each side of the harbour. There were also two centres for community gatherings—the Orange Lodge and the Wigwam.

As the years passed, the island residents started relocating to the larger centres in the bay and up to mainland Canada. With Premier Joseph Smallwood's resettlement program introduced, the once prosperous community faded into history.

On Thursday, September 22, 1983, I loaded up Father's old eighteen-foot wooden speedboat and headed out the bay to Surgeon's Cove Head Lighthouse. Randy Dawe from the Marine Aids Office had phoned a few days earlier informing me of a work shift at this lighthouse. Principal lightkeeper William (Wil) Chipp was retiring on Friday, after working decades on the secluded Cape St. John Gull Island and now on Surgeon's Cove Head. The Cost Guard needed a relief lightkeeper, and I gladly took up the offer.

My solo boat cruise out to Exploits Lighthouse was a little unnerving. I had never travelled that long water route before. The few times I had visited Exploits Island were out from the port of Lewisporte, miles away, and this route was foreign to

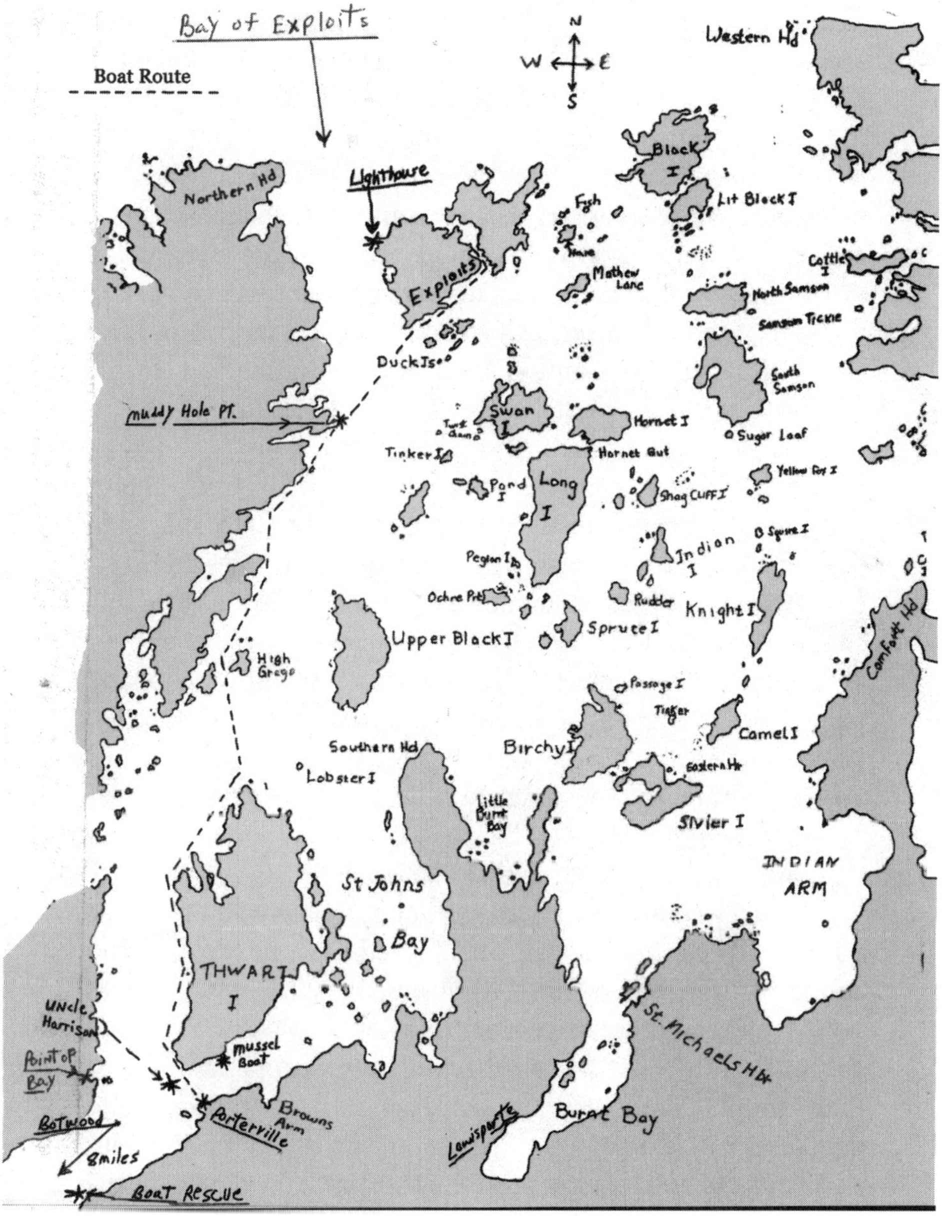

me. I had steamed around Thwart Island a few times but never "out the bay" to the edge of the ocean, which was a good twenty miles away. Back then, living up in the bay, as we were, that was like another planet for us. I motored out with no radio, and it seemed to take forever. I did not own a boat, so I took Father's old twenty-five-horsepower Johnson, which was not running the best. My father was not big on maintenance—as long as the motor on his boat, farm tractor, or other equipment was running, that was good enough! The main throttle or tiller handle did not work properly. I could steer the boat, but I could not adjust the speed of the motor. To do that I had to reach back to the rear of the motor and adjust another short lever. Not ideal when carrying out a shift change in the gurgling seas in the gulch under the steep cliffs of Surgeon's Cove Head.

The notorious "gulch" was well-known around the Bay of Exploits, but very few boaters had ever entered its inner chambers. The gulch was a small notch carved about 100 feet deep in the sheer cliffs below the lighthouse. This is where we completed our shift changeover by hoisting up our essential monthly supplies. You had to carefully inch your way in there in your speedboat and hook the cable onto your net full of supplies and reverse out of there as soon as the load was winched up a few feet clear of the boat. Sounds easy, but it certainly was not.

The unique gulch was surrounded on three sides by sheer cliff face, so much so that it hardly received any sunlight. There was only enough space for one boat to go straight in and reverse straight out. Directly above, approximately 200 feet, was a large red spar and boom, constructed from heavy pipe and connected by cable to a diesel-powered winch. The set-up was bolted into a large concrete block and kept in place with several galvanized guy wires. It was a three-lightkeeper operation—one man running the winch and cable up and down, the second lightkeeper would be two-thirds of the way down the cliff with a view of the gulch below, and the third man in the boat. The second man would pull on the long rope attached to the boom and swing the heavy boom out from the cliff so it was dangling over the churning waters below. Then he would signal or radio instructions to winch down or up. If the sea conditions permitted, the man in the boat would gently manoeuvre into the gulch far enough for the large hook or net to be removed from the middle of his boat. He almost had to put the bow of the boat on the jagged rocks to get room to snatch the netted load.

The lightkeeper in the boat would have his boxes of supplies in a squid net with an eye hook, all ready to snap on, then motion to the man on the cliff to raise up. That guy would relay the message to the lightkeeper operating the powerful winch. When the net was just above the boat, the boat operator would back out and sometimes wait for a second load, depending on how much cargo was being brought to or from the lighthouse.

It was a tricky and dangerous operation. If there was the slightest amount of sea, the gulch was like a flush box. Years later, one of my supervisors in St. John's told me the Coast Guard broke every safety rule in the book carrying out this shift changeover. Most of the time we could not enter the gulch, which meant we had to throw our boxes ashore to a lightkeeper clinging to the side of the cliff like Spiderman. We would transfer the boxes, then two keepers would carefully jump out of the boat, and the two keepers departing jumped into the moving boat. That was also extremely dangerous, because the rocks were always wet, slippery, and sometimes covered in ice or snow. To add to this, we were always wearing heavy, bulky survivor suits, and the speedboat was always in motion—bobbing in and out, up and down with the relentless waves, wind, and sea. Not a place to screw up. I know of one of my co-workers who misjudged his jump and ended up in the frigid Atlantic Ocean. He went under, but luckily, his partner grabbed him when he popped back up. A close call indeed.

If conditions were too rough to throw our boxes ashore, it meant we had to take all our monthly supplies into the harbour and store them in Richard Wells's stage. Then, slowly, we had to carry our knapsacks and our boxes by hand on the hour-long hike approximately three miles across the island to the lighthouse. This usually meant a couple of long trips a day, and it could take the next two or three days to transport all of it. Thankfully, I only had to do this on two or three changeovers. There was nothing easy about the life of a lightkeeper.

Surgeon's Cove Head Lighthouse and paper boat

Eventually, I navigated my way out to the distant island and the lighthouse, where Calvin Moores met me down near the ocean's edge. When he discovered my tiller was not working properly, he cancelled the idea of me going into the dangerous gulch and winching all my supplies up from the water's edge. Luckily, the sea conditions were calm, so I threw my boxes out of the boat to Calvin perched on the side of the cliff. He carefully packed them on the rugged rocks up away from the sea's swells. I then took my speedboat around the island and into the harbour, where I moored it off. Then I made the long walk out across the island to my work site, the lighthouse.

I had arrived a day early because I did not want to be late for my first shift as a lightkeeper with the Canadian Coast Guard. Luckily, I got a chance to meet and spend the night with veteran lightkeeper Wil Chipp. That night I listened to

Wil's old lightkeeper stories till the late hours. It was an exciting day, but I was glad to be there at the station and beginning my career as keeper of the light.

My shift was twenty-seven days instead of the normal thirty-two. After working over three decades, Wil wanted to work right up to his very last scheduled day, refusing to use up his holidays or sick days for those last four or five days. Wil Chipp made the long trip from his home in Tilt Cove to work those last few shifts here. A true dedicated lightkeeper.

Wil Chipp and Calvin Moores

Some of the lightkeepers from the past who worked here were Richard Lacey and his son Archibald (1912), Ambrose Manuel and his son Reginald (1938), Clyde Purchase, Anthony Winsor (1947), Gus Jefferies, Hollett Hutchings, Lawrence Rumbo, Edmen Budwall, William Chipp, and Calvin Moores. The regular relief lightkeepers were Ed Loveless, Eric Dove, and Gord Jones. Others who filled in were Dave Fudge, John Mudford, and Hardy Burry. The principal keeper was Lloyd Lilly, and Arch Budgell was the assistant principal keeper. A few years later, Carl Greening joined the staff there after doing a lateral transfer with Jack May. Years later, Darryl Marsden filled in for me while I was on leave.

I worked my very first shift as a lightkeeper with Calvin Moores. He carefully showed me the daily routine involved with the running of this lighthouse—the important checks on the diesel motors, batteries, the daily weather reports to Comfort Cove Coast Guard Radio, the operation of the large spar/boom and diesel winch, plus all the regular maintenance. Calvin was an excellent instructor and a wonderful man. He loved food, and he loved his gut. I had brought a box full of fresh home-grown veggies, right out of my father's fertile gardens—don't say Calvin didn't love my Porterville turnips! He said they were the sweetest turnips he had ever tasted, and he always raved about them, even years later during our VHF radio chats.

This light station was a large site. The present double dwelling was built in 1960 for two lightkeepers and their families. It was joined together by a doorway and sat on a full eight-foot above-ground concrete basement. There were two kitchens, two bathrooms, two living rooms, and several bedrooms on each side. There was plenty of room for us lightkeepers. We had our separate bedrooms and a couple of bedrooms for visiting techs. We had a storeroom that was fully stocked with everything from paint to screws, hose clamps, light bulbs, and cases of cleaning spray and powder. You name it, we pretty much had two of it at this station. It was like a miniature Home Hardware store.

We mainly used the west end of the dwelling closest to the light tower. The basements had a couple of large deep-fridges, a furnace, and our large water cistern holding tank located between the two basement areas. The basement on the opposite side was our workshop. We had a workbench, some wood and lumber pieces, and a variety of tools. Outdoors was the old cast-iron light tower with the main light sitting at the top. It was a beautiful large light made of heavy brass and thick glass lenses. Located to the right of the tower was the engine room building, which contained the three hard-working Lister diesels and generators. Next to this building was a small but heavily built drop pad for helicopter use. To the left of the light tower was another small building that stored the videograph and foghorn system and an old diesel motor called the HA unit. This old motor was left from decades ago and could still be used for a fourth backup generator. If the Lister motors went down—and believe it or not, there were times when all three failed—this old HA unit had to be started up to keep the main light shining. This was a tricky motor to start up. It had to be decompressed and cranked over by hand, and several levers were shifted and thrown for this unit to take over the required power load. To run the diesel generators non-stop, there were three large fibreglass fuel tanks containing 2,000 gallons of fuel in each. They required refuelling twice a year.

Just behind the dwelling and up the grade a little was our large helicopter pad. We usually stored a couple dozen drums of helicopter fuel on the edge of this pad. Farther down the hill was the large spar and boom and diesel winch. Here we stored dozens of drums of diesel fuel for the Lister motors and generators. (Some years later, the CCG ship *Sir Wilfred Grenfell* would pump our fuel up into our large holding tanks, eliminating the use of all the forty-five-gallon drums.) Our eighteen-foot government speedboat was on another large wooden deck. Next to the winch was a small red wooden shed, which contained a spare outboard motor with gasoline and oil, ropes, nails, and bolts. The spar and boom were mounted on the very edge of the cliff that dropped off, straight down to the dangerous gulch, approximately 200 feet below. Just up from the winch were several small gardens of soil where the lightkeepers grew potatoes and a few other vegetables.

On the logbooks, the two lightkeepers took turns working officially every second day, unless we were working on a big project or repairs. This was the common schedule on the remote island lighthouses. On my day off, I would often take the long walk across Exploits Island into the harbour. The well-worn trail crossed the rugged island from the lighthouse into the harbour ending in Butt's Cove near the government wharf. It was always a challenging walk because it was uphill when you left the lighthouse and uphill when leaving at the opposite end. The walking trail roughly followed the old telephone/snowmobile trails that intersected in many places, confusing many hikers. You walked around a few small ponds and bogs on this route, and you were continually strolling uphill or downhill, around trees, and over rocks. If the temperature was warm, you could not stop because the flies or stouts would eat you alive. You just kept on moving and walking, and I often carried a skinny limb to swat the flies away. It was always a good hike, and after a while, you got in the groove.

In September 1983, there were still several part-time residents staying there in their cabins or in their original clapboard saltbox houses. At the time there were seventy-five to eighty cabins scattered throughout the eastern and western sides of the harbour. Most property owners had a family connection with this community. At this time of the season, they enjoyed the peacefulness of Exploits, catching a few fish, picking a few berries, or doing some wharf maintenance.

That first fall, I walked miles and miles around the old harbour and over the hills, checking out all the sites. I explored several interesting old graveyards, reading the snippets of history carved into the weathered headstones.

I made a point to visit a few of the local folks during my shift. I visited Harold Sceviour and his wife, Madeline, a few times. Harold had a neat six-wheel ATV, which he used around their property doing odd jobs. I remember helping him pick mussels in it at low tide one day and getting a flat tire. I repaired it for him because he was not able to do it. He was really grateful for me repairing his tire and gave me one of his highly prized "homebrews." I drank the nice cold beer with him and headed out for my long walk to the lighthouse. I crossed the concrete bridge, then booted out through the woods, bound for the light. Well, I am not sure what was in Harold's tasty homebrew, but I flew out through the twisty trail in record time that afternoon. I also paid Richard Wells and Lydia a few visits. They lived on this isolated island year-round. Every visit I had with these fine folks was great. I always left their house feeling blessed and certainly more informed.

In a short time, my first shift as a lightkeeper for the Canadian Coast Guard was over. I returned to my home in Porterville in October just in time to go moose hunting with my dear father, Max. We were partners. For the next several months, I waited to get a call back for another shift at the lighthouse. That did not happen until the spring of 1984. That was when I took a one-week shift in May with relief keeper Eric Dove from Crow Head. In early June, I got another one-week shift with my long-time friend Ed Loveless from Lewisporte.

The next month, lady luck was on my side, I was offered a lightkeeper position at the magnificent Long Point Lighthouse on Twillingate Island, and that established my new career.

3 Long Point Lighthouse, 1984

Long Point Lighthouse is located at the head of Devil's Cove on Twillingate Island, approximately one mile from the small fishing community of Crow Head. It has been sitting there on duty, guiding marine traffic safely throughout Notre Dame Bay, since 1876. The lighthouse sits 300 feet above sea level with a square concrete light tower, red in colour with a white dome top, at almost thirty feet high. The white light flashes every five seconds with a normal range of twenty-one nautical miles. The original main light apparatus was made by the Chance Brothers of Birmingham, England. The fog-horn, which blasts for four seconds and falls silent for fifty-six seconds, was installed in 1920. Finally, the lighthouse was connected to the main electrical power system in 1972. Prior to that, the station generated its own power. The station also had a radio beacon on site. This is the type of beacon that transmits a radio signal (the letter "L") that is picked up by radio direction-finding systems on ships and aircraft. During World War II, pilots used this radio beacon to take directions by radio compass.

Early in July 1984, my supervisor, Randy Dawe from the Marine Aids Office in St. John's, called to offer me four weeks' work at Long Point Lighthouse. Lightkeeper Allan Roberts was taking his holidays beginning July 11. Other lighthouses in this bay had their holiday shifts covered by other relief light-keepers. I needed whatever work was out there, so I agreed. Allan was departing on the end of his Tuesday shift on July 10, so I drove from Porterville down to Long Point on Monday and Tuesday for several hours of orientation with him before he left.

Long Point

Allan had worked at Long Point since around 1969. He had previously worked several years on Bacalhao Island Lighthouse, which was a few miles southeast of there. He was also a World War II veteran who had proudly served his country overseas. Allan meticulously showed me the ropes in operating this important lighthouse—the daily checks, the required maintenance, the paperwork, and the extremely sensitive clock adjustments on the radio beacon. Quite the amount of information to take in when I was still a rookie lightkeeper in the system. I had only six weeks of experience from working on Exploits Lighthouse, and Long Point was quite different than that station. There was only one lightkeeper here, and all responsibility fell on me.

The dwelling house was originally built for two full families to live on site year-round. The large two-and-a-half-storey house was split down the middle. Over the years, a couple of renovations were carried out on the dwelling. In one half of the house, there was your regular kitchen, dining room, living room, and on the second floor were three bedrooms and a bathroom. It also had two more small rooms on the top floor in the attic or crawl space. It had an identical set-up on the opposite half of the dwelling. Two full houses in one, plus an office built on the southern end, which housed the radio beacon. There was a large, twenty-foot hallway leading from the main house to the light tower with an exterior door for tourists to access. The light tower entranceway had a large, red, 300-pound cast-iron door, which led inside the 108-year-old structure. Inside was a dark and cold time capsule, with walls built out of neatly stacked bricks that were reinforced with a foot of concrete. Allan informed me the brick walls had cracked during the aftershocks from the famous 1929 earthquake that occurred off the south coast of Newfoundland. Mounted up on the brick wall was a lovely old wooden oak rack containing about three dozen signalling flags, which were used for communicating with passing ships a lifetime ago.

On the rough brick floor were several iron weights connected to a cable that led up and disappeared into the landing overhead. The old lightkeepers would hand-crank these heavy weights from the floor, up to the bottom of the main light floor, using the powerful brass gear system similar to a grandfather clock. As these weights would gently float downwards to the brick floor, it slowly rotated the main light, which sat on a large bowl of mercury. Originally, the weights had to be cranked up every ninety minutes. Later, the gear ratio was changed so it required cranking every eight hours. Thank God those days had passed! During my work period there, a small electric motor rotated the powerful 500-watt bulb for mariners to observe.

Leading up to the top of this tower was a beautiful spiral oak staircase that twisted its way to the top. Notched into these wooden steps were the footprints of the old pioneer lightkeepers who climbed these stairs many times a day—trusted old lightkeepers like Samuel Roberts, James Henry Preston, and J. T. Preston. In 1932, Jack and George Roberts took over duties, and later, Edgar Sharpe from 1950 to 1980. Allan Roberts and Bert Hamlyn also worked there, making it a three-man station. Other relief lightkeepers who worked there were Cyril Dove, Eric Dove, Paul Fudge, and Gord Jones.

There was a large white fog alarm building perched at the very edge of the cliff near the dwelling. This building was constructed in 1944 and contained two large green air compressors that powered the mighty air horn. Long Point's foghorn was extremely powerful, with an audible range for at least ten miles. Also in this room was a large four-cylinder Lister diesel motor and generator, which were wired to start up whenever there was a power failure. Power outages were common due to the extremely high winds on this hill and the nasty salt spray in the air. The motor was also on a timer—it started up once a week and ran for fifteen minutes just to keep everything oiled. Connecting the main dwelling to the fog alarm building was a unique wooden tunnel stretching approximately 125 feet. There was another lightkeeper's dwelling built in the parking lot in the 1960s for the third lightkeeper. Bert Hamlyn and his family lived there for six years while working at the station. Later, this dwelling was closed. During this period, the Canadian Coast Guard supplied a 4x4 Jeep at the station for the keepers for their own use and for transporting their children down over the slippery, dangerous hill so they could attend school in Crow Head.

In the early 2000s, a craft shop began operating out of this abandoned lightkeeper's dwelling.

Also at the light station was a small, one-bay garage, an oil shed, and two old outhouses, one that was still used by the general public. There was a work (tool) shed, a large 1,000-gallon diesel fuel tank, and a radio beacon tower. In addition to this, Comfort Cove Coast Guard Radio had just had a new, sturdy 270-foot-high VHF communication tower erected by LeBlanc & Royle in the parking lot. It was equipped with a trailer full of high-tech electronic equipment and its own diesel generator system. This was being installed and hooked up during my first summer there. Long Point light was quite large and an extremely busy light station.

On a sunny Wednesday morning, July 11, 1984, I proudly took up duties on the beautiful Long Point Lighthouse in Twillingate. I will never forget that day. I was so happy and honoured to run this classy lighthouse. Long Point was a picturesque setting with the bright red and white lighthouse sitting on the edge of the cliffs overlooking the blue Atlantic Ocean—postcard perfect, with occasional icebergs drifting past and humpback whales playing nearby. It was pure paradise when the weather was favourable. I soon learned this lighthouse was the pride of Crow Head and Twillingate Island. This majestic old lighthouse was held in high esteem and had guided the local fisher persons and hunters through these dangerous waters for over 108 years. Long Point was their lifeline and their crown jewel attraction in the rapidly growing tourism industry on the island.

The previous lightkeepers who worked Long Point were accustomed to the lifestyle of extreme winds and rough sea conditions around this rugged island. It was strongly embedded into their DNA. Now I, Barry Porter, was responsible for running and maintaining this grand old light station. For over a century, most of the previous lightkeepers had been from the much-respected Sharpe and Roberts families of Twillingate Island. To add extra pressure on me, I was the first proper "outsider" to work as keeper of the light here. I had absolutely no family connections with Twillingate! I was a farmer's son from "up in the pond"—that is what the locals called the area up in the bay where I came from.

My shift ran from 0800 to 1600 hours (8:00 a.m. to 4:00 p.m.) seven days a week. It was a one-man station. Every day,

I commuted from my lovely little hometown of Porterville down to Long Point Lighthouse, which was on the extreme tip of Twillingate Island. I soon settled into the regular duties at my very own lighthouse, and things went very well. At the beginning, the residents of Crow Head were not sure about this outsider looking after their lighthouse. Back then, I was driving my cool black customized Chevy van with the chrome rims, side pipes, and fat tires. My commute to work was quite long for Newfoundland standards—it was about an hour and a half one way, sometimes longer, depending on traffic and weather conditions. I would leave home at 6:25 a.m., and by around 7:50 a.m. I would be cruising up though the narrow main street of picturesque Crow Head. Even at that early hour, half the older retired fishermen in town were out standing on the sides of the road having their regular morning chat. When they saw me approaching in my van, they froze in their tracks and stared at me. I'd see a scattered old guy check his watch as if checking to see if I was on time! It was funny, but it did not bother me. The same thing would happen when I drove down to the post office or when I departed after I had worked my daily shift—they would just stand there looking at me. They did not have any idea who was in charge of their beloved Long Point.

Slowly but surely, the residents got to know me at the local stores, the garages, and the post office. I remember giving old Harvey Sharpe of Crow Head a gallon of glossy Coast Guard red paint. Harvey was a local colourful character and getting up there in age. He had walked all the way up the hill to the station for a chat with me and to ask me if I had any paint to spare. Many times, I also gave well-known local fisherman Fred Sharpe rides home from uptown or from the Anchor Inn back to his small house in Crow Head. Fred never did own a car but was a nice fellow who had fished all his life and had hands on him as big as a bear's paws. He told me a few old stories about life on isolated Twillingate Island long before the causeway opened up the island to increased traffic. After some time, word spread that this new lightkeeper, this Porter guy, was not that bad and was actually a good man. Eventually, I earned the local residents' approval, which was important to me. I was proud to be taking care of this majestic old lighthouse, and I carried it out to the best of my ability.

One person I never did get approval from was the lighthouse inspector at the Marine Aids Office. This guy was originally from Twillingate but was now living and working in St. John's with the Coast Guard. For some reason, he did not like me one bit, maybe because I was an outsider, or maybe because I was young blood. Who knows? Part of the inspector's job was to check on every lighthouse in Newfoundland and Labrador once a year. Back then there were still fifty-six manned lighthouses in the province. This inspector would drop by Long Point Lighthouse unannounced almost every month. Any weekend that he returned home to Twillingate, he would carry out an intensive inspection of my lighthouse. He would thoroughly go through my logbooks, all my entries, walk through every building, every room, and inspect my inventory as if looking for something.

My summer university students who were taking visitors on guided tours would often observe him from the light tower. The inspector would park down in the lot, tucked in with the dozen cars already parked there. Then he would sneak around the grounds, "inspecting," and finally he would come and meet with me. Finally, one day after several inspections and unable to find anything out of order, he said to me while he was leaving, "Never sign off your logbook with 'All OK,' because there might be a light bulb burnt out down in the dirty gravel crawl space below the floor!" He would also phone me at the lighthouse from his St. John's office a few times a week, and it was always five minutes before my shift ended or five minutes after my shift had started—checking to see if I was at work, I guess! I was a rookie lightkeeper, so I tolerated this for a while. Then one day, when

I'd had enough of this harassment, I phoned my supervisor in St. John's, and the annoyance from Mr. Inspector suddenly ended.

With the fishing season in full swing that summer, the marine traffic was busy around these turbulent waters. The local fish plant was at maximum production, and there were small open speedboats mixed with the odd old trap skiff fishing everywhere around the lighthouse. There was a steady flow of longliners entering and exiting the safety of the Twillingate harbour. Off in the distance, coastal boats, large paper freighters, and fuel tankers were steadily shipping in and out of the busy seaports of Lewisporte and Botwood. All this traffic used Long Point Lighthouse as a beacon, an important landmark.

On the light station's grounds, the tourists were everywhere. I was amazed by the number of tourists who made the effort to drive or hike up the twisty gravel road to visit beautiful Long Point. Hundreds and hundreds every day, and thousands every week, would walk around the parking lot and throughout the lighthouse grounds taking photos or just taking in the beautiful scenery. There was a steady stream of large, chartered tour buses visiting almost daily, many from the mainland, but the local McCarthy's bus tours were also regular visitors. Some days we would even have three tour buses visit the lighthouse. Most of these visitors would come inside for a tour up the beautiful light tower and gaze out from the top. Some were just interested in a chat with a "real life" lighthouse keeper. The mainlanders especially loved this lighthouse and the surrounding rugged scenery. I used to say, if you were born and raised in Saskatoon, Saskatchewan, you would be blown away by the natural beauty around here. Most of us locals are guilty of taking our natural Newfoundland landscape and lifestyle for granted. I am so blessed to be able to call Newfoundland and Labrador my home.

I feel the lighthouse gods tested me early in this shift. Two weeks on the job, on Tuesday, July 24, a vicious lightning storm hit the island. It knocked out the main power leading into the lighthouse. A powerful lightning strike blew up the transformer in the parking lot, knocked out my radio beacons, and fried my telephone. Luckily, my VHF line to the Comfort Cove Coast Guard Radio station still worked, so I was able to report the problems through the radio operators there. A few days later, I also discovered my important foghorn was damaged from that storm. It had a different sound, which meant more calls, plus a "notice to shipping" stating that Long Point's foghorn had a different characteristic had to be broadcasted. Luckily, my backup diesel generator automatically fired up as programed and kept the main light lit. The following day, two technicians from Comfort Cove Coast Guard Radio, Jack Edison and Lloyd Horwood, arrived at the station and repaired my radio beacon. I would get to know these guys quite well over the coming years. Due to other storm damage around Twillingate Island, it took almost three days before the power company arrived to repair the damage up on the hill. Each day I had to manually pump in extra diesel fuel into my "day tank," but my old diesel generator operated perfectly, and the main light shone. Terra Nova Tel finally repaired my telephone line on the third day. Later, on July 31, a Coast Guard helicopter landed on the large pad and dropped off technician Paul Neil to repair my damaged foghorn. It took several days for all the repairs from the lightning strike to be completed, but finally, all was back to normal. Quite the introduction to my new job here—welcome to lovely old weather-beaten Long Point!

Thankfully, those first months there I had two excellent university students, Paul Dove and Derrick Dalley, working with me to deal with the large volume of visiting tourists. In no time, summer flew by, and I'd had a successful summer season running this popular light station. I carried out the regular lightkeeper duties plus those involving an endless stream of tourists who explored the lighthouse. Along the way, I received some positive reviews on my work record. One day in August, a lady's handbag was accidentally left on the rocks near the light tower. I picked it up and checked inside for some identification, hoping it was owned by someone local. I discovered it belonged to a lady from the mainland along with its bundle of cash, credit cards, and medications. I promptly turned it in to the local RCMP detachment in Twillingate. Several months later, I received an alarming letter from the Department of Justice in Ottawa. It was from a Supreme Court judge . . . and it was his wife's handbag that I had turned in to the police! He sincerely thanked me and informed me he had written a complimentary letter to my superior, Ian Gall, in St. John's weeks earlier. Around the same period, I worked several extra hours one weekend to help a Coast Guard technician who was out from St. John's working on the new trailer belonging to Comfort Cove Coast Guard Radio. Apparently, he also forwarded a good word to my superiors, which is helpful when you are a rookie lightkeeper.

This was around the same time the previous lightkeeper and a fine man, Allan Roberts, decided to pack it in and retire. The positive feedback on my work record at Long Point certainly did not hurt my work resumé. What was supposed to be a four-week work period for me turned into four very enjoyable years with the Canadian Coast Guard at this beautiful lighthouse and the fine folks of Twillingate.

Once Allan retired, I continued working the set schedule of seven days a week. The station required one eight-hour watch daily, fifty-six hours a week, year-round, with no days off, and strangely no overtime. Due to the fact my first six months were considered a probationary period, I did not accumulate any holidays for this period. This meant I worked every day for eighteen months without getting one single day off. As crazy as it sounds, that was the schedule if you were a lightkeeper who worked on a "land" lighthouse. (Only the federal government could get away with this work schedule—compared to the island lighthouse shifts, which were thirty-two days on and thirty-two days off, plus holidays.) Island lightkeepers received ninety per cent of their pay rate, whereas I received one hundred per cent of my salary.

During those early months at Long Point, I was doing a three-hour commute every day. The drive was approximately 112 kilometres one way, but I had to drive through fifteen different communities, which meant I was burning through valuable time and fuel. It was difficult, but I needed this job and needed to keep my foot in the door with the federal government, so I sucked it up and paid my dues. Finally, after several months, my superiors in the Marine Aids Office in St. John's decided to allow me to live in the old lighthouse. This gave me a break from all the driving. It was a win-win for me and for the Coast Guard. This meant far less driving for me, and if some marine emergency occurred after 1600 hours (4:00 p.m.), I would be on site. Not to mention that I would be unofficial security for the station, because from time to time local cars would hang around in the parking lot late in the night.

Now, it was just me and my faithful lighthouse beagle, Gypsy, living in this beautiful century-old lighthouse with ten bedrooms sitting on the very edge of the Atlantic. I moved in with my belongings, set up my home stereo and a bunch of plants, a few pictures, and made it home. I picked one bedroom (out of a possible ten) on the second floor. This room had an electric baseboard heater—several bedrooms had no heaters. The bathroom was also on this floor. The main kitchen area had an oil range for heat, and there were a few baseboard heaters spread throughout the house. The old house was drafty and difficult to keep warm during the coldest part of the winter. I remember one night I left a glass of water near the window in my bedroom. It was a cold and windy January night. The next morning when I got up to start my day, I reached out for my glass of water, and the glass was skimmed over with ice! A tad chilly, but the old place had character. It was now my home, and I made the best of it.

Over the years, I took the opportunity to check out every nook, cranny, and crawl space. I would put on my coveralls, take a trouble light with a long extension cord, and explore the dark crawl spaces and the hidden attics of this landmark. I never did find any treasures, but I found it all extremely interesting—how they built dormers and a roof over the original old roof years ago, the coal pit in the basement, and more. I have to say this old house was built solid. The wall studs, rafters, and roof truss were all cross-braced and reinforced with heavy lumber. It was a testament to the quality of workmanship put into this dwelling to withstand the elements for the past hundred years.

Nobody had lived in the old dwelling since previous lightkeepers Edgar Sharpe moved to Crow Head and Allan Roberts relocated to Wild Cove many years earlier. To this day, I am the last lightkeeper to live in the beautiful old Long Point Lighthouse!

It was also around this same time that I fell in love with a beautiful little pharmacist, Alice, who worked at Twillingate Pharmacy. She became my wife a few years later.

Allan Roberts and Barry Porter

Soon, the fall season rolled around, the weather began to change, and winds started to increase. I had never experienced such strong winds as I did on the top of that hill. Almost every day it blew a gale from some direction. There was no windbreak there, just the raw Atlantic wind biting into my face and body. Even the telephone repairmen had bolted extra straps onto the doors of their service vans to prevent the wind from blowing them open and causing damage. Allan once told me a story about a time he and his family had been in town visiting and shopping when a vicious storm hit the island all of a sudden. He returned to the lighthouse, and due to the extreme winds, he had to crawl from his car to the dwelling. Once there, he gathered a long piece of rope and fastened it to the house and onto his car. Then he carefully helped his wife and children slowly navigate from their car to the safety of the dwelling while clinging onto the rope for dear life. Now, that is windy! I used to say the only windbreak at Long Point was Ireland.

Fall meant turr-hunting season in Twillingate, and the local men had their guns and their boats ready. When the winds were from the favourable direction, look out—the hunters would be out by the dozens. This was an eye-opening experience for me. To say the Twillingate residents liked hunting those feathered little birds was an understatement. Every morning at the start of my shift, I would climb up the old oak stairs and spy out over the rough seas with my binoculars, checking the weather conditions and marine traffic. The bird hunters were already out there, bobbing through the sea swells and zigzagging about. There were so many boats, they would assemble in lines in a staggered formation and shoot just behind the neighbouring boat. I could not believe my eyes.

From the tower, I could see flocks of turrs flying south along the shoreline or the tide rips, cutting inside or outside of dozens of trigger-happy hunters. It was no problem to hear their shotguns firing from up on the hill. These hardy men were not afraid of a bit of salt spray or wind in their faces.

They loved this annual hunt. I have seen hunters out in forty- to fifty-mph winds, tucked behind a point of land or a small island, getting a little shelter from the unrelenting wind. The local men lived hard, worked hard, and were professionals when it came to harvesting turrs, ducks, seals, or fish. It was a way of life for these tough islanders.

Environment Canada's weather station,
the foghorn building with a big sea on

From the comfort of the upper level of my light tower, I could see hunters in their speedboats all the way from Western Head to Twillingate Island and down eastward toward Bacalhao Island. When conditions were favourable, many mornings I counted over 125 speedboats out hunting in these dangerous waters. I must say, I admired their drive and desire to go out on the sea to shoot a few turrs regardless of the conditions. I was glad, and even amazed, that nobody drowned during my watch at Long Point.

I made many good friends while working on the light, one of which was artist Ted Stuckless. He was well-known for his incomparable paintings of old traditional Newfoundland. Ted was a night owl and did much of his creative work in the wee hours of the night. I spent many hours sitting in Ted's upstairs studio sipping on a beer and discussing life and the mysteries of the universe. I always enjoyed my visits there along with the chance to meet new people. On one of my visits, I encountered one of the most interesting and best speakers I have ever met in my life.

It was a cold Christmas Eve, Wednesday, 1986, when I passed Ted's studio on my way to the Bank of Nova Scotia. I had planned to drop in with a little gift after I did my banking. I had gotten off work a few minutes early to catch the bank before it closed for a few days during Christmas. The staff locked the door behind me, as I was the very last customer allowed in. I patiently waited my turn and then carried out my banking and wished them all a merry Christmas as they locked the main door behind me. I hurried back to Ted's studio, where a handful of my buddies had already gathered. As I walked to the side door, I noticed this odd-looking grey car parked out front. It was a Porsche stuffed full of video cameras, tripods, and tapes. I entered the upstairs chamber to see a few of my friends engaged in a major debate. The ringleader was none other than the famous and eccentric Geoff Stirling, the owner and founder of the NTV broadcasting station, CHOZ FM, and the *Newfoundland Herald*.

I gave Ted his bottle of Cabot Tower, then proceeded over to see what Geoff was having to say. He was front and centre, commanding everybody's attention as he spoke about everything from powerful business companies up in Canada like Molson to the big banks to world peace. Geoff had a gleam in his eye and was on a roll. I had never seen anyone so passionate and knowledgeable. For forty-five minutes Geoff had us captivated with his interesting stories, when suddenly he stopped in mid-sentence. He said, "Oh my, I have to go to the bank, but I'll be back." I chuckled and told him he was out of luck because I was the last customer there and they had locked the door behind me. Undaunted, Geoff raced down the stairs and disappeared.

We were enjoying our beers when about twenty minutes later Geoff reappeared with a smile from ear to ear. He told me he had gotten in and completed his banking, no problem. I was amazed. I guess he had gone to the front doors of the bank and caught a few workers finishing up their Christmas Eve social inside. Being very rich and powerful, I guess, old Geoff must have flashed his special banker's smile and was able to get inside!

Life on Long Point

Living up on the very crest of Long Point was challenging. Besides the relentless winds there, just to drive up over the steep, twisty gravel road was an ordeal. In the winter, contractor Lester Sharpe would do the snow clearing for the Coast Guard, but the hill was often very icy. There was an old wooden box full of salt halfway up the steepest part of the hill, so occasionally I would have to manually salt the road in that area. Over time, I had the driving up this problematic hill figured out to a science. I had to hit the bottom of the hill at top speed to be able to make it up over the steepest section. I learned that if I spun out, it was better to turn my vehicle around on the hill instead of attempt to back down. Each winter, I would notice new dents, scrapes, and paint carved into the guardrails.

I remember a January afternoon in 1987 when two of my friends, artist Ted Stuckless and photographer Charlie Falk, walked up the hill to visit me at the station. Charlie is pretty laid-back, but I could tell he was not himself when he arrived. They had just attempted to drive up the hill in his brand new Toyota 4Runner and spun out three-quarters of the way up the most difficult section. While attempting to reverse down the hill, he lost control and ended up scraping and crunching against several rough lengths of the guardrails, damaging the entire side of his new rig. Not a pretty sight.

With winter season came my extra ice reports, which were separate phone calls in to the telegraph office in St. John's, who then forwarded a telegram directly to Montreal Shipping Company's office in the busy seaport of Botwood. Montreal Shipping was the company exporting all the paper products from the Abitibi-Price pulp and paper mill in Grand Falls–Windsor. For many years, the company had an agreement with the working lightkeeper to send a daily, detailed telegram of the local ice and weather conditions. It was very important for their shipping schedules. I would describe the percentage of rough ice, grey or white ice, first-year ice, and strings of open water along their main shipping route. There were "paper boats" passing by the unpredictable waters off Long Point on a regular basis. I was new, but I provided these important reports, as I thought it was part of my job. The next summer, I received a cheque in the mail from the company thanking me for my services. Allan had failed to tell me about this little side payment, but I gladly carried on this tradition for the four winters I spent here.

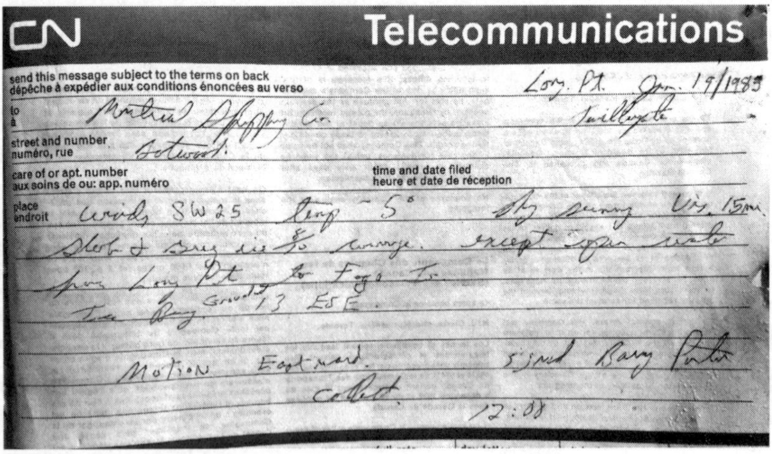
CN Telecommunications

send this message subject to the terms on back
dépêche à expédier aux conditions énoncées au verso

to
à

street and number
numéro, rue

care of or apt. number
aux soins de ou: app. numéro

time and date filed
heure et date de réception

place
endroit

CN telegram sent through Long Point, 1985

Along with the winter season came sports. I joined the local pickup hockey team at the old George Hawkins Arena in town. That was a great bit of fun, a good mixture of skilled and semi-skilled men having a good skate and a few laughs. The men were a great bunch, and they accepted me into their little group, which I appreciated. I also got involved with other things around the town of Twillingate, like Melv Sharpe's fitness gym in Wild Cove, and I played some badminton at the town gym. I also fought countless battles of Ping-Pong against my buddy Robin Vatcher at his newly constructed home. We had a small crew, but man, we had many epic games there!

Emergency light, main light, and ship

Due to the fact I worked seven days a week year-round, every Thursday my schedule allowed me two or three hours off to run errands like buy groceries and do my banking. Many times, I did not take this time off—it depended on the weather and what was happening at the lighthouse. When I did take advantage of this break, I would go cross-country skiing or hiking the many miles on the remote trails and barrens. I soon discovered there were many lovely hidden paths throughout

Twillingate Island, old walking trails that were used by the first settlers a few hundred years ago. I also went skating on a few of the ponds near the Royal Canadian Legion and near Crow Head. Great times were had, and I made memories and friendships to last a lifetime, all the while keeping the light shining at good old Long Point Lighthouse.

Postcard photo

Other memories from Long Point include climbing the new 270-foot-high VHF communication tower in the parking lot. This tower was extremely high and quite unnerving, but I did climb it four or five times. The first exciting climb up was with one of the Coast Guard riggers, Lee Chaffey, when he and Sid Smith were bolting on ice shields to protect the important clearance lights. That was thrilling. I strapped on the safety belt, hooked it to a safety track, and slowly climbed up inside the triangle-shaped tower. It was quite the climb—and the first time I had ever attempted anything like this. The view at the top was amazing. You could see for miles back over Twillingate Island and all around the bay. Looking down, straight down, was scary—the trailer, fence, and cars in the parking lot looked like little toys.

There was an added optical effect because the ocean was another 300 feet below the small parking lot. So, I was perched inside a cold, steel structure almost 600 feet above sea level.

The tower and communication trailer were secured by a locked chain-link fence for which I had a key. Part of my job was to carry out weekly checks on the diesel generator and its batteries. Climbing the tower was not in my job description, but the view was worth it. I took my Nikon camera with me on each climb to capture some photos of the old lighthouse. Due to the large guy wire extending from this tower, it was difficult to take a good photo without getting a cluster of wires in the photo. Unless, of course, one was inside this ugly steel tower. I would wait for ideal conditions—little or no wind—and catch the favourable lighting to capture my prized photos. I also climbed it once with low fog banks sitting around the cliffs and the sun shining brightly on the lighthouse. A few years later, from two of these hard-to-get photos, I printed off approximately 10,000 postcards and several hundred fridge magnets and sold them at local craft shops.

March 26, 1987, was the very last day I climbed the tower, because that time I ran into a problem up there. Not a good spot for trouble. I had reached the very top, taken a few photos, and when I decided to climb down, I could not move. I was stuck for some reason. My safety belt had locked up inside the safety track. The brake was hooked and would not let me descend one inch. Holy smokes—I was stuck, clinging on at 600 feet above the sea! This was not an ideal situation. However, after some fiddling around and much sweating, I discovered how to resolve the dilemma. I had to carefully remove my safety belt from around my waist while hanging on at the very highest section of the tower. I carefully disconnected it from the brake system on the safety track that ran the entire length of the tower. This system prevented you from falling if you slipped or lost your grip. It was a weird, uncomfortable feeling to be up there completely untethered—not a place to get weak, faint, or to panic. After a few deep breaths, I reattached the belt around my waist, refastened it into the track, and breathed a sigh of relief. Taking one final look around, I carefully descended halfway down and took more photos. I learned that this was the best angle to capture the lighthouse. I then continued my descent to the bottom, finally setting my two feet on the gravelled parking lot. That was when I retired my tower-climbing career forever.

I had a close working relationship with Comfort Cove Coast Guard Radio staff while I worked there. Besides my daily weather and ice reports with the several radio operators, I would also have the occasional private chat with the operators on the radio at Long Point, and I would sometimes drop in while driving past their station at Loon Bay Hill. I was once invited to a little Christmas lunch there with all the staff. While I worked at Long Point, the CCG Radio operators were John Earle, Bill Strong, Jeff Lush, Gordon Carter, and Jim Cramm. I had many good talks with these fine men while working at the lighthouses. Comfort Cove CCG Radio station also had several highly trained technicians on site who kept the radio systems working during my time. They were Jack Edison, Lloyd Horwood, Len Woodford, Nigel Thornley, Dave Slade, Keith Beaubien, and later, Brian Greene. With the new communication tower built near the Long Point Lighthouse, a couple of these techs would pay regular work visits to their equipment trailer next to the VHF tower. There always seemed to be some piece of sensitive radio equipment that would

View from VHF tower 270 feet above parking lot

require some adjustment or replacement. The techs would make the weekly drive down from their Comfort Cove station to Long Point, then drop into my lighthouse for a cup of tea, lunch, and a chat. It was always good to see the boys, especially during the cold days of winter. They were always welcome.

After their expensive and massive tower was powered up one night in the middle of a snow and ice storm in early 1985, I ran into a serious problem. I was watching TV with my lighthouse beagle next to me, when suddenly I heard glass breaking. I walked out to the north end of the dwelling to find a small pane of glass broken out of one of the windows in the spare kitchen. It was windy, but I hadn't thought the wind was strong enough to break glass. I patched it up with some cardboard and returned to the comfortable living room. A repair job for tomorrow, I figured. About an hour later, I heard another smashing sound. What the heck was happening? Was it a prankster or a ghost?

I went out into the other living room, which was not being used, and sure enough, another window was broken. This time I saw a chunk of ice melting on the floor. A few minutes later, I heard a smack against the outside clapboard. It was ice melting, blowing off the large VHF tower next door, and striking up against the dwelling. Remarkably, weather conditions caused ice and glitter to freeze onto the higher sections of the tower and its guy wires. When the temperature warmed up a little, the ice would fall off, and if the winds were strong enough and coming from the right direction, it would force strings of ice to rain down on the lighthouse. This was extremely dangerous for me and visitors to the parking lot. If a piece of ice falling from 300 feet hit you in the head, it could easily kill you!

The next morning, it was safe, so I walked around inspecting the damage to my dwelling and my truck. Luckily, only a couple of windows were broken. I decided I had better inspect Comfort Cove CCG Radio's trailer directly under the tower. Unlocking the door, I looked inside the radio equipment room, and to my shock, the ceiling was leaking. I could see water running down through the plywood ceiling splashing all over the high-tech equipment. It was coming from the melting ice and snow overhead. The ice protection that was added to the roof of the trailer was inadequate, and falling ice had penetrated through the roof, causing the leaks. There was over $160,000 worth of communication equipment sitting there, stacks of electronics with water splashing overhead. It was a scary sight. I promptly reported the damage to Comfort Cove Coast Guard Radio station and reported it to my boss at the Marine Aids Office. I also informed them about the window damage to the dwelling.

Well, this was the fastest time I ever saw the Canadian Coast Guard react. The Comfort Cove Radio techs were on site in no time, spreading a $10 roll of plastic over the sensitive radio equipment, and it saved the day. Also, the CCG carpenter shop in St. John's rigged up several nice storm windows made of wire mesh to protect my windows from ice damage. They were shipped out to me in a few days, and the ice protection on the roof of the trailer was also reinforced. Fortunately, all this worked out, and there was no more ice damage.

A lightkeeper was on watch!

Note: A few years later, the Canadian Coast Guard removed the large communication tower and erected another tower, just south of the lighthouse, across the bog on the top of another rocky hill. It was located a safe distance from the visiting general public.

Lightkeeper Jack Roberts

Mr. John (Jack) Roberts spent most of his life at Long Point Lighthouse, right up until he retired as lightkeeper. His father was the previous lightkeeper there, and young Jack worked with him and later proudly took over the principal duties. This was a common process throughout the lighthouse world in Newfoundland. The positions were often passed down from generation to generation. When I took over lightkeeper duties on the hill, John Roberts was known as "Old Jack" Roberts. He lived in a beautiful large garden in Wild Cove only a few miles from the lighthouse. I noticed he would drive up and circle the parking lot almost every day, sometimes twice a day. He drove a huge brown Chrysler New Yorker and always took time to stop and gaze out over the ocean. He would never get out of his car, and he would never come up to visit the lighthouse.

One day, after seeing Jack many times on the lower parking lot, I asked Allan Roberts why he did not drop in. Allan said that Jack was a private man and that he missed Long Point so much it was too painful for him to visit. He and his wife, Hettie, had never had any children—the lighthouse at Long Point was his baby.

Allan proudly told me a story of Jack carrying out a rescue back in the 1950s. There were a couple of seal hunters in trouble on the rough ice just north of Long Point. The tide and winds had slowly shifted, and the pack ice had suddenly become unsafe. Jack spied this from the tower, quickly grabbed a length of rope, and proceeded down over the snow-covered bluff, then raced out over the ice to the hunters. Allan said the ice had gotten so loose and dangerous that Jack had to wear snowshoes to walk out to the men. Once there, he tied the rope around both men and assisted them back to the icy shoreline. They were wet and cold but very thankful.

A lightkeeper was on watch.

Long Point Lighthouse had a long-running tradition with the local seal hunters, and an important life-saving one at that. Little did I know that one day I would have to continue this tradition. When Mother Nature would occasionally co-operate, the bay would be stuffed solid with rough Arctic ice for miles and miles, with herds of fat harp seals all around. When this happened, the brave local seal hunters would be twitching to go out swilin'. The rough Arctic ice would be pressed so tightly against the cliffs around the island, the seal hunters could walk out a few miles over the bleak white icescape. I would observe this hunt from the top of the light tower or from the couple of observation stations attached to the ends of the dwelling. There were two wooden ledges built for placing your binoculars on and providing some shelter from the harsh winds.

These skilled and determined hunters would slowly navigate their way out from the rocky shores of Crow Head, Sleepy Cove, and Wild Cove. This was dangerous and difficult work. They would zigzag their way out through the rough ice dodging ice boulders as big as trucks and the odd growler or iceberg. Sometimes they were forced to climb around huge pressure ridges of ice protruding upwards like chain-link fences. This happened when the ice had been crushed together by moving tides and winds. The ice here could be fifteen to twenty feet thick, according to the Canadian Coast Guard icebreakers with whom I had contact. Not to mention the hunters would have to keep an eye out for the odd slippery, snow-covered hole where one could easily disappear into the freezing ocean!

When the seals were plentiful, there would be dozens of hunters out on the ice floes off Long Point. They would spread out in all directions like ants on a mission. Due to the unpredictable weather, the time window for this hunt was always limited. Being the only lightkeeper on the hill, I would always pay extra attention to the hunters and to the ever-changing local weather and ice conditions during this traditional hunt. The Twillingate men have been carrying out this hunt for hundreds of years off Long Point. It came naturally. It was a way of life for them.

March 1987 was an extremely bad month for shipping. The Arctic ice had been jammed solid around the bay for several weeks. One of the largest icebreakers with the Canadian Coast Guard, the *Sir John Franklin*, had been working in this area for weeks. On March 10, I recorded several longliners and a paper boat stuck in heavy ice a few miles northwest of Bacalhao Island, which were visible from Long Point. There was tremendous outside pressure on this ice. No shipping was happening in this bay until a change in the weather.

On this sunny day in March of 1987, I observed many seal hunters harvesting a few harp seals off the lighthouse. The entire Notre Dame Bay was still packed in solid with rough ice—right to the horizon and beyond. The forecast called for a snowstorm moving in by night, and today was the calm before the storm. There was not a draft of wind, a great day to be sealing. Almost too good.

I finished my lunch and decided to walk to the top of the light tower for another look out over the ice floe. Shortly after spying out with my binoculars, I could see small, hairline cracks forming throughout the white landscape. It was like cracks spreading through a car windshield. Being perched at 335 feet above sea level, I had the vantage point to see the subtle changes in the ice conditions. In contrast to the hunters standing at ice level, they would not be able to see the magnitude of the problem developing under their boots. The pressure that had kept the ice glued to the rocks for the past few weeks was suddenly slacking off. The winds and tides were shifting ever so slightly. This caused the pack ice to ease off and open up cracks and grow leads of sea water. These cracks can grow to great lengths in a short time—a few feet at first, then hundreds of feet.

Once I observed these cracks spreading across the ice floe, I had to warn the hunters of the impending danger. I raced down over the spiral staircase and ran to the fog alarm building as fast as I could. I swiftly fired up the powerful foghorn manually. The motor kicked in and filled the large air compressor tank within a couple of minutes. The old horn blew out the loudest blast I have ever heard. It echoed out over the ice pack for miles and miles. The hunters took notice—it was a calm, sunny day with visibility over twenty miles, and suddenly the Long Point foghorn goes off. Thankfully, all the local hunters knew this was a warning. If the foghorn blasted on a clear day, it meant real danger.

Immediately, every hunter turned and started walking back toward land as fast as their legs could take them. Most men dropped the several seals they were dragging right on the spot and hightailed it toward shore. I let the horn sing out its warning cry for about five minutes, then shut it off. I returned to the top of the tower again, and by now I could see that many of the cracks had grown into small leads of open water and were growing larger by the minute. This made it difficult for the men on the ice. They would have to walk several hundred extra yards or even half a mile to get around certain ponds of this frigid water. It looked like most of the hunters were making their way back to dry land. By now, word had spread around town, and several local men had driven up to the parking lot and were spying out over the chain-link fence with their binoculars. They observed this life-threatening race against time before their very eyes.

Right in the middle of all this action, the big yellow search and rescue helicopter suddenly flew over my head, flat out, by only a hundred feet. Excellent timing, I thought. I radioed the pilot to inform him of the dangerous situation occurring off Long Point, but the pilot told me they were flying north to the St. Anthony area. They were tasked to a rescue mission up there. The ice had similarly broken off from shore, and there were a couple of stranded hunters on the ice floes. With a snowstorm approaching, this could be very serious. The pilot informed me that if I needed assistance later, they could help on the return flight to their home at 9 Wing Base in Gander. Luckily, the SAR crew were not required here.

Later, I spoke to a couple of hunters who had successfully walked into Sleepy Cove Park. They said they had come upon a large, narrow string of water too long to walk around. Luckily, they had a jigger and line with them. They managed to get on a small pan of ice and skilfully throw the jigger across the narrow body of water. The jigger hooked, and they carefully pulled their ice raft across the sea water and continued their walk back to the rocky shores at Sleepy Cove. A close call.

Long Point and lead of open water in the Arctic ice, 1988

My trusty old foghorn had performed its job flawlessly. This was the first and only time I ever had to carry out this traditional foghorn manoeuvre. Thank God all the seal hunters made it back to their beloved Twillingate Island. I thought old Jack Roberts would be quite proud of me.

I must add my own interesting Jack Roberts story here. It was mid-March 1988, a year after my foghorn-and-seal-hunter event. I was off work, on sick leave, in the James Peyton Memorial Hospital in Gander recovering from sinus surgery. I had some minor complications and had to spend a week in there before I was released. At the tail end of my stay, Old Jack Roberts was admitted to hospital and was placed in another room not far from mine. Apparently, Jack had fallen and broken his hip. He was now eighty-five years old and living alone. By this time, all the nurses knew I was a lightkeeper working at Long Point, so they informed me Jack had been admitted. He was in fragile condition when he arrived. He had fallen and had to crawl across the floor to the phone and call for an ambulance.

After almost four years working at Long Point, I still had never actually spoken to this gentleman. I was somewhat shy, and he would only visit the parking lot. The next day, I decided it was time to visit Jack's room and introduce myself to him. He did not say much—he was still in extreme discomfort—so I returned to my room. One of the nurses told me Jack had only one request when he arrived—he wanted to be able to see the water. So, they gave him a room with a view of the huge Gander Lake in the distance. Nice call, I thought.

Later that night, I heard a commotion out in Jack's room. I was feeling bored lying around, so after a bit of time passed, I walked out to the nursing station. They informed me Jack was not very well. His vital signs were failing and he was going downhill—he was dying. Now it was close to midnight and all was quiet on the ward, so I asked the nurse if I could go to his room and sit with this legendary lightkeeper from Long Point. They gave me permission. The poor man was all alone—he had no family there. I felt sad for this man, who was all alone in this very foreign environment. I entered his dimly lit room and sat there for a long time as he slept. There was not a sound, so I started speaking "lightkeeper talk" to him. I said, "Jack, the fog is rolling in, and you have to go down and start up the foghorn." I continued speaking this unique Long Point lightkeeper lingo to him—icebergs, turrs, seals. After a while, I heard a few mumbles from the dear old man, but that was all. Before I left, I placed a little coloured photo of Long Point Lighthouse on his bed table. It was a photo I always carried in my wallet. A gift for him when he woke up—if he woke up.

The next morning, while I was waiting for my tasty hospital breakfast to be delivered, the nurse who was about to go off shift came into my room and said to me, "Barry, I don't know what you said to Mr. Roberts last night, but he has made a marvellous recovery, and he loved the photo you left him."

I was discharged that very day and returned to Long Point to resume my lightkeeper duties. Dear Mr. Jack Roberts recovered in Gander Hospital and lived out the rest of his years in the long-term-care ward of Notre Dame Bay Memorial Hospital in his beloved Twillingate—with a lovely ocean view.

Long Point Lighthouse, Continued

Saturday morning, May 17, after working a long night shift, I was getting ready to leave the station at 0800 hours. I had planned to drive back home for the evening and return for my regular Sunday shift. That May in 1986 was a hot and dry month in central Newfoundland. Before I left, the radio announced two small forest fires, one near the Catamaran Provincial Park, and the other up around the Peterview and Norris Arm North area. Taking note of the continued dry forecast and the wind direction, I decided to throw the light station's heavy gas-powered water pump and hoses in the back of my pickup truck—just in case!

I drove home to Porterville and had a short nap. When I woke around noon, the word around town was this little fire had grown into a serious forest fire and was burning toward the Burnt Arm and Laurenceton area. That afternoon, I drove up to Burnt Arm on my motorcycle to see for myself. There were a couple dozen residents standing in shock, looking across the peaceful cove at this vicious fire brewing on the opposite side. The fire was steadily growing and getting out of control. In another hour or so, all residents of Laurenceton, Brown's Arm, and Porterville were ordered to evacuate. Cars, trucks, and campers stuffed full of personal belongings made a quick escape from the communities. Even the senior citizens living at North Haven Manor in Lewisporte were bused out to Gander and Grand Falls due to poor air quality and the fire threat. A handful of us men stayed to fight for our homes that we had built from hard work and sweat.

By midnight, exactly sixteen hours after I threw the water pump in the back of my truck, I was standing on the roof of my house watering down my shingles with cold salt water. I had my water pump sucking up the salt water from the harbour, and I was soaking my roof and all the grounds and trees around my property. The wind was driving the fire toward Porterville, and my house was one of the first in its path. Standing on my roof in the darkness gave me a surreal feeling. I could hear the fire roaring off in the distance like a monster or like Niagara Falls. At one point I heard a blood-chilling scream echo out over the hills. Some poor moose or black bear must have gotten trapped and died in the blaze. What an eerie cry it was! Earlier that evening, my cousin told me many types of wildlife were racing across the road and through the woods up on Laurenceton Road.

Early on Sunday morning, Neil Porter, with his powerful yellow Cat D6 tractor, plowed a huge firebreak across the western side of my property, flattening my lovely spruce and fir trees just sixty feet from my back steps. They had to be removed to create an important firebreak. Then I fired up the water pump again and flooded the freshly cleared soil with salt water. At the same time, Bill Sceviour took his farm tractor to the farmlands and plowed long trenches in the many acres of fields—anything to slow down this raging fire. It was serious.

Helicopter next to my house with water bucket

It was a stressful time—my peaceful little community was under attack. It looked like a war zone. The sky had a sickly orange glow to it filled with smoke and noise. There were two large water bombers and two helicopters, flat out scooping up tons of water from the harbour, straight out in front of my house. They were buzzing around and dumping loads of salt water across the threatening fire edge. Regardless, the southwest winds continued to push the horrible fire toward my little Porterville. Finally, by late Sunday afternoon we got a much-needed break. The wind suddenly died down, then slowly changed direction, blowing in from the east. What a relief! This terrible inferno had burned a ten-mile stretch through the forest and around ponds, frying everything in its path. When it finally stopped, it was only half a mile from my home.

On Monday, a forestry crew and a few of us men spent the day attacking the remaining hot spots up in the Sparrow Cove area. We used shovels and water-filled extinguishers on the small pockets of fire still smouldering down in the ground. Finally, on Tuesday morning, May 20, I drove down and took up my duties again at Long Point, along with my well-used Canadian Coast Guard water pump. I felt totally exhausted. I had hardly slept since my short nap on Saturday. What a difficult way to spend the popular May long weekend!

Barry Porter using CCG water hose on new firebreak

Having just returned from a California bike tour, the summer of 1987 was another warm season and an eventful one at that. For three years now I had been loyally sending my monthly "whale reports" to Dr. Jon Lien's whale research group at Memorial University. Dr. Lien was a popular professor at MUN and in 1979 had created the Whale Research Group. It was an educational and conservation campaign that ran the official marine animal release program around the province. Dr. Lien was a world expert on humpback whales and in removing these large beasts from the tangles of cod-fishing gear. He was known as the "Whale Man." I had always recorded great detail during my numerous whale sightings and hoped that my information was going to good use.

On the morning of July 20, a fisherman contacted me about a large humpback whale that was trapped in his fishing gear down off Herring Neck. I felt I should do something, so I phoned Dr. Jon Lien's office. I informed him about this trapped whale, and he said he would check it out. Later that evening, after work, I was uptown, and someone told me Dr. Lien was in Twillingate and was staying down in Sleepy Cove Park. So, I figured I would drive down to the park and finally meet this interesting man. When I found him, he and a summer student were in a small campsite with his pickup truck and a small rubber Zodiac. They were set up for the night with their sleeping bags on the damp grass. His summer student, who was assisting him, was from Quebec. They had no tent, no shelter, just a wide-open space, and were about to sleep under the beautiful skies of Sleepy Cove. After a short chat, I invited them to come up and stay overnight at my lighthouse, since I had ten bedrooms in the place. Thrilled, they took me up on my offer and spent the night. Dr. Lien lived and breathed whales—they were his true passion. We spent hours and hours talking about humpback and minke whales while sipping on a little dark rum into the late night. The next morning was an early rise. I cooked them a tasty breakfast, and then the Whale Man and his student drove off on another whale-rescue mission down in the waters near Herring Neck.

That same summer, a local contractor was hired to replace the weathered shingles on the dwelling. The old red shingles were stripped off and new roofing nailed and cemented back in place. During this job, the roofers ran into some rot in places, and a small section of the roof had to be replaced. When they had the roof exposed, I climbed up to look at the condition of the roof and the attic hidden inside. I admired the detailed woodwork the original carpenters had put into building this solid roof. The thick, heavy rafters had sturdy wooden cross-braces fastened throughout the entire roof—built solid to withstand the extreme high winds around this rugged hill. The construction of this lighthouse over 100 years ago was a skill, a work of art you never see these days. The roof was only exposed for a few hours, but before the hole was sealed up again, I placed a "time capsule" inside. I tucked it in between another old original dormer that had been built over when an extension was built on back in the 1920s or 1930s. The time capsule was a bottle containing a letter I wrote telling a little history of Long Point, a list of some of the lightkeepers, and a new loonie coin. The loonie had just been introduced that year. I also placed an unscratched instant lotto ticket inside the container. Maybe another fifty or 100 years from then, some carpenter or an interested lightkeeper would discover my time capsule during another roof repair project at beautiful Long Point!

Another interesting character I met during my time working at Long Point was the famous captain Peter Troake. Captain Peter was best known for being the skipper of the life-saving Newfoundland medical ship the MV *Christmas Seal* from 1950 to 1970. He was awarded the Order of Canada in 1987 for his contribution in the field of health. Captain Peter's family were known as hard-working, dedicated fishermen, hunters, and spokesmen for the industry and its rich heritage.

Every season when the Arctic ice was in the bay and the boats were out seal hunting, Captain Peter would phone me at the lighthouse two or three times a week inquiring about the amount of Arctic ice, how far it was offshore, how many boats were out, and the number of seals. Usually, our conversation would turn to him telling me some amazing story from years ago. It might be when Peter was stuck for days in the rough ice up in White Bay, or maybe harvesting thousands of seals out in the middle of the main herd. Every story he told me was thrilling and epic. On days when there was little or no ice around, he would phone me, and as I reported it to him, I would hear a click just as the last words left my lips. It was funny—he would not even say goodbye, just hang up. I looked forward to his stories, and one day in the spring, his son Jack and grandson Gary (who was a friend of mine) visited the lighthouse. We had a great old chat that day, and it was a treat to finally meet this saltwater legend in person. He was a fascinating character.

Christmastime was never a holiday at Long Point Lighthouse. The lightkeeper was required to work an eight-hour shift every day. Each year, I cut a small Christmas tree and placed it in my living room there, because I would not be spending much time back home in my house in downtown Porterville.

December 30, 1987, I was invited to a big family supper at my parents' home. It had been snowing all day but not enough to prevent me from driving up for one of Mother's delicious cooked turkey meals with all the veggies and trimmings. I was so looking forward to this meal I could taste it. There would be around fifteen of the Porter clan there. Supper would be around 6:00 p.m., so I left Long Point at around four thirty. I was driving my trusty grey Toyota 4x4 pickup with my old Ski-Doo strapped down in the pan. I planned to do some snowmobiling around the remote areas of the island. After lifting my dear, crippled beagle aboard, I jumped in. I planned to stay the night and return early the next morning. By now it was dark and still snowing. I booted it down the steep hill and through Crow Head—there was very little traffic on the go. I guess I was a bit anxious to get home for Mother's cooking—I was cruising into the winding turns of Wild Cove a little too fast for the driving conditions. The speed limit was fifty, but not on this evening.

Suddenly, I spied a dark figure in the distance in front of me in the middle of the roadway. I touched my brakes, but nothing happened—the pavement was pure grease. It was an older gentleman clearing snow out of his driveway and scooping it across to the opposite side of the road—Mr. Wilson Guy, a well-respected and retired businessman around Twillingate. Getting closer, I had very little room or control to manoeuvre around him. I must have caught him off guard, because he stood there like a deer in my headlights. Desperately trying not to hit the poor fellow, I tried to gear down and gently brake at the same time, but it was useless. I knew I had to hit the ditch. Skidding past Mr. Guy, I busted through the snowbank and landed in the ditch with a mighty thud.

What a smack! It felt like my truck was wrecked. When the snowflakes finally settled, I helped my poor, scared beagle off the floor. She had landed upside down with a thump, but none the worse for wear, just a scared look on her face. I slowly climbed out of my truck just as Mr. Guy walked over to check on me. I was shaken but okay, and the most important thing was Wilson was untouched. I checked my truck for damage but could not find a scratch. The biggest issue was that I had flattened both of my front tires from the impact. I also noticed the two skis of my snowmobile were bent and my pan was dented from my Ski-Doo almost coming through my front seat.

As I chatted with Mr. Guy, in the back of my mind I could picture my hot Christmas supper going down the drain, but it could have been so much worse. Amazingly, just like Santa to the rescue, Brian Guy arrived on the scene in his payloader. He had been out clearing snow and was returning home for supper. I knew Brian through the hockey league I was playing with. He quickly hooked a strap to my truck and towed me to his garage, which luckily was only a few hundred feet down the road. Within minutes, Brian had my two tires inflated, and I was back on the road again in record time. As I was driving, I relived the accident in my mind. I could not believe what had just happened—one minute I was skidding out of control into the ditch, and the next I was back to driving as if nothing happened, all thanks to the Guys. What a Christmas evening after all. As it turned out, I was late for turkey supper by only ten minutes. Peace on earth!

Working at this tourist magnet during the summer months, I had the privilege of supervising and working with several talented summer students. They greeted the tourists and conducted daily guided tours up to the top of the light tower while telling them the rich history of Long Point. Divided into groups of eight to ten, thousands of tourists from all over the world made the climb to the top, observing the important main light and the breathtaking view from there. To name just a few of my students, there were Paul Dove, Derrick Dalley, Tracy Jenkins, Brenda Grimes, Patty Cooper, Barry Hicks, and Nancy Hamlyn, all great individuals who went on to become educators, chemists, health care workers, lawyers, and even a politician. We had fun and made special memories during those sunny summer months on the hill.

After four great years running this historic lighthouse, I felt it was time to move on. It was a difficult decision, because I loved it there, and Long Point and the Twillingate residents had been good to me. I had met many fine people, and I admired their way of life on this island.

Porterville was my home, and I had a house there that I built and had spent very little time in these past four years. I requested a transfer to an island light station that offered thirty-two days on and thirty-two days off. Jack May was working on Bacalhao Island Lighthouse at the time, and he wanted off, so we made a lateral transfer. On June 10, 1988, I received word from the Marine Aids Office that my transfer was accepted, and I would be finishing up in a couple of weeks. During my last week, I said my goodbyes to the friends I had made during my stay there. Several folks dropped by the light to wish me well, and my closest buddies had a party for me. A few days before I left, technicians Len Woodford and Dave Slade from Comfort Cove Radio surprised me by driving down and barbecuing a freshly caught salmon with me. On June 25, Saturday morning, I packed up all my personal belongings, locked the door to my favourite lighthouse, and returned home, ready to start another chapter in my career.

Barry Porter and Comfort Cove Coast Guard radio techs
Dave Slade and Len Woodford

Last supper at Long Point: Barry, Gypsy, and Alice

4 Life at Bacalhao Island Lighthouse, 1988

After spending four years stationed at beautiful Long Point Lighthouse on Twillingate Island, I was making the switch to Bacalhao Island. After looking across the eleven miles of blue ocean toward the station every day, I was now going to take up a new position as lightkeeper on this remote island.

Bacalhao Island Lighthouse was established on December 6, 1894. The island is located approximately three miles northeast of Herring Neck Point and just over four miles west of Change Islands in Notre Dame Bay. The light tower is on the highest point on the island, 348 feet above water. The iron tower was manufactured in St. John's by Victoria Iron Works. It had light characteristics: flash, white, normal range of twenty-one nautical miles. Description: circular tower, red and white spiral, cast iron with a red dome. Foghorn: blast three seconds, silence twenty-seven seconds. The light is located near the western entrance to Hamilton Sound, which is the body of water that most ships take when travelling into or out of Notre Dame Bay. This route takes marine traffic south of Change Islands and Fogo Island, saving approximately two hours and valuable fuel. Otherwise, they would have to cruise northward outside of Fogo Island and the Little Fogo Islands.

The permanent lightkeepers here were Ralph Hurley (principal keeper, 1967–1991), Harvey Walkins (assistant principal keeper, 1966–1991), Les Powell (1973–2001), and now me. I had made a lateral switch with Jack May—I replaced him there, and he took over my duties at Long Point Lighthouse. Jack had only worked about one year here, but he was not fond of work on this island. Some of the lightkeepers from the past included John Kearley, Edward Hussey, Bennett Stuckey, Raymond Miles, Cyril Cutler (1963–1966), Heber Stuckey (1963–1966), Allan Roberts (1963–1969), Eric Fudge (1963–1983), Wilson Guy (1969–1970), Harold Farthing (1970–1972), Stan Cabot (1972–1973), and Carl Greening (1984–1987). Later, lightkeepers Stu Welshman and Clayton Bowers worked there until the station was de-staffed. A few of the relief keepers who worked there over the years were Ed Loveless, John Card, Paul Fudge, Eric Dove, Gord Jones, and Brian Smart.

The original lightkeeper's dwelling was built up on the top of the hill on a landing near the light tower. It was a beautiful two-storey dwelling connected to the light tower with an enclosed wooden tunnel leading up to the tower. The lighthouse operated seasonally, shutting down during the winter when the bay was packed with Arctic ice. Ralph Hurley informed me the original dwelling was sold to Raymond Miles for $25. He took it down in 1965 and reused the lumber to build a house. The new, smaller bachelor dwelling was built on the island and opened in 1963. This was a much smaller building than most lightkeepers' houses. Along with the engine room and foghorn building, it was located on the west side of the island down near the ocean's edge. It is only 75–100 feet above sea level.

In a bad storm in late fall, I've seen four to five inches of slob ice built up on the clapboard outside my bedroom. It wasn't a good feeling trying to get to sleep and hearing the salt spray hitting the outside of the dwelling only inches from my head. I know of a couple of times when, with the rare combination of high tides, sea, and vicious winds, the ocean rose enough to wash over the cliffs and damage our sturdy walkway leading out to the foghorn building. That was scary!

The house had a full eight-foot basement that was above ground and sitting on cliff rocks. The main floor had the kitchen, dining room, and living room in the middle in one open large, square room. There were two bedrooms with two bunkbeds and two closets per room on the north side—these were shared by the four lightkeepers. The bedrooms were small with built-in wooden bunks that had several wooden drawers under the beds. There was one spare bedroom on the south side for a visiting technician or a relief lightkeeper. Also, there was a standard bathroom and a small room at the back wall off the main living area. This was where the mobile telephone and our first aid supplies were located. Downstairs, half of the small basement contained two deep-freezers, the furnace, a few supplies, and all our outdoor and work clothes, including coveralls and rubber clothes. There was a large wooden box for storing our vegetables, and a dartboard owned by Les was set up. The other half of the basement was occupied by our freshwater storage cistern.

Digging a well for drinking water was impossible at this station and at most lighthouses because they were built on solid rock. All the water we used for drinking, cooking, and washing was rainwater. It was collected from the oversized wooden eavestroughs built around the roof. All rainwater was channelled down into the basement, where it was filtered through a large compartment full of silicon sand. From there it would filter out to storage in our concrete cistern. It looked like a small swimming pool in our basement. It worked fine, as long as you did not waste water, especially during the winter months.

If we were lucky, sometimes we would get mild weather in late January or early February and be able to top up our supply. Back up over the walking trail was a little spring of water that drained from a small pond a few hundred yards beyond. The previous keepers had built a miniature wooden dam there to control the flow of water. During one of those mild days, we would have several hundred feet of black, two-inch waterlines that we fitted together to direct some of this surplus water down over the rocks and into our filtration system. This little top-up of water was a blessing that got us through the long, lean, rainless winter months. If we did not get this extra water, our laundry and bathing would be limited.

Bacalhao Island dwelling and sheds

There was a medium-sized helicopter pad next to the engine room building. Between these were our two main large storage tanks that supplied fuel for our important diesel generators. These large red tanks each contained 2,000 gallons of diesel fuel. There was a lovely white clapboarded storey and a half–storage shed just down under the hill near the dwelling. A steel track or tramway led from the ocean's edge up past the shed. Bolted into the rocks near the ocean was a large, steel spar and boom used to unload the station's annual supplies out of a barge from one of the Canadian Coast Guard ships that would service the lighthouses. We would load a small, flat trolley with cases of paint, cleaners, rope, toilet paper, etc., then use our gas-powered winch to pull the trolley up and down the rust-red steel tracks from the water's edge to the storage shed. We would also send back all our empty drums of fuel or motor oil onto the barge using this spar and boom and return them to the CCG ship. The station's supplies were dropped off there once a year, in the summer, when sea conditions were suitable. This was always a big production on the station. Later, in the early winter, we would have to climb down over the slippery rocks and chop off the excess ice buildup on the spar and the guy wires with an axe. It was amazing how quick the saltwater spray could build up on the cables. I have seen ice three feet thick frozen onto the one-inch guy wire. Thankfully, a few years later, we stopped using the spar boom and winch and relied on the Coast Guard helicopter to sling our supplies onto the helicopter pad. This system worked much better and was so much faster and safer. Every time we operated the old winch-and-cable trolley system, it was an accident waiting to happen.

Oil drums on trolley

Just a few hundred feet south of the boom/spar area was a small cove. It was somewhat sheltered from the northerly winds but only partly from the common swells. This was where we carried out our monthly shift changeovers when conditions were favourable. Boxes of food (frozen and fresh), books, and bags of clothes were thrown ashore like basketballs.

Spar and guy wires in storm

Canadian Coast Guard helicopter dropping off fuel drums

Then, four lightkeepers would make the switcheroo—two keepers leaping onto the wet rocks, and two lightkeepers jumping back into the bobbing speedboat. This lightkeeper waltz took place through sun, rain, wind, fog, or slop snow. When a sea was running, the trick was to jump out of the speedboat when it was riding up with the swell. You had to time your jump perfectly—if not, you could end up in the Atlantic. When seas were too rough, we carried out the changeover on the back of the island, hoping for calmer waters at Bottle Gulch. For the arriving lightkeepers, this meant having to make several trips across the island carrying all your monthly supplies to the dwelling. We would use knapsacks and our homemade wooden handbar stacked full with our boxes. Transporting all our supplies across the island was never much enjoyment, and it would happen quite often in the fall of the year, when the seas were working against us. In the winter months, our changeovers were completed with the aid of a Canadian Coast Guard helicopter.

Guy wire, iced, and John Card

Bottle Gulch was on the back side of the island facing the Hamilton Sound and Change Islands. A small growth of healthy fir trees in the valley led to the gulch area. This spot was a little notch carved out of the cliffs. We stored our new eighteen-foot "government" speedboat there. Also there was a nicely painted boathouse, a boat pad, a set of steps, and an old wooden ladder leading down to the edge of the bone-chilling sea. We had another spar and boom set up there, which was connected to a winch by a long cable. This winch was an old cast-iron, two-man manual winch. It had two long handles sticking out from opposite ends for cranking purposes. It was bolted down into a concrete block and rocks, put here back in 1894, and it worked amazingly well.

Bottle Gulch from chopper (Photo courtesy of Gordie Simmons)

John Card with boat winched in mid-air

The gulch had cliffs located on three sides. It could be a calm oasis or an extremely dangerous spot. The gulch was on the protected side of the island, away from the northern winds, but often the seas would churn around this little cove like a broken flushing toilet. When the sea conditions were favourable, we would lower the speedboat down for shift changes, to go out for the odd jig of fish, or to hunt a seal. If the seas were civil, there was no problem—it would be a picnic. If there was a moderate sea running, you had to be careful and quick on your feet. Usually it was a two-man operation, but if the seas were calm, one man could do the boat launch.

The boat would normally be tied down on the pad near the boathouse. Our first move was to winch the boat up approximately a foot off the pad, then we would swing the boom and boat out fully by pulling on the ropes until it was carefully positioned directly above the gulch and the sea below. Then we would tie the boom in position with ropes so it did not swing in by the wind or by the strain of its own weight. We would cautiously winch the boat down closer to the edge of the moving ocean. It was always a strange sight to see a shiny white eighteen-foot fibreglass boat hanging in mid-air like a leaf blowing in the wind. Once the boat was in place, I would climb down the rickety old steps and make the giant leap right into the dangling boat. From here, it was all about timing. I had only a few seconds before the seas would again wash around the gulch like a whirlpool. I had to make sure everything was in place for the next important manoeuvre. First, the speedboat had to be pointing straight out of the cove, the drain plug had to be inserted, and the paddles, gaff, or ropes had to be in place, unable to get tangled. The little space I was standing in had to be clear and safe. Patiently, I would watch the sea conditions around me and the incoming swells. It was not scientific, but it seemed that after seven swells washed in around the gulch, sometimes there would be a little break, a few extra seconds to make my move. When the cove was calm, I would shout out to the lightkeeper manning the winch up above. He was out of my sight, operating blindly. He would then quickly lower me and the boat down, the last couple of feet, into the churning ocean. With my heart pumping, every second counted. Like a pit stop racing crew member at Indianapolis Motor Speedway, I would quickly pull out the choke on the motor, squeeze the rubber primer ball on the fuel line, adjust the throttle, and pull the twenty-five-horsepower Evinrude outboard motor to life. As soon as it sounded like it was running, I would detach the big hook and cables, snap it in gear, and escape out of that saltwater flush box before the next swell rolled in. Mission accomplished!

Bacalhao Island was a beautiful little island measuring just over two miles long and approximately a third of a mile wide. There were a couple dozen small ponds ranging in sizes. Also, there were several large bog areas with deep sinkholes, a few small valleys where large, healthy fir trees grew freely, and other places where stumpy, wind-beaten spruce trees struggled to survive. They were probably hundreds of years old and only three to four feet in height, tangled like thick steel wool. There were the rare patches where the elusive bakeapples grew but also large areas scattered across the island where you could fill your bucket with tasty marshberries or partridgeberries. There were valleys where gales of northern winds funnelled though, leaving rocky walkways

Lightkeeper Ralph Hurley in CCG boat in the gulch

embedded like cobblestones. Toward the eastern end were sea arches, caves, sea stacks, and another small, rocky archway inland. Then there was Bacalhao Harbour, a sheltered but rocky cove. It was the only harbour on the island. There was a long, narrow entrance leading into it, which was wide enough for a single speedboat. Inside was this little haven shaped like a bowl. There were a couple of old, abandoned hunting shacks, built during the glory days of seal hunting a decade or two ago, tucked into the trees.

There were numerous interesting rock formations spread throughout in some of the most obscure nooks and crannies, some hidden by sheer cliffs with only one life-threatening route into it if a certain lightkeeper dared. Just up the path from Bottle Gulch was a small, protected area with something rare—topsoil. Here we farmed a few fresh vegetables every summer—a few potatoes and carrots. The more vegetables we were able to grow, the fewer we had to carry out in boxes to the station. For a rugged rock set in the Atlantic Ocean, there were countless interesting things going on here.

On the days when there were no projects to work on or a technician needing a helping hand, I would take time to explore the island. I walked, climbed, and skied miles and miles over its rocks, every shift, for the four years I worked there. I scaled cliffs and crawled through crevices that no man had seen in years. After many of my hikes, I would often return with one of those large orange floats with me, the ones used on fishing gear or for bumpers on boats. I would find them sitting in remote coves or wedged under huge rocks somewhere. The other lightkeepers were not scouting over the rocks or climbing the cliffs like me. Most of the others were older and had no interest in exploring. Lightkeeper Harvey Watkins used to call me a "mink."

I found over a dozen of those orange floats, some faded to white from being trapped under a rock for years. I gave several of them away and kept a few for my own use. I remember once even trading two or three large floats with a fisherman in Herring Neck for a salt beef tub of fresh cod tongues. The combination of coves, cliffs, ponds, bogs, and wooded areas made traversing the island fascinating, challenging, and enjoyable. It was a good workout for my body and for my soul.

It was a sunny Friday morning, July 15, 1988, when I met up with relief lightkeeper John Card in Merritt's Harbour. This was my first time meeting him. We loaded the speedboat with our boxes of supplies, everything required to survive on the island for thirty-two days. Because I was going there for my first time, I had extra gear this trip—a dozen cardboard boxes neatly tied up—including my food, clothes, bedding, a little twelve-inch TV, CB radio, antenna, books, and of course my trusty Nikon camera. I took my camera everywhere. I had my small ghetto blaster, too, because I liked to have music with me.

Summer hike down over the island

John and I steamed out from the protection of Merritt's Harbour and into the wide, choppy ocean. We passed by Berry Island, where I spotted an abandoned fishing shack, and then proceeded on to the mysterious lighthouse island. We landed in the little cove beneath the station for the shift changeover. This was my first time setting foot on Bacalhao Island.

I was looking forward to seeing a new lighthouse with new routines and schedules to learn. I settled into the life there well. Two lightkeepers were on the station for thirty-two days, then off for thirty-two days. The thirty-two days off were always the best. We were paid for our days off, which was good, plus I was entitled to four weeks' holidays per year. Our annual pay was on the low side of the Canadian Coast Guard pay scale, and peanuts compared to the pay the rotational workers receive these days, but our benefits with the federal department were good.

I was responsible for every second day on the station. My shift was two eight-hour turns every second day. I would go on shift at 0200 hours (2:00 a.m.), work till 1000 hours (10:00 a.m.), then go back on 1400 hours (2:00 p.m.) to 2200 hours (10:00 p.m.). Then, technically, I was off the next day. I would record the weather conditions, take note of any marine traffic, and check the main light and the engine room. Everything was documented into the lightkeeper's logbook. Our main light up in the light tower, the fog alarm, and the dwelling were all powered by a Lister diesel motor generator.

There were three Lister motors at this station, three cylinders rated at eighteen horsepower. Attached to each motor was a remote oil reservoir that contained twenty-five gallons of oil. This, along with an excellent cooling system, meant these dependable motors could run for months. Amazingly, I've seen the odd one run non-stop for over a year. They were the heart of the station, operating twenty-four hours a day, seven days a week, month after month. It was crucial that we check the Lister motors every four hours. I would get dressed and scamper out across the path over the wooden ramp in the rain, snow, wind, fog, and sometimes during a bad storm I would duck buckets of salt spray while heading to the fog alarm building. Once inside, I would put on my ear protection, as the roar of the Lister motor was deafening. I would give the complete unit an inspection because "strange" things could happen when it had been running non-stop for months. I have seen fuel lines break and squirt greasy fuel out all over the floor, clamps vibrate loose, oil leaks, exhaust hoses break, you name it. The well-run motors would almost always require a little oil wipe-down with a clean rag. Often, oil would seep from minor gasket leaks. I would do regular checks of the large batteries and top up their water levels when required and inspect the cooling system. There were two other Lister motors for backup sitting side by side. If the main unit shut down for whatever reason, a backup motor was programmed to start automatically within minutes. Most times they did, but occasionally there would be trouble, and I or the other lightkeeper would have to go into the engine room and start the backup Lister manually. The never-ending chug, chug, chug was always echoing out from the engine room. The light must shine!

Also located on this island were two range (navigational) lights. These were coloured lights mounted on two high towers and powered by solar panels. These two important range lights aided ships when cruising in through this route. We were responsible for maintaining the large batteries at the base of the towers and occasionally replacing a burned-out bulb in the range light.

Usually, the lightkeeper who was off-duty that day was responsible for cooking the dinner. Every day we had a tasty cooked meal for dinner. I must add, the older lightkeepers had a set, regulated menu at this station. They were not fond of diverting from this regimented schedule that had been established here for decades. Fish had to be on Friday, Saturday was soup day, and Sunday was a full cooked dinner—either a chicken, roast of beef, or pork. Monday was frozen chicken and chips, Tuesday was Jiggs' dinner, Wednesday was pork chops or sausages and potatoes, and Thursday was a Jiggs' dinner again. I will never forget that menu. Every now and then, I had to change it up slightly.

When there was work required, you worked along with your partner. Regardless if it was your day off, if there was work to be done, we did it—whether scraping and painting on the dwelling, moving a forty-five-gallon fuel or oil drum, or painting the light tower.

Bacalhao Lighthouse was always kept in top condition. Dear old Ralph made sure of that. It was a clean station—the house and engine/foghorn building were swept and mopped regularly. The day or two before our shift changeover, we would make an extra cleanup effort throughout. Everything would be spotless when we left the island and the incoming lightkeepers took over.

The maintenance of the station was also important. It had to be—if not, the harsh winds and salt air would show wear and tear on the oil-painted clapboard and railings in no time. This entire light station had a two-year schedule, which meant every building (including the dwelling and light tower), every rail, fence, and wooden stairs were scraped, primed, and painted with gallons of glossy Matchless marine oil paint. Winter months were the period to complete all the inside painting. For some strange reason, paint rollers and trays were never ordered for the station—whenever we painted the interior walls or floors, the oil paint was always applied by brushes and lots of elbow grease! Every shift, we would be assigned certain projects. I know a lightkeeper who would put off his share of painting until the last few days on the island. Then he would spend hours slapping on the oil paint, day and night, finishing up his portion of the work. It was amusing to watch.

When working outdoors, we had to work around the rainy and frequently windy days. That was always a challenge on this weather-beaten island. The most important marine aid at this lighthouse was the main light tower. Perched on the top of the hill, it measured twenty-five feet high with a wide red and white spiral band painted down through it like a giant candy cane. At the base of it was a small, white, clapboard wooden shed. Being surrounded by salt water and spray, the tower, especially the white parts, quickly turned to a rusty stain colour.

Painting this unique light tower was always a big production. First, we would have to carry gallons of red and white paint, brushes, ropes, and rags, along with a ladder, up to the top of the hill. Then we would have to climb up an aluminum ladder with a chipping hammer, a gallon of primer and a brush, and hang on for dear life. I would tie the ladder on so that, hopefully, if would not slip on the round tower. I'd attach another piece of rope around my waist, tie that to the railing above me, and hope to God I did not fall! Looking back and being wiser, I realize now that we broke every safety rule in the book while painting this old light tower. I guess we had no fear back then. It was expected of us to complete this tedious paint job, safety or not, because that was how the lightkeepers had done it for the past century. The lightkeeper would have to chip off all the rust and the blisters of swollen paint, then apply an ugly rusty coat of primer onto the freshly chipped cast iron.

I would let it dry for a day or so, then return to apply the bright red and shiny white paint to it. To do this, I would hook the cans of two different colours of paint onto a rung of the ladder and start from the top, just under the circular walkway, slowly painting my way to the bottom. The red and white swirl was terribly sensitive to paint. I would be working with two wet edges of fresh oil paint, one red and one white. You had to be careful, because if one tiny drop of red paint dropped off onto the wet white band, then all of a sudden you had pink paint! Gradually, day after day, we worked our way down to the base of the old tower, onto the rocks that were spattered with paint from previous lightkeepers. When it was completed, the tower looked brilliant. This gleaming red and white spiral tower looked like a giant candy cane sitting on top of this barren hill. It was a lovely piece of artwork.

Left: Barry painting light tower on ladder Right: Tower painted

During my four years working on Bacalhao Island, I am proud to say, I painted that beautiful beast of a light tower twice, along with the help of another lightkeeper. Besides having to work around the uncertain weather conditions, sometimes other challenges popped up. I first helped paint the tower in May of 1989 with Ralph. We had excellent, calm weather that month when we were preparing to start this painting job. In a short time we had carried all the paint supplies up to the top of hill. Soon, I discovered my co-worker was colour blind! He could not distinguish the difference between the ugly primer paint and the bright red paint. I could not believe it at first—I thought he was joking—but old Ralph did not joke around. I had a difficult time convincing him not to use that primer for the glossy red finish. He was convinced the cans were labelled incorrectly. After some friendly debate, he finally believed me—I think. By the end of our shift, we had the light tower completely repainted and had it looking brand new. We were very proud of our paint job.

Two years later, the large light tower was due to be painted again. The white was getting rusty from two years in this salt environment. Relief lightkeeper Gord Jones was working with me this time. My regular partner, Ralph, had retired after two decades of dedicated service. It was late July when the weather finally co-operated, and we got geared up to paint this structure again. We had all the paint, brushes, ladders, cleaners, and rags in place. We had opened a few cans of primer and were stirring up the paint when, unexpectedly, my buddy disclosed to me that he was afraid of heights. What? He was not joking. My good buddy Gord was dead serious. I will give him credit, though—he did try. He struggled to climb up the short ladder, a few feet off the rocks, but he was shaking like a leaf. I could not have this—it was now a safety issue—so I told him to forget it. I ended up painting the entire darn tower, from the tip of the weathervane on top right down to the bottom—well, except for the bottom five or six feet of the structure. Gord did a great job painting that section! The paint job was completed on August 13, 1991. The old light tower glistened in the sun again with a new, glossy coat of paint on a red and white spiral. It looked absolutely beautiful once again.

Bacalhao Island, Highlights

It was December 19, 1988. I kissed my wife, Alice, goodbye and climbed into the Canadian Coast Guard helicopter, which was already starting to rev up. We lifted off from the government wharf in my hometown of Porterville, bound for Bacalhao Lighthouse. This was my first helicopter ride to the island. All my previous trips were by speedboat. We flew down over country that I had never seen before from the air. It was interesting to look out over the ponds, bogs, and woods road that I had often snowmobiled through over the past few years. In about twenty-five minutes, we touched down on the helicopter pad on Bacalhao Island. My co-worker had been dropped off an hour earlier. This was going to be my first Christmas spent on this isolated island surrounded by snow covered-cliffs and icy seas. I was sitting in the middle of the Atlantic Ocean on a lonely rock for the next thirty-two days. I was there from December 19, 1988, to January 20 of the next year. This was a new experience, but I settled in.

I always loved Christmas, but spending it on Bacalhao Island was going to be a challenge. I boxed up a few decorations and brought them out with me in the helicopter to try to spread some Christmas spirit at the lighthouse. The weather was so cold, windy, and damp you could hardly go outdoors, and some days I didn't. There was almost no marine traffic around and the days were short, but the nights were long. A few days into it, I knew it was going to be a long, dreary shift on this lonely island. I would try to make nightly radio contact with Alice back home, but it was such a long distance for the CB radio system that many times there was too much static to carry on a sensible conversation. That became frustrating after a while. I would make daily radio contact with the lightkeepers on Surgeon's Cove Head Lighthouse through the VHF radio. That was a blessing, because I knew they were also working through Christmas. Our other co-workers over on Cape John Gull Island Lighthouse had closed for the season the previous week and were now sitting comfortably at home. The lucky dogs!

There was enough snow on the ground to turn everything white, but there was little Christmas spirit here. My co-worker on this shift was much older than me, a nice guy, but he was incredibly old-fashioned. He believed Christmas had no place at work. This was my work, but it was also my home for thirty-two days.

Christmas was getting closer by the hour, so the heck with it—I made the decision: I am cutting a Christmas tree and putting it up! I really needed to. On December 21, I took my axe and trotted back over the barren land to a little wooded area in search for a tree. There wasn't exactly a Christmas tree farm on Bacalhao, but I managed to cut a suitable one. Perfect! I let it dry off, then mounted it in a customized salt beef bucket, and placed it by the back wall in our kitchen area.

Christmas tree

I did not know what skipper thought of it, but he was only filling in there for a few weeks. I have had a real Christmas tree every year of my life, even years ago when I lived out in the bleak northern area of Thompson, Manitoba. It gets cold up there, and pretty trees are difficult to find. Even there, I took a day off work, and my buddy and I managed to cut a skinny tree in frosty, minus-forty-degree conditions. To this day, I still cut my own real tree every Christmas, and I plan to until I am too old to do so. It is an important part of my Christmas tradition.

I decorated my little five-foot Bacalhao Christmas tree the best I could, and it looked beautiful. The other lightkeeper said that was a first for there. Apparently, no lightkeeper had ever put up a tree in this dwelling. By now it was December 23, Christmas music was all over the radio, and Christmas shows were on TV. It was good, even if I was watching the shows on the lighthouse's pitiful little black and white twenty-inch TV. But I was getting the blues, the lonely homesick Christmas blues. I was stuck on this godforsaken rock missing the woman I loved—missing the Porter family clan, missing the Christmas food, and parties that I knew were happening all around.

It was time for a walk. I bundled up and went for a nice slow trot up to the "mountaintop," to the light tower. The fresh air filled my lungs, and the view was amazing from up there. It reinvigorated me. Up there, surrounded by the harsh, unforgiving landscape, there was still a beauty about it, and it felt good for my soul. Later that evening, I had a good talk on the radio with my buddy Gord Jones, who was working up on Surgeon's Cove Head. I knew he felt much like myself, as we were both working through the Christmas holidays.

Early on Christmas Eve morning, I took my turkey out and sawed the bird in half with a nice sharp handsaw from the shed. I left one half out to thaw for roasting. Later that afternoon, I went for another walk down toward Crow Head. The hike over the slippery rocks and through the snow-covered trees helped me fight off the Christmas blues and refresh my head. Then it was Christmas Eve night. I poured up a drink of rum and went down in the basement and had a game of darts by myself. I think I won. It was a lonely old night, and I was just killing time, throwing a few darts, and listening to the radio. The program drifting out of the radio that night was *Night Lines* out of CBC Winnipeg with host

Ralph Benmergui. It was an excellent music show. I'll never forget when he played the song "River" by Joni Mitchell. The timing, my mood—it hit me hard. A few lonely tears rolled down my cheek. I was missing my Alice. A little later, I got my act together, left the dull, mournful basement, and went back upstairs. I then put a few gifts under my little Christmas tree—gifts that Alice had given me—and I even placed one there for skipper. Then I called it quits and dived into my cold bed.

Dwelling surrounded in ten-tenths coverage in Arctic ice

I woke up Christmas morning in no real rush to get out of bed. There was a blizzard on outside, a gale of strong southeast winds, visibility zero in snow, and minus four degrees. Slowly, I got up my nerve and crawled out of my bunk. I got a cup of tea, then opened a couple of small gifts from my sweetie. Later, I cooked and served a delicious turkey dinner with all the trimmings. It was good, but it was not like Mother's Christmas dinner back home. That night I talked to Alice on the mobile phone, and later I phoned my dear mother. That made me feel better inside.

Boxing Day came, and I went for another walk out through the barren, snow-covered landscape. By the next day, the Christmas spirit was quickly fading around the station. I was also getting sick of hearing my co-worker grumble about having a Christmas tree at the lighthouse. He would even comment about it to his buddies on the CB radio. Later that afternoon, I grabbed my tree and threw it, still half-decorated, out over the cliff into the salt seas below. Christmas was over, period. Two years later, I did the same darn thing all over again. Peace on earth!

I was three-quarters through my lengthy shift on Bacalhao Island when I started to count off my days. I would hardly look at a calendar until I was a few days over the halfway mark. That was in my constitution out there. Winter months were always the longest, especially on this remote island. Sometimes, if you were lucky, the Marine Aids Office would send out a couple of technicians to repair the furnace or install a new Lister motor. In that case, the men would usually have to stay at the lighthouse for a few days. To have company and another person to talk to was always a pleasant change. Nighttime meant a few entertaining games of cards and stories. This social interaction was always good for the mind. It really helped break up the long shifts, especially during the stormy winter season. Many months, we would not have a visitor or even sight a ship or a speedboat—nothing but a white landscape of rough Arctic ice as far as the eye could see. As old Skipper John would say, "A solid jam of ice and a black tick of fog." Often, the only life I saw was a scattered crow or seagull. Even they looked like they were sick of the winter season.

The spring of 1989 was a bad one with considerable amounts of Arctic ice hanging about and many days of terribly damp, foggy days. One day, May 18, happened to be sunny with blue skies and calm winds on the island. Status quo, day in day out—soon I would be going back home to my loved one.

Barry Porter hiking during the winter

I was cleaning up the dishes after our cooked dinner when, suddenly, out of nowhere I heard the roar of a helicopter landing on our helicopter pad. The pad was seventy-five feet from the dwelling, and the house vibrated every time a helicopter visited. Strange, there had been no radio call on the VHF, just touchdown! I eagerly scooted out to see what was happening. Visitors, oh joy! I stood back a little and waited for the helicopter to shut down and for its long blades to stop rotating. I did recognize the pilot as Kenny, but I could not see his co-pilot. Then this person exited, and it was the one and only Charlie Falk from Gander. It could not be old Chuck, could it? What a pleasant surprise! Charlie was an old biker friend of mine from the motorcycle club days in the 1970s. Charlie was a bit of an eccentric guy. He had a long beard and often travelled with his pet rat or pet crow. An interesting character but the best kind! He was also one of Newfoundland's best photographers and operated a busy photography shop in Gander called Falk Foto. After they climbed out of the rig, to my surprise, a lovely lady with long, flowing hair stepped out from the rear door. Wow! I could not believe my eyes. She wore bright red lipstick and was covered in a full-length fur coat. After spending almost thirty days on this rock, surrounded by strings of Arctic ice stretching out for miles, she sure looked beautiful to me. We chatted, then I invited them to come inside for a cup of tea. We had a good talk, but the gorgeous woman did not say a word, just smiled and looked pretty. It worked for me, but I wondered, was she a TV star or a model, and what the heck was she was doing out in the middle of this ice-infested world? Details were scanty but no big deal, I was more than happy to see another human being at this point. After tea, they jumped aboard the shiny red helicopter, and in a flash, off they flew. They had big smiles on their faces, and they certainly put a big smile on my face as well. It was definitely the highlight of my spring shift!

A year or so later, I was visiting Charlie in his photo studio in Gander, when suddenly he called out from his back room. There he produced several glossy eight-by-ten photos from that magical day. The mystery lady posed professionally with the bright red and white helicopter. The contrast of the ruggedness of the background, made the photos look spectacular. Rumour has it the "special" photo shoot had taken place that day near a light off Lushes Bight. Charlie certainly had the eye for snaps. The unofficial word was the Canadian Coast Guard had sent Kenny out to check on some of the smaller navigation lights in part of Notre Dame Bay. He just happened to bring a couple of passengers with him for company—his good buddy Charlie and the mystery smiling lady. Charlie then informed me that the quiet, pretty lady was an exotic dancer visiting from Quebec and performing at the famous Flyers Club in Gander. What a treat for the boys! And a treat for this lightkeeper.

May 24 was my thirty-third birthday, and I was spending it on the island without loved ones, but at least I had a warm day with not a draft of wind. For a treat, I went out seal hunting for the first time in my life. Ralph gave me a hand lowering down the government boat, and I soaked down around the eastern end. The sea was flat calm like a mirror. The bay was scattered with loose pans of Arctic ice and the odd humpback whale swimming by looking for lunch. I was a couple of miles just northeast of the island, and my landscape was almost surreal. I slowly manoeuvred around the pristine ice, taking in the beauty and also looking for the elusive seal. I saw a few, but they disappeared before I could get a shot. In no time, another seal popped its head up out of the water. I quickly turned the boat toward the shiny black target and fired off a shot—I didn't touch a thing. I made a couple more attempts, but no luck. Steering the boat and shooting at the same time was difficult when you were a rookie. So, I called off my great seal hunt trip and decided to soak back toward Bacalhao Island.

As I approached the end of the island, a large humpback whale came to the surface. I had my Nikon camera with me, so I attempted to get a close-up photo. I observed the beast for several minutes from a distance. This animal was huge. It was bobbing gently in the water when it slowly dived in under, so I quickly steamed over to where it disappeared and left my motor idling. They recommend that so the whale knows exactly where you are located in case it resurfaces near you to take another breath. The ripples left in the ocean where the humpback dives is called the footprint. I sat in the middle of it in the eighteen-foot speedboat, watching the ripples extend many feet out from my bow and stern. This whale was massive.

I suddenly felt like a tiny, baby pimple in this flat, wide ocean. This began to spook me a little—I was out of my comfort zone, so I decided it was time to move on. As I gave the motor a little throttle, I glanced out over the gunnels of my boat and saw the large white section of the humpback that is under the side fin. It was right there, swimming just under the surface, maybe curious what this birthday lightkeeper was up to. Due to my close encounter with this large creature, I called off my excursion and headed back to my home port of Bottle Gulch. There, I slowly winched the government boat back in place on the boat pad. What a day I had spent soaking about on the ocean! Conditions could not have been better. It was another thrilling experience, being up close with Mother Nature. Priceless.

The summer of 1989 was an excellent one for me. I carried out something I believe I am the only man ever to do on Bacalhao Island. It was early Friday morning, August 18, when I cruised into the town of Herring Neck harbour to pick up my girlfriend. I had left the island early because I was concerned there appeared to be a sea making. I picked up my sweet Alice, and by 10:00 a.m. I was safely back in Bottle Gulch with the government boat resting up on the boat pad. By lunchtime there was a big sea running, and I would not have been able to land there, but the early boat ride worked out perfectly. It was nice to have my soulmate on the island with me for a few days. Saturday was a lovely sunny day, so we packed a picnic and walked down across the island to the tiny, secluded Bacalhao Harbour. Sunshine, blue sky, and calm winds made for a peaceful and tranquil setting. There was a slight wash around the smooth rocks from the previous day's sea.

While relaxing there having a little snack on the edge of the ocean, Alice spotted a clear plastic bottle floating around in the narrow cove. She noticed something in the bottle, so we threw rocks to splash it closer until she reached out and grabbed it. Then she unscrewed the stopper and read a message inside the bottle. The main part of the message read, "I love you," and, "Will you marry me?" Thank goodness she said yes! I'd say this was the first official proposal ever made on Bacalhao Island.

Earlier, without Alice knowing, I had hiked down over the island to Bacalhao Harbour. I planted the bottle on a rocky edge, knowing the tide was rising and, maybe in a few hours, this "love note bottle" might float into the bottom of the tiny harbour. Luckily, my plan worked flawlessly. If it hadn't, I could have accidentally proposed to someone over on Change Islands. The next day, I transported Alice back to her car in Herring Neck. On my return to the island, I stopped on Young Grassy grounds and jigged five nice cod-fish. I was an incredibly happy lightkeeper. I was getting married!

During the fours years I worked on the island, I carried out changeovers from Herring Neck, Merritt's Harbour, Salt Harbour, and once or twice we had to leave in boat from Pikes Arm, because the wind and sea were just too rough to safely depart from Herring Neck. We travelled in eighteen-to-twenty-foot open speedboats to a classic old twenty-nine-foot wooden trap skiff owned by the Card family. Any changeovers from Porterville were always carried out by Canadian Coast Guard helicopter.

Friday, December 8, 1989, was an eventful changeover for Ralph and me. We were due to leave the island, and Harvey and Les were scheduled to work the Christmas shift there. We had phoned the Marine Aids Office in St. John's a few days earlier and requested a helicopter for that day. It was always a gamble when the chopper had to fly all the way from St. John's that time of the year. Weather and schedules were always a concern. That day there was a storm headed our way. By mid-morning, we received word that the helicopter was not flying. Ralph informed Harvey there was no helicopter, so it was now on to Plan B. They had to move fast because the forecast was poor. A snowstorm was racing our way and coming closer by the minute. The incoming shift lined up John Card to bring them out to the island and return us back using an eighteen-foot open speedboat. Considering we knew the storm was bearing down on us, we should have cancelled the changeover, but the older, experienced guys said they could pull it off in time. The sky was getting dark and ugly when John landed the two lightkeepers down in the cove. We transferred all the boxes and bags as fast as we could, but always being cautious, on the slippery rock. Nobody wanted to end up in the ice-cold Atlantic Ocean that day.

By now, it was getting late for shift changeovers by an open boat. It was approximately 2:00 p.m. when we departed the icy rocks in the cove and were headed to the safe harbour of Herring Neck. We were only 500 yards out from the cove when the snow and wind hit us. It came on fast and hard—blinding, sideways snow and rough seas within minutes. I pulled up the hood on my yellow, Coast Guard–issued rubber jacket, turned back-on to the northern winds, and hung onto the seat for dear life. The distance from the southwestern end of Bacalhao Island to the Starve Head, which opened to Herring Neck harbour, was just less than three miles. Visibility was reduced to about a hundred feet, but I put my trust in the two experienced men with me. We should pass Berry Island midway during our trip in. This rocky island measured approximately one mile in length and would provide us with much-needed shelter from the terrible northerly winds. I was getting cold and damp by now, and it was becoming a miserable boat ride.

We punched our way along through salt spray blowing over us, along with the blinding snow, but no sign of Berry Island yet. We continued slowly in this set direction, but I could tell from the men's faces there was trouble. We continued cruising into the unknown and still no sign of Berry Island. I was growing concerned as we slowed down to a crawl. Then, finally, they said we were off course. It could easily happen in poor visibility with snow biting into your face. We were lost! This was before cellphones or GPS, but not before compasses.

However, the “captain” never bothered to bring his compass. Old-school thinking, “Nobody needs that foolishness!” Well, it would have helped us that stormy afternoon lost in the horizontal snow. We could not see any landmarks anywhere due to the thick blowing snow. We could not tell if we were headed south or west. We were in a white cloud of snow and freezing rain. I said I noticed, when we were steaming, the track of water behind the motor was not straight—it appeared we had been veering slightly to the west. That meant we would have passed north of Berry Island, missing it completely.

We regrouped, gathered our thoughts, and set off again. Now paying the strictest attention to our direction, we inched along. After battling the harsh elements for over an hour, we finally sighted land. Hooray! Ralph and John knew every inch of every rock around there but could not recognize where we were. With the snow blocking out the background landscape, every rock and cliff looked the same. They still did not know where we were. We slowly soaked along the shoreline until there was a slight improvement in the visibility, when suddenly, skipper recognized a landmark. Praise the Lord! Our spirits lifted. We had tracked to the west, headed toward the main causeway that connected to Twillingate Island. We were off course by a mile or two. Things were looking up—we were not totally frozen yet, and the main thing was we still had fuel for our outboard motor. We cautiously continued following the shoreline and finally found the entrance before we tucked into the back of Merritt’s Harbour. What a relief when we tied up the ice-covered boat to the wharf!

Man, I was mighty glad to get on dry land that cold December afternoon. It could have turned out so much worse. With that frightening and exhausting boat ride behind me, I headed home to good old Porterville for Christmas.

Visitors to the remote island of Bacalhao were rare, but they were always welcomed. Located as it was on the edge of the often-turbulent Atlantic Ocean, not many people dropped by. I could count on my two hands the number of visitors I saw during my four years on the island. It was a warm, sunny day in July on my first shift when some of the family members of relief lightkeeper John Card visited. They came out in the family's big trap skiff. It was a huge wooden motorboat measuring twenty-nine feet in length.

Much later, on March 14, 1989, we had a visitor from Ottawa—the Deputy Minister of Transport, Mr. Ron Jackson—and he was accompanied by Mr. Ray Browne, the Regional Director of the Canadian Coast Guard from the Southside Coast Guard base in St. John's. They were travelling by CCG helicopter. First, they visited the icebreaker *Sir Humphrey Gilbert*, which was escorting the Fogo Island–Change Islands ferry. From there they flew to Bacalhao Lighthouse for a little tour. It was nice to meet Mr. Jackson and Mr. Browne. I would meet Ray many more times during my career. We always had a friendly relationship. We had our lighthouse freshly cleaned and mopped from top to bottom for this visit. I heard later that, aboard the icebreaker, the ship's crew had repainted the exact route Mr. Jackson would walk—only from the flight deck to the bridge and back. I'm sure it looked in top shape.

A visitor known as the "Young Puffin" from Change Islands visited by speedboat on August 12,1989. After a year of communication with Glen Hurley through the CB radios, it was good to finally put a face to the voice I had been talking to. On June 12, 1990, we had more visitors. It was a nice day, and I had just spent the morning planting four beds of potatoes in the little garden over near Bottle Gulch. When I walked back to the station for lunch, Fisheries Officers Harvey Horwood and Clarence Mitchell had just landed down in the cove. I invited them in for a cup of tea and a chat. They were out on patrol from Twillingate. I knew both men, and it was good to see them. During my previous four years working on Long Point Lighthouse, I had played hockey with these guys. They were local hockey legends there.

A year later, I was working with Gord Jones for a shift, and we had the most visitors ever. On July 31, 1990, Fisheries Officers Wilson Jenkins and Allan Vincent paid us a visit. August 1991 was beautiful weather-wise throughout my shift. Gord and I kept busy painting and doing maintenance. We had been carrying several 100-year-old bricks from the original old house, up near the tower, down near the new dwelling. It was August 10 when we constructed a small barbecue pit down on the only grassy knob around the dwelling. We had just finished placing the last brick when Dr. John Sheldon and his wife, Kathy, paid us a visit. It was nice to see them—he was a popular doctor in the New World Island Clinic. He moored off his beautiful sailboat, the *Shel Duck*, and paddled in. We had a pleasant visit with them. Only days later, on August 13, Bill and Pansy Strong also visited. Bill was a radio operator at Comfort Cove Coast Guard Radio. I had been talking to him daily for several years with weather and ice reports. They were in their lovely black and white sailboat named *Kocomo*. Bill had skilfully built this large sailboat by himself next to his house in Lewisporte. A few days later, Lightkeeper Arch Budgell and his wife, Bonnie, visited on August 14. Arch wanted to see the place after many years of talking to the lightkeepers on this island. Our final visitors were on August 17. Brothers Terry and Earl Fancy from Lewisporte dropped in en route to Change Islands. That is my complete list of visitors for the four years on the island.

The year 1990 started off with great news for me. After working unofficially full-time (without a break in service) since I went to Long Point Lighthouse in July 1984, I finally became a full-time federal employee. I had been signing the government "work term" papers every six months for more than five years, and finally the Canadian Coast Guard were hiring me. Due to the ever-constant "lighthouse automation" threat hanging over lightkeepers, they were reluctant to hire another keeper into their system, even though I was paying in to my union dues and pension plan. Eventually, word came down from the big boss in Ottawa to hire me. I joked that Prime Minister Brian Mulroney had to sign it off.

Later, in July, Alice and I got married in the little white United Church in downtown Porterville. A few days after, we lovebirds departed on a honeymoon motorcycle tour to the mainland. With a "Just Married" sign attached to my bike, we cruised through the Cabot Trail on Cape Breton, then over to PEI, and on to my buddy's place in Whitby, Ontario. Then we returned driving through New York State, Vermont, New Hampshire, Maine, and finally back to Newfoundland. Then it was back to "keeping light" on Bacalhao Island.

On Sunday, September 16, 1990, I walked up over the big hill near the light tower for a good look around the seascape. The great Newfoundland fiddle player Rufus Guinchard had passed away a few days earlier at age ninety-one. I had seen Rufus perform and met the dear old man a few times at various folk festivals in Newfoundland and Nova Scotia. I enjoyed his music, so I decided to build a little tribute in memory of him. I built a naked man on the western end. (A naked man is a stack of rocks piled on top of each other three to four feet high, visible from the sea. It is sort of like an Inukshuk but not quite.)

Wednesday, April 24, 1991, I flew out to Bacalhao Island and took up duties with Ralph. The past few days, hundreds of seals had been taken by the local sealers. The weather and ice conditions had been ideal for seal hunting. They were harvesting quite a few seals off Exploits Island and Twillingate areas. Many thousands of harp seals were in the area. Even Ralph had been out the previous week and managed to get sixty-seven seals. There were quite a few hunters out, scooting everywhere around the island in speedboats.

The day I flew out, I noticed several snowmobiles parked at the ice edge approximately two miles south of Bacalhao Island. The ice was packed solid from halfway out to the island. The eager hunters would tow their boats out over the sea ice using their snowmobiles, then push their fibreglass or aluminum boats into the ocean and cruise out through the ice floes hunting for hours. The bay was mixed with Arctic ice and thinner local ice with about six- to seven-tenths coverage. This seascape was changing every hour and every day. The hunters had to be on their toes. The seas were wild with the ever-changing leads of open water and the unpredictable weather.

On Thursday, we received news about some bad luck one of the sealers had had. Mr. G. Brown had pulled his speedboat out to edge of the ice with his brand new Ski-Doo and parked it. From there he pushed off and had gone out hunting for hours. During the time he was out sealing, a slight sea began to make—not very much, but enough to slowly start breaking off the ice edge, piece by piece. It slowly chewed into where the snowmobile was parked. Sure enough, when the hunters returned, no Ski-Doo was to be seen. The ice edge had been reduced by a few hundred feet, and the machine was now sitting on the bottom of the Atlantic Ocean. Quite the loss! I heard later that Mr. Brown hired a diver to go down and look for the machine, but I didn't hear if he successfully retrieved his saltwater snowmobile. He might have taken a few seals that day, but luck was not on his side.

During my summer holidays in 1991, my regular partner, Ralph Hurley, retired after working almost twenty-five years at his beloved lighthouse. Harvey Watkins, who worked on the opposite shift, also retired at the same time. My new co-worker was Gord Jones. I had first gotten to know Gord when I was working at Long Point Lighthouse at Twillingate. I had worked a few shifts with him before, but now he was regularly filling in on Ralph's shift.

John Card, Rodney Card, and Gord Jones
leaving Bottle Gulch on Bacalhao Island

The foggy, rainy days of fall were upon us. After thirty-two long days, Gord and I were preparing for our end-of-shift changeover. We worked together the best kind, but after our shift on this island, we were both anxious to return home to our loved ones, even though this was only going to be a half-shift home. The last couple of days we were kept busy cleaning the station and watching the dreaded forecast. Changeover day finally arrived on October 22, 1991. Early that morning we had received word from St. John's that the helicopter was not available due to poor weather, so we lined up John Card to carry out the station changeover. There was a big sea running, and it was getting worse by the hour. It was so rough that John, accompanied by his grandson Rodney, steamed out in their huge wooden twenty-seven-foot trap skiff. She was a noble beast. It was too rough to carry out the changeover down in the cove, so we had to carry our gear across to the back of the island to Bottle Gulch. There, the seas were not quite as dangerous, and we carefully exchanged boxes and bodies from land to boat. We were lucky because the winds were increasing and the seas were growing. It was always a major relief to complete one of those shift changeovers safely, and the best thing was we were headed home!

Gord's Search and Rescue Mission

For years I watched the bright yellow search and rescue helicopters buzz past the lighthouses at which I'd been stationed—be it the old classic CH-113 Labrador or the newer, flashy CH-149 Cormorant helicopter. They were known as the SAR unit of the Royal Canadian Air Force, based out of 9 Wing Gander, Newfoundland Labrador. These highly skilled, dedicated search and rescue helicopter crews flew in the best but more often in the nastiest weather conditions around the province. Often when they flew past my lighthouse, they were on a routine training flight, but many times they were on a mission to save a person's life. From time to time, I would have radio contact with the SAR helicopters, maybe providing current local weather conditions and sometimes assisting them in a real search taking place in the wild seas or ice not far from my lighthouse. Never did I dream I would have to call this elite search and rescue unit for help right there at Bacalhao Island Lighthouse!

It was early Monday morning, January 6, 1992, changeover day, when I received word from our Marine Aids Office in St. John's that there was no Canadian Coast Guard helicopter available for us that day. This meant another frosty changeover in an open speedboat—if conditions were safe. This certainly was not my favourite method of transportation in the winter months. I knew the lightkeepers on the opposite shift had just punched a long, hard Christmas shift out on Bacalhao Island and were eager to get off that isolated rock. I threw my boxes and luggage aboard my truck, said my goodbyes, and promptly made my one-hour-and-twenty-minute drive down to Herring Neck, where relief lightkeeper Gord Jones was waiting for me. As luck would have it, retired lightkeeper Harvey Watkins had his speedboat all ready for the changeover job. Sea and weather conditions were fairly good, considering it was January month.

All went well as planned. Harvey transported Gord and me out from the shelter of Salt Harbour, past Berry Island, and to the snow-covered island of Bacalhao. In about half an hour of steaming through the frigid air and the chilly Atlantic waters, we landed safely in the cove just under the dwelling that would be home for the next thirty-two days. In this slightly sheltered cove, we carried out the monthly "lightkeeper waltz" over the ice-covered rocks—cardboard boxes full of supplies and lightkeepers in bright orange survivor suit drifting through the chilly air in perfect sequence. Cirque du Soleil would be proud of our coordination. Lightkeepers Les Powell and Ed Loveless were more than pleased to be headed home and for us to take over their duties.

I was working another regular shift with my co-worker, relief lightkeeper Gord Jones from Twillingate. On Tuesday, January 14, we performed something that I think was never carried out on the island before. We played a game of pond hockey! We made a snow scraper and, along with a shovel, carefully cleared off a large section of ice on the small pond on back of the dwelling. We fabricated a goalie stick out of some lumber, and then we managed to have an entertaining game of hockey. The Red Wings versus the Habs, live at Bacalhao Arena! I had skated on this pond a few times by myself in previous winters with my stick and puck, but this skate was special. I had a human goalie to shoot on. It was a great bit of fun. During a dark, cold shift in January, fresh air, a bit of exercise, and a good laugh were good for your spirits and your soul. It was a great day.

Pond hockey

Later that day, just as the sun was sinking, we watched the long-used Newfoundland coastal boat MV *Terra Nova* pass by our light headed down into the Hamilton Sound. It would be her last trip in Newfoundland waters—the word was it had been sold and was cruising to the warmer waters of Central America.

Throughout the past few days, the waters around the island were rapidly filling in with thick slob ice. We now had approximately two-thirds coverage in new grey ice with small lakes of open water mixed within. Several hours after the *Terra Nova* steamed past, a freezing rainstorm system moved in, reducing visibility to zero. Luckily, the foghorn kicked in properly—sometimes ice froze onto the visibility sensor window (called a videograph), resulting in foghorn malfunctions. This undesirable freezing rain continued all through the night and into the next morning.

When daylight broke, I could see that the entire light station was covered in a shiny layer of ice. The walkway from the dwelling to the fog alarm building and to the helipad had a half-inch of glistening ice covering everything. Even the pebbled walking path from the basement door to the fog alarm building was coated in ice. It was dangerous to walk anywhere outside of the dwelling, especially when one had to check on the diesel generators in the fog alarm building. I had never seen conditions like this before. I could almost lace up my skates and glide around outdoors. I also noticed the top section of my CB antenna had snapped off overnight from the extra weight of the ice buildup.

Gord was the chef on this ugly day. He had cooked a delicious roast beef dinner for us. One thing was certain, when you are away from home and stuck out on a lonely island, you need good food in your belly! I was finishing cleaning the dishes when Gord decided to take out the daily garbage. From the corner of my eye, I saw him grab the old red metal garbage bucket in the hall and head toward the basement stairs. These glossy grey wooden steps led down to the open basement and to our main exterior door. I turned back to my dishes in the sink when I heard a scream, then several thumps and knocks. Holy smokes! What happened?

I rushed over to the head of the stairway to check it out. Gazing down, I could see Gord's twisted body lying at the bottom of the steps. It did not look good as I quickly descended the stairs to check on my buddy. His colour was white, and he was in pain, so much so that he was urging! Gord, a big, heavy-set boy, some would describe as "shart and t'ick." He had taken a terrible fall. Somehow, he missed the first step and tumbled down the entire length of the stairs, landing on the solid concrete floor below.

All of us lightkeepers are trained in first aid. First, I made sure he was breathing and then checked for blood or any other obvious injuries. He was complaining of back pain, so I dared not move him for fear of a possible spinal injury. He was conscious, and his gagging slowly subsided, but he was still in extreme discomfort. I talked to him and tried to comfort him, but I was limited in what I could do. After checking Gord over, I decided I had to make a call for help. I rushed upstairs and called Comfort Cove Coast Guard Radio and informed them there had been an accident and requested a search and rescue helicopter. Then I returned to the basement with a warm blanket and placed it over my co-worker. I had also cranked up the thermostat to push some extra heat into the cool basement. Within minutes, I heard our mobile telephone buzzing upstairs, so I swiftly booted up the stairs again. It was a medic from Search and Rescue, 9 Wing Gander requesting details of Gord's accident and his current condition. I gave the medic all the details, and I informed him of the dangerous icy conditions presently on Bacalhao Island. He told me the good news was that the search and rescue team was on its way.

During all this drama, I also phoned my supervisor, Mr. Randy Dawe at the Marine Aids Office, and informed him of the incident at the station. I then returned to Gord's side to monitor his condition and to keep him company. I felt useless. There was nothing more I could do—except . . . I got my ghetto blaster and played some music for my injured co-worker. I picked out my favourite mixed tape of the Beatles and John Prine and pressed play. That was the best comfort I could give my old buddy at the moment.

While waiting for Search and Rescue to arrive, I kept talking to Gord and assured him everything was going to be fine. I also cleaned up the garbage that was scattered all over the basement floor from Gord's failed "triple Salchow" down over the basement steps. The waiting seemed like forever, but an hour or so later, I heard the familiar loud chop, chop from the big Labrador helicopter approaching. The massive helicopter hovered above the dwelling for a few minutes, then called me on the VHF radio. The pilot informed me they would not be able to land there because our helicopter pad was too small for the huge CH-113 Labrador. This twin-engine helicopter weighed 24,300 pounds and measured eighty-three feet in length from blade tip to blade tip. To add to their concerns, there was a strong crosswind blowing, and the helicopter pad was covered in glitter, not to mention there was a large cliff face mere feet from the eastern end of the helicopter pad. They would have to go to their Plan B.

Left: Search and rescue helicopter Right: Gord in stretcher

The noise coming from this large rig hovering overhead and the downwash from the blades was quite powerful. Within a few minutes, I saw a SAR medic winching down on a cable from the side door of the helicopter onto the icy pad. Then a stretcher came down, and finally the second medic was lowered down and placed his two feet on the slippery pad. This was like something out of the movies. I just stood back and took it all in. With a thumbs-up from the medic, the mighty Labrador swung away, disappearing behind the icy cliffs. Carefully, I led the two medics over the frozen walkway to the dwelling basement door. With their shiny helmets on and their cool little mics still attached, they rounded the back to the basement door and entered.

Once inside, the two medics quickly got down to business. They were professionals on a serious mission. Gord was thoroughly checked over, then a neck brace was fastened onto him. They carefully moved him onto a backboard, and we gently placed him into the wire cage stretcher. There, he was strapped, Velcroed, and then doubly strapped down. He could not move—he could barely blink. While the medics were attending to my injured co-worker, I received another phone call from our Marine Aids Office. My supervisor informed me I had to leave the lighthouse with the search and rescue crew. For safety reasons, I was not allowed to stay at the lighthouse alone. With that, I quickly packed a small bag and returned down to the basement, where they were preparing Gord for transport. Three of us then carefully carried the heavy stretcher containing Gord out to the pad, stepping ever so carefully along the icy path. Once there, one of the medics radioed the helicopter to return. All this time the Labrador pilot had been flying around the back of the island, just killing time while waiting on word from the medics and also burning up valuable fuel.

As the mighty Labrador helicopter quickly returned from back over the cliffs, I crept back to the side of the dwelling. There, I watched this amazing real-life movie take place in front of my eyes. Occasionally, I would snap a few photos with my camera just to prove this was really happening. To see this highly skilled search and rescue team do their magic up close was thrilling. The Labrador hovered approximately 100 feet above the pad, then lowered a cable down, which they attached to the stretcher. Suddenly, Gord was being winched up toward the noisy helicopter while a medic was holding onto a rope to prevent the stretcher from spinning with the downwash from the powerful rotor blades. In no time, Gord disappeared into the safety of the large Labrador. Then the other medic quickly zipped up and tucked into the side door like Spiderman. Quite impressive, I thought. By now the orange sun was beginning to set behind the distant hills of Twillingate Island. It was getting windier and noisier as that bright yellow beast swirled above my head. The lone medic, Tom, and I stood on the cold helicopter pad. Now what? Then I watched Tom snap the tiny cable onto his sturdy harness. I was getting nervous. Bad thoughts were racing though my head. Could this slight, skinny cable hold the weight of us two men? Before I could chicken out, Tom placed a life ring around me, under my arms, and shouted to me, "Hold on to your nuts!" I was about to say "What?" when he wrapped his two legs around me, and up we flew, spinning in the frigid winter wind. I was terrified. I remember glancing down and watching the helicopter pad shrink in size the higher we winched up. Quite the ride! Once inside the Labrador, they slammed the side door shut, the yellow beast tipped, and off we flew. I took one last peek out through a side window to see lonely Bacalhao Lighthouse sitting there without its keepers of the light. The first time in decades.

They flew Gord and me straight to Notre Dame Memorial Health Centre on Twillingate Island, which was approximately nine miles to the west. Darkness had set in when we gently touched down at the hospital's helicopter pad. Gord was quickly wheeled into the hospital, where he spent the next two days recovering from his fall. I thanked the search and rescue team for their fantastic service. I had arranged a ride with my Twillingate friends John Chipman and Brian Greenham, who were waiting nearby. My buddies drove me up to the Causeway Motel, where we met up with my wife, Alice. She had driven down to meet us.

All ended well, and I managed to get a couple of bonus days at home during a long, dark January shift. Due to poor weather, a Canadian Coast Guard helicopter was not available until noon of Saturday, January 18. That was when pilot Gordie Simmons picked me up in the Canadian Coast Guard Helicopter 126 at Porterville's government wharf. I returned to Bacalhao Island Lighthouse with relief lightkeeper Eric Dove from Crow Head. It was the first time working with Eric since the spring of 1984 on Surgeon's Cove Head, Exploits Island. We finished the remainder of our scheduled shift without any accidents. This was quite a thrilling start for the new year of 1992, and I had more adventures to come!

Wildlife on Bacalhao Island

Wildlife abounded on and around this little island sanctuary. It made no difference whether it was the spring, summer, fall, or winter season. I would make regular excursions down through the island, over the rugged rocks, across the bogs, till I ran out of land down at the eastern end. From there, historic Change Islands looked like it was only a good swim away. Hiking or cross-country skiing across the diverse landscape of Bacalhao Island was great fun and always challenging. On one of my earliest hikes across this interesting rock on July 22, 1988, I climbed to the top of a high cliff named Round Head for the first time.

While sitting on a rock taking in the tranquil landscape, I sighted a large pod of orca whales swimming below the cliff on which I was perched. It was an amazing sight, approximately twenty animals bobbing along with their dorsal fins riding high. They appeared to be headed south toward the Hamilton Sound run. This was a thrill, my first-ever sighting of killer whales. Back in 1988, orca sightings were rare compared to summers nowadays, when they are a little more common, maybe due to the changing water temperatures and food supply.

Dolphins, minke, and humpback whales were a common sight here right from the kitchen window. Every time I went for a hike across the island, I would encounter something interesting or unique. Often, I would see a flock of saltwater ducks or dozens of turrs sitting in the frigid water.

One calm day on April 27, 1990, I observed approximately twenty ducks riding out the cold wind tucked in near Kier Rock on the eastern end. Later, when I returned from my long walk, I was surprised to see another 200 ducks sitting in the cove in front of the dwelling. Time after time I would go down across the island, slowly pacing my trek through the rocks, bushes, and the bogs—not a living soul around me for miles, just myself, enjoying the wonderful peacefulness, when suddenly two or three ptarmigans would flutter noisily up from under my feet, almost giving me a heart attack! They sounded like a Cormorant helicopter taking off and always spooked the living daylights out of me. In the winter months, these birds would magically turn pure white, blending into the snow seamlessly.

A few times during the long winter shifts, I also had the delight of coming across two big snowy owls down across the island. They were huge white feathered beasts. I don't know who would be more startled, the owls or me! I would be quietly skiing along, and sometimes I would get so close to them that I could actually hear their wide wings cutting through the cold, crisp winter air. They were quickly trying to gain altitude and getting away from this foreign creature on skis. There on this deserted island was the first time I ever observed these graceful birds. It brought me pure enjoyment to see the variety of birds that frequented Bacalhao Island. Eagles, puffins, crows, saltwater pigeons, curlews,

Lightkeeper Harvey Watkins cleaning cod

owls, gannets, ospreys, kittiwakes, and seagulls were common sightings on this not so lonely island.

The waters around Bacalhao Island were always abundant with codfish. From time to time on a good day, we would winch down the Canadian Coast Guard speedboat and run out to the fishing grounds, called Old Grassy or Young Grassy, to catch a fresh cod for supper. That was always a treat out on the island!

One species our little Bacalhao Island went without was the rabbit. There were no bunnies running around here, unlike most other islands in this large bay. We would talk daily to the lightkeepers up on Surgeon's Cove Head on Exploits Island, and they would tell us great stories about all the rabbits, how plentiful they were this season or how big the critters were. Catching two or three bunnies a day using only a few rabbit slips was common. Exploits Island was a large, forest-covered island, and with only one or two hunter-lightkeepers there, the rabbit population was always healthy. I had first worked there for a shift in 1983 and had seen for myself that the rabbit leads through the bush and woods were like highways. The rabbits had been using the same paths and leads for decades. I had hunted a few rabbits in my time, but I had never seen rabbit leads like those on that island, which were located not far from the dwelling.

When the hunting season opened, look out for the wicked rabbit stories on the VHF radio airwaves, even if they were sometimes embellished! We totally enjoyed it—it added to our nightly entertainment. After a few years of listening to all these exciting Exploits Island rabbit stories, I started thinking. The American bison was imported to Brunette Island on the south coast of Newfoundland in 1964, moose were introduced to the Howley area in 1878 and 1904, red squirrel in 1963, and the snowshoe hare in 1864, so why couldn't a few local, furry rabbits be imported to Bacalhao Island?

Between the two lighthouses, we devised an elaborate plan—and a "top secret" plan, at that—to increase the bunny population on Bacalhao Island. Our skilled co-workers on

Surgeon's Cove Head, Ed Loveless and Arch Budgell, would keep any of their trapped rabbits that were still alive for possible exporting to Bacalhao Island. The great hunters would check their slips every day throughout their shift. Most times, any rabbits they found in the slips were stone dead, but every now and then they would catch a live one. In those cases, the lightkeeper would have to gently remove the rabbit slip from the traumatized bunny, stuff it into his knapsack, and return it to the lighthouse. There, the keepers had made up a large homemade rabbit pen using duct tape and the thin wood and wire from fruit boxes. They kept the bewildered wild rabbits in the spare basement, out of sight, in case they had visitors.

This important rabbit recruitment went on for several days. Our fellow lightkeepers were on a mission. Each night, we would get a rabbit update from the lightkeepers-turned-rabbit-specialists on the CCG Radio. There was no privacy on our VHF radios. Back then, one-third of Notre Dame Bay's residents had their own VHF or CB radio in their kitchen, and they all listened to the fishing boats or the lightkeepers at the lighthouses. We were aware of that, so our rabbit conversations were carried out in code. It was funny, but it helped break up the long winter nights on the isolated light stations.

The rabbits were kept for such a long time, they had to start feeding them and giving them water. After all, healthy, strong rabbits were part of the contractual requirements. We were told one night that two or three rabbits escaped from their custom-made pen, and the boys had to chase down those wild critters dashing throughout the basement. Oh, what fun that must have been! Another big problem was they had no idea what sex the bunnies were. There was no point in sending down all male rabbits, so they had to catch a few extra just to improve the odds of getting mixed sex.

Finally, after exercising much patience and care, there were seven frisky rabbits ready for relocation. Luck was on our side this shift. The Canadian Coast Guard helicopter was stationed on the icebreaker *Sir John Franklin*. The ship was escorting paper boats in and out of Botwood, and the helicopter would carry out daily ice surveillance flights. When the timing was right, the lightkeeper on Surgeon's Cove Head radioed the pilot requesting that a special package be dropped off to us on Bacalhao Island. This was something we had never ever requested before, but it was on his route, so a few hours later, the helicopter landed on their pad at Surgeon's Cove Head. Our buddy lightkeepers were right there to meet it, placed our precious boxed cargo in the rear compartment, and off they flew. Our friendly pilot had no idea he was delivering a box full of bunnies! Fifteen or twenty minutes later, the helicopter pilot radioed to inform us he would be landing at Bacalhao shortly.

Ralph and I scurried out to the helipad and retrieved the large box from the noisy helicopter. We stood back, gave the pilot the thumbs-up, and off he lifted, continuing his ice patrol. I could feel the cardboard box vibrating with the extra roar of the helicopter taking off. I guess our new rabbits were excited after their first helicopter flight. I know I was bubbling with excitement as we carried the box full of Exploits-bred rabbits. We went back to the foot of the large hill, the white and red spiral light tower sitting a few hundred feet above us. This was an ideal location, with friendly bushes and many stumpy, dwarfed trees. I had prepped this location for the official day of our rabbit release program. A couple of days earlier, I had painted up a nice sign and nailed it to a tree. It read, "No Hunting / Rabbit Haven." I had also set up my video camera on a tripod, because I wanted to capture the first moments of the dear rabbits' freedom.

Our new furry friends were getting anxious. I could feel quite a lot of movement in the cardboard box. We placed the box down, slowly untied the rope around it, and gently opened the cardboard flap on one end. Then, like the *Apollo 11* lifting off, rabbits started flying out of the box! The first two or three bunnies went straight up in the air about eight feet, never touched a thing, and were gone like a missile, out of sight! We just about died laughing. The remaining three or four cute bunnies leaped out of the box and looked at us as if puzzled, wondering what the heck had just happened. After a few minutes, they regained their legs and cautiously hopped over to the wooded area in their new Rabbit Haven. After all these years, on a chilly day in February of 1990, the island of Bacalhao now had a colony of rabbits roaming free to their heart's desire—all credit going to the hard work of the two lightkeepers on a distant island. Thanks, and a job well done all around!

On a cool October 2, 1991, I was halfway down across the island with my beloved eleven-year-old beagle, Gypsy, picking a few partridgeberries, when suddenly she went nuts, barking. She tried running the best she could, but it was difficult for her with her back injury and the rough terrain. To my amazement, she had flushed out a fox! Where did he come from? He appeared to be a dirty grey in colour, and wet. The fox must have arrived on the island when the Arctic ice came down several months ago. Maybe he smelled the new rabbits freshly imported to the island. The odd polar bear was known to come ashore from the Arctic ice floes in Fogo or Twillingate areas, so I guessed an Arctic fox could make the same incredible voyage south on the ice pack. During all my walks down through this island over the previous three years, I had never seen a fox or even a track.

As the weather changed and it cooled off, food became less plentiful for Mr. Fox to find. By early November, I started noticing the fox standing off about 100 feet from the dwelling. He would appear around dinnertime each day. I guess he smelled the good cooking being carried out inside. I would take my bones and scraps and throw them out across to the pathway toward the fox. Sure enough, he would ever so slowly walk in to eat it. Every dinnertime, I would look out the window, and Mr. Fox would be patiently waiting for those tasty, hard-to-find treats. I threw scraps out for days. Each time, I would throw them a shorter distance. Over time, the fox would slither in closer and closer to retrieve the delicious chunks of

Arctic fox

food. He would snatch them and circle back a few feet, then eat. His coat of fur appeared to be changing colour. Day after day, I would talk and whistle to Mr. Fox as I carefully lured him closer to me. The fox would flatten itself right down onto the ground and ever so slowly inch in to retrieve the food scraps. It was such a beautiful sight, but the fox still had a wild gleam in its eyes. The poor animal was obviously hungry. By now it was feeding only a few feet away from me. If I blinked or moved ever so slightly, it was gone in a flash. It had turned, as if by magic, from a dirty grey to having a pure white coat of fur that would fluff up in the gentle winds. A pure Arctic fox, the first one I had ever seen. Then, to my surprise, on November 29, the fox returned, but this time it was accompanied by a baby Arctic fox! "He" was really a mother fox! What a surprise! She must have arrived on the island pregnant and given birth there. Good old Mother Nature at her finest.

A few days later, on December 1, I finally managed to feed the mommy fox from a fork in my outstretched hand. Now, that was super cool. Over several weeks, I had slowly gained the trust of this wild animal. I used my video camera to record this feeding triumph.

I continued to feed this ball of white fur from a dish. I would whistle and talk to her continually. We had named her Chips, and her baby was named Ding. The baby would never come in for food—the mother would carry it back to her pup. This continued until I left the station for my shift off. When I returned weeks later, I resumed feeding mother fox again. I don't think the other lightkeepers took part in feeding the animal. On January 18, I noticed the mother fox carried her food dish away. That was odd.

February 4, 1992, was my changeover day, and that was the last time I saw my foxes. I flew back home to Porterville, and during my lieu days, I got a transfer to a new lightkeeper position at Surgeon's Cove Head Lighthouse on Exploits Island. After four years, I was finished working at Bacalhao Lighthouse. I am hoping that, in a perfect world, the rabbits, the Arctic foxes, the ducks, owls, and all the rest coexist in the peaceful sanctuary of beautiful Bacalhao Island, in Notre Dame Bay, Newfoundland, Canada, Earth.

Bacalhao Island Lighthouse was de-staffed in December 2001, and the dwelling and all sheds were later torn down and removed. A lightkeeper was not on watch!

5 Surgeon's Cove Head Lighthouse, 1992

A lightkeeper position became available on the Exploits lighthouse early in January 1992, so I applied for a transfer. Surgeon's Cove Head Lighthouse was much closer to my home, thus making shift changeovers easier, plus it offered an improved radio connection to my radio system at home. Not to mention there was a small community in the harbour for roughly three-quarters of the year. After spending four years on isolated Bacalhao Island, I was ready for a change.

On Wednesday, March 11, at 2:30 p.m., the CCG helicopter picked me up at the government wharf in Porterville and flew me to my new job on Surgeon's Cove Head. After landing, I dropped off my several boxes at the lighthouse and then jumped back into the chopper to fly to Bacalhao Lighthouse. My transfer was approved while I was home, and I still had several personal items left back there. I flew to the lighthouse for the last time and quickly packed up the remainder of my belongings. I filled up a few boxes and said my goodbyes. I haven't been back to the island since.

On my return flight that afternoon, I observed hundreds of seals scattered all over the place while we buzzed along just feet above the rough pack ice. We had one more stop to make first—we had to land aboard the powerful icebreaker *Sir John Franklin* for refuelling. We landed on the ship's small helicopter pad on its retractable hangar at the stern of the ship. That was a rare and thrilling experience for me, especially while the ship was still crashing through the bay ice heading toward the port of Botwood. The flight deck crew were professional—

three flight deck crew members all dressed in fire-repellent suits, helmets, and fire hoses in hand, and a safety fence was put in place. It was like a pit stop at a Formula 1 Auto Race. They refuelled our helicopter, and with a hand signal, off we went again. Minutes later, the pilot landed me on the Surgeon's Cove Head Lighthouse helipad, where I joined my new work partner, Arch Budgell from Campbellton.

Preparing to land on icebreaker *Sir John Franklin*

It felt good to be working back there again—it had been eight years since I first worked as a relief lightkeeper there, but this time I was returning as a proud full-time lightkeeper. The opposite shift included lightkeepers Lloyd Lilly and Carl Greening, both from Lewisporte. I unpacked my supplies and belongings and picked out my bedroom. I settled into life on Surgeon's Cove Head quite well.

My first official thirty-two-day shift went fast considering it was winter. It was a busy shift with visitors dropping by on snowmobiles almost daily, along with my many ski trips across the island to the harbour and beyond. I basically worked every second day during the month there on shift. On my days off while on the island, I would often snap on my cross-country skis and go wherever I could. I skied in around Peyton's Pond, which was an important water source providing gravity-fed water to dozens of cabins on the eastern side. Another day, I skied into the harbour, then went eastward through the woods and bogs until I broke out on the opposite side of the island in Tom Wall Harbour. That was interesting. I could see the old woods trails cut into the thick woods and notches worn into the bogs by the island pioneers from a hundred years before my time.

Skiing on Exploits Island

During that part of winter, the Bay of Exploits was packed full of Arctic ice. When the ice conditions were somewhat safe, snowmobilers from Lewisporte, Campbellton, and Summerford areas visited the island almost daily. Some travelled as far as twenty miles over questionable sea ice. Many had cabins in the harbour and took this short window of opportunity to transport supplies or cut firewood or do repairs. Often, they would make the ride out across the island for a visit to the lighthouse. Our first brave group of winter visitors came on March 17 and 18, 1992. Don Manuel, Frank Janes, Carlton Wheeler, Ross Winsor, Hardy Burry, and Wally Snow dropped by for a little tour and a welcoming cup of tea. A few days later, the Cuff brothers visited. Compared to the countless lonely winter days I had spent at Bacalhao Lighthouse, I thought this was wonderful, and all were welcomed. On March 20, I was in the harbour and helped Arch's brother Gilbert put out his herring net through the ice. We cut several holes into the bay ice and set a net over near Garden Cove in bitter minus-twenty-degree weather. That was a first for me, an enjoyable experience.

Snowmobile visitors

The Canadian Coast Guard icebreakers were regularly escorting oil tankers full of jet fuel into the port of Lewisporte, supplying the Gander International Airport, and fuel for the Irving Oil depot in Botwood. Plus, paper boats were steadily shipping paper out of Botwood from the busy paper mill in Grand Falls–Windsor. These large ships all required icebreaker assistance during the heavy ice season. We lightkeepers constantly kept the snowmobilers informed of any new channels cut by the mighty icebreakers. Depending on their route, occasionally they would cut off certain communities from crossing over the ice to visit Exploits Island. Then the residents would complain to the CCG in St. John's, the politicians, lightkeepers, and even to radio talk shows. It was a constant dance between the icebreakers and the snowmobilers.

By Tuesday, April 7, 1992, we were islanders again. A big sea had made overnight, and just like that, the swells broke up all the pack ice that was surrounding the island. This cut off all snowmobilers who were planning to visit the island for the remainder of the winter.

My first shift was almost complete, so I skied into the harbour one last time. On that visit, I discovered Richard Wells had several sweet baby lambs bouncing around his yard on their little hoofs. They were beauties. While in the harbour, I also took time to nail a window back in place at my buddy Dave Locke's cabin. I had noticed a few days earlier the window had blown open during our last snowstorm.

Arch and Gilbert Budgell during shift changeover

Cabin security and emergency repairs were one of the volunteer services Arch and I carried out in the harbour during our regular visits. Over the years, I have nailed windows or doors back in place that had shifted or had blown open. I poured salt down toilet bowls to prevent freezing solid, disconnected waterlines before frost, bailed rainwater out of boats, and cut several loads of firewood and dropped them off at my friends' cabins. During the off-season months, it was only Richard and Lydia and us lightkeepers out on the island daily, so we liked to keep an eye on the many cabins, sheds, and wharves and inform the owners if something was damaged or out of order.

I didn't mind doing any of this, because the cabin owners were always good to me. I received countless rides in speedboat from the harbour out to the lighthouse from many of them. After spending my "off day" in the harbour, doing a project at the cabin or helping somebody out, a boat ride out to the cliffs beneath the light was much appreciated—so much better than the sweaty one-hour hike back to the lighthouse with hundreds of flies buzzing around me!

By April 10, my first shift was completed. We had a total of fifty-seven visitors at the lighthouse during my thirty-two-day shift on the head. I could not believe how many people made the nail-biting voyage out over the Bay of Exploits ice and then across the island on their snowmobiles to pay us a visit. It certainly broke up the usually long boring winter shifts. I had seen more visitors at this lighthouse during my first month than in the four years I worked at Bacalhao Island Lighthouse! Soon, the Canadian Coast Guard helicopter picked me up and took me home to my dear wife, Alice. A few days later, I flew up to my buddy's home near Toronto, Ontario, for a week-long visit and radical change of pace.

By Tuesday, May 12, duty called again, and this time I hired Val Tucker from Lewisporte to transport me out from Embree to the lighthouse for a shift changeover. Usually we carried out shift changeovers using our own speedboats, but often in the early spring or late fall we had to hire a speedboat and its operator. The other regular boat operators we hired for this important job were Gilbert Budgell and Wally Snow, but most often it was Ford Rideout from Embree. Ford was our go-to guy. He could manoeuvre his Sea Runner fibreglass boat around the rocks, and especially inside the treacherous gulch, better than anyone around.

My first winter and spring shifts on Surgeon's Cove Head went great. I really enjoyed it there. On May 24, I celebrated my first birthday at this light by myself again, thirty-six years young. On June 11, I planted five beds of potatoes and a few carrots and cabbage on the limited decent piece of soil on the head. A few days later, my shift was up, and it was time to return home to Porterville.

It was a short shift home, and I was back on the island again for work by Monday, June 29. This time I was in my own seventeen-foot speedboat, the SS *Beagle*, and I had company with me. I brought my wife, Alice, along with my old beagle, Gypsy. Alice had taken a few days off work from the pharmacy and came out with me for her first visit to the lighthouse. Unfortunately, the weather was terrible during her stay. We had rain, fog, and northeast winds with four-degree temperatures every day. It was good to have my sweetie with me during this stretch of terrible weather. I must add, Alice was over seven months pregnant and getting bigger by the day.

Finally, the weather broke on Sunday, and the sun appeared. Alice had planned to return home that day, July 5, so I had a ride lined up for her with a friend in Exploits Harbour who was headed back to Lewisporte after the weekend. However, there was a problem, because a big sea had made overnight and the cliff rocks were awash with churning seas. Alice would not be able to make the dangerous jump into a waiting boat with her big, lovely belly. This meant a long, challenging walk for her and me across the island.

We were packing, up preparing to tackle this hike, when suddenly, out of no where, a bright red and white Canadian Coast Guard helicopter dropped down on our pad for refuelling. This was excellent timing, and the pilot was good old Gordie Simmons. I explained the predicament we were in and asked if Alice could possibly get a ride. Gordie said it was not a problem, that it was only slightly off his planned route. About thirty minutes later, the chopper lifted off with my happy and pregnant wife, leaving my dog Gypsy with me. Gordie gave Alice a first-class private ride into Porterville's government wharf, her one and only helicopter ride ever. She jumped out and smiled proudly as she walked down the roadway wearing her knapsack, Floater coat, and rubber boots. It is funny, but I returned the favour a few years later one day while I was driving into Gander. Alice and I were leaving Lewisporte when I passed this older guy hitchhiking on the side of the road. I had only caught a glance, but it looked like Gordie. I turned my truck around and went back, and sure enough, it was Alice's helicopter taxi pilot. I gladly picked Gordie up and gave him a ride into Gander. He was hitchhiking his way back to St. John's.

With the improved weather back on the lighthouse, we started scraping, priming, and painting the large dwelling. Gallons and gallons of white oil paint would be used for this job, and we had cases of it in stock. That July, there were dozens of beautiful icebergs all around the bay. During this month, I hammered a wooden spike into a piece of vacant land in the west side of the harbour. With the help of Richard and Madeline Sceviour, I had spent months tracing down the family of the original landowners. The piece of land I acquired had been used by Cecil Stride and family, who had left Exploits Island for Ontario in the 1950s. The family gave me permission and their blessings to build my own cabin on their old property. (Thank you, again.)

Around this time, the northern cod fishery was suddenly shut down by the federal government, shocking the whole fishing industry and all Newfoundlanders. This also meant much less boat traffic on the waters around our lighthouse.

I was back on Surgeon's Cove Head by mid-August, wrapping up the last bit of summer maintenance that was required. I had started working on the foundation on my cabin in the harbour. I always said building a square cabin on a round planet was the hardest job in the world. Thankfully, my buddy Rod Wells helped me level up and square off my foundation. Rod was one of the best carpenters around, and he was born on this beautiful island.

Longliner hauling cod trap near lighthouse

On September 2, well-known Newfoundland fiddler Émile Benoit passed away. I was always a fan of his music and had watched him perform at several folk festivals over the years and met him once at the Atlantic Folk Festival in Nova Scotia. So, the next day, I walked across the gulch to the headlands and built a naked man (a small rock tower) in his honour, much like the one I had built for Rufus down on Bacalhao Island two years earlier, almost to the day. On

Sunday, September 6, relief keeper Eric Dove replaced me a few days early because Alice was about to have our baby. Sure enough, a few days after I arrived home, Alice gave birth to a bouncing baby boy, Dylan, in Gander hospital. At the ripe age of thirty-six, I became a father for the first time. Man, was I ever proud! I even bought a box of cigars, because I thought that was what a new dad was supposed to do. It was amazing to witness the birth and the life created. I was awestruck and will never forget that day.

Barry Porter and Rod Wells working on cabin foundation

A few weeks later, while still on my lieu days, in early October I hired Melv Day and Ivan Lockyer from Brown's Arm to help me build my new cabin. I had most of my materials out there and had the foundation and floor joist in place. We all stayed at Wally Snow's cabin nearby for a few days. After two long days of hard work, we had the cabin almost completely closed in with plywood. Then a tropical storm hit the island overnight. It blew a living gale! Wally's whole cabin was shaking like a leaf in the vicious wind. That night we thought it was going to blow off the large rock it sat on. We had seventy-five mph winds with gusts to ninety mph from the north-northeast. It was the worst storm I had experienced on Exploits Island. As daylight broke, I looked out from Wally's cabin across to my new cabin, and things did not look right. At first, I could not believe my eyes. My new cabin had been moved! The strong wind funnelled in through the narrows and got in under my cabin, lifted it up off the concrete blocks, and threw it about eight feet closer to the beach. My cabin was heavy, well-constructed, and measured approximately twenty feet by twenty-four feet with a half-loft and two-by-six walls. What a disappointment after all that difficult work! I almost cried.

The water in the harbour was fully adrift with salt spray. It was wild. The strong winds and driving rain were relentless for days. A large shed collapsed down in Lower Harbour that morning as well. We did not feel safe at Wally's small cabin, so the boys and I walked out across the island to the lighthouse in wind and rain. We stayed there for a night, safe and sound. The next day, October 8, Winston Butt's large old two-storey shed blew down in Butts Cove. The next day, the wind died down, but there were still big seas, so we packed up and returned home, leaving my cabin in a mess. I remember cruising over mountains of sea, even south of Muddy Hole Point, rowing into the bay. I was disappointed, but a week later, I returned to the island with ropes, straps, jacks, block and tackles, and with the extra help from Bob Shepherd and Wally Snow, we pulled my "wounded" cabin back to its original location and slowly jacked it up till it was level again.

Later that fall, on Tuesday, November 24, 1992, Arch Budgell and I were involved in the strangest marine rescue I ever witnessed on the light. It was a cold, clear night with light winds and an extreme big sea on. All day there were huge swells rolling in the Ships Run. At approximately 2300 hours (11:00

p.m.), we received a radio call on the VHF on the Canadian Coast Guard channel 19. Over the airwaves came a desperate cry for help!

A voice cried out, "We are lost, we are going to die!" At first, we could hardly believe our ears, but we could tell by the tone of the voice this person was scared and panicking. He said they almost crashed into the jagged cliffs under Northern Head. This was the massive headland just across the Ships Run, less than two miles northwest of our lighthouse. We talked to the guy operating the radio in the boat and slowly got him to calm down. He informed us they were in a sixty-foot longliner from Labrador with two men aboard and were headed to the marine centre in Triton, which was located about twenty-two miles to the west in Green Bay. By now, Jeff Lush, who was the radio operator working at Comfort Cove Coast Guard Radio station, had heard all the commotion on the Coast Guard channel, and he broke in to speak to us and the distressed boater. The boat operators were baffled and very difficult to communicate with over the radio. The guy did not want to talk to Jeff or any CCG ship, so Jeff let us deal with the confused man. Comfort Cove Coast Guard Radio said they would monitor the situation but also requested a Coast Guard ship that was in the bay to be on standby.

The boater said they had no marine charts, no radar, just a regular road map, and once they passed south of Cape John Gull Island, they panicked. Over the next three to four hours, we communicated with them and slowly guided their vessel eastward across the Ships Run while they battled the large swells. I remember Arch and I standing out on the edge of the cliffs using our portable VHF radio and a powerful spotlight assisting the lost boaters. After some time, the longliner got closer to our lighthouse, and we instructed them to cruise southward along the side of the island. We were in constant radio contact. Finally, they got into the safety of Exploits Harbour. There they tied up at the large government wharf for the night. Another sea disaster averted, but quite the thrilling late night for us!

The next day was Arch's shift off, so he left after breakfast on his usual walk into the harbour. He had plans to visit the boaters we had assisted a few hours earlier. To his surprise, when he got to the wharf, nobody was there. For some reason, the longliner had left bright and early before Arch had had a chance to meet them. Not only that, they did not even untie their ropes. Oddly, they chopped both the bow and stern lines with an axe, leaving their ropes still attached to the wharf. The following day, I walked in and saw the chop marks on the wharf rails for myself. Very strange, but true. I am not sure what the crew on that boat was up to that night or what was going on, and I will never know, but I do know we kept them safely off the rocks that mysterious night in November. A lightkeeper was on watch.

The year 1993 brought another good winter for skiing and for snowmobile visitors. February 25 was changeover day, time to return to work. During this shift, on March 3, 1993, we had visitors from the Canadian Coast Guard Engineering Department checking for mercury and lead levels. They collected soil samples from around the station. Over the many decades, most of the lighthouses around the island had some issues with contamination and pollution. Large amounts of lead paint were used, and quantities of diesel, motor oil, and gasoline were stored on site, along with some discarded batteries and used motor oil. Later, the CCG began an intensive process of cleaning up the light stations around the coast. All garbage and contaminations were removed, and new topsoil was flown in and seeded, and eventually new grass emerged. I must admit, the environmental cleanup team did an excellent job on this project on the head.

The mystery boat

On March 10, I skied and climbed up to the highest piece of land on Exploits Island—Man of War Hill, 553 feet above sea level. On other trips I skied out to the cove that is named Surgeon's Cove, and another day I explored Gull Island Cove. Both remote coves had a history of families who once lived there many decades earlier. Later, our annual snowmobile visitors began arriving on the island and riding out to the lighthouse. One of our first groups to visit this winter turned out to be my relatives. My dear Uncle Harold Porter and my first cousin Ron, along with Kevin Manuel, George Winters, and Pete Seaward, dropped out on March 13.

For the next few weeks, we had several groups of visitors. On one occasion, Arch and I invited Wally and Maisie Snow, and of course Richard and Lydia Wells, out for a big cooked supper. I was chief cook that day and put a special effort into cooking up a big pot of Jiggs' dinner with all the trimmings. I was excited to have company, especially when the mayor visited by snowmobile. Richard and Lydia visited rarely because it was a tricky ride across the island in the dark on their two little Elans. I put out the entire feast for my friends, and we were just sitting down, when Richard suddenly stood up and went to the cupboard and grabbed a mug. He then went over to the large pot and asked, where was the pot liquor? Holy smokes! In all the preparation, I had inadvertently poured all the delicious pot liquor down the kitchen drain. When I told Rich that, the look on his weathered face was of shock and disappointment. He was flabbergasted. I will never forget it. We had a great supper and a game of darts afterwards. Fun times.

Winter shifts on Surgeon's Cove Head were such a contrast to the four winters I spent at Bacalhao Island Lighthouse. The routine work of winter cleaning and painting inside was the same, but here we would get visits from snowmobilers. During a few of my visits into the harbour that month, I helped Wally Snow haul out several large wharf sticks to be used at his cabin. Another time, we installed a new, larger picture window with help from Ross Winsor and a very sharp chainsaw. Zip, zip, and we had the window installed in record time. That winter was a short season for snowmobile visitors. The bay ice became unsafe toward the end of the month, and once again we were isolated islanders.

A couple of days later, it was cleanup time again. We would always spend our last two days at the station scrubbing the large dwelling from top to bottom. The place was always sterile when we departed and returned home. I used to joke that you could perform open heart surgery on our basement floors. It was a well-known fact that our principal keeper was a little obsessive over cleanliness. I must admit he ran an extremely tidy and well-equipped light station. Ask any technician or staff on the southside Canadian Coast Guard base. They all knew about our clean station, especially our glossy kitchen and living room floors. The Honourable Brian Tobin, Minister of Fisheries and Oceans, flew out and visited our station once when he was a member of Prime

Minister Jean Chrétien's cabinet. This light station was one of the CCG jewels out of the many isolated lighthouses around the province.

On Wednesday, April 28, I boarded the helicopter and flew back out to the lighthouse for another shift. We were surrounded by quite a bit of pack ice, and the bay and coves to the south of us were still packed in solid. Due to the heavy ice conditions, there were no boats or hunters during our first few days. However, late one afternoon, there was a knock on the back door. Strange, because we had not seen a single boat our first couple of days on shift. Two men had landed down in the gulch and walked up the steep ladder and steps. They came in and had a chat with Arch and me. I recognized one of the guys, Rick, from Lewisporte. He was accompanied by another man who owned the boat. The men said they had launched their boat from Twillingate because most harbours in the bay were still packed with heavy ice. They said they were not hunting seals, just out touring around and sizing up the beautiful bay. Rick asked us dozens of questions during their visit, many of which were odd. They questioned the accessibility of certain coves, the boat traffic, and even the amount of surveillance by the Coast Guard. Strange questions at the time, but I did not think much of it. Just another curious boater, I figured. At least not until six months later, when in October 1993 one of these men was involved in the massive thirty-ton hashish drug bust in Ireland's Eye! This was a small, resettled island just off the coast of Clarenville, similar to Exploits. Coincidence, or not?

Footnote: On March 26, 1997, forty kilos of cocaine (worth over $8 million) were seized in the paper boat *Abitibi Orinoco* in Botwood. This large ship passed under my bedroom quite regularly at the lighthouse. Later, in September of that year, another eight kilos of cocaine were also discovered in the ship *Abitibi Claiborne* in Quebec. This ship was headed to Botwood but at the last minute was diverted to Port Alfred,

Abitibi Orinoco in ice being escorted by the *Sir John Franklin*

Quebec, due to the local stevedore workers' strike in Botwood. I also know of a story from this time period of two stowaways from Columbia/Venezuela who were discovered in one of the paper boats during a winter trip headed to Botwood. They had hidden in its steel hull down in South America. When the ship entered the ice-packed waters of Notre Dame Bay, they were forced to come out of hiding due to the cold winter temperatures. I'd say some interesting cargo passed by our lighthouse over the years!

For some reason, winter was always late retreating from Exploits Island. It was like it had its own separate climate bubble. During this shift, on Monday, May 3, 1993, Arch and I snowmobiled across the harbour ice to his cabin. The ice was dark and scary with large holes in it from the fresh water and snow melting and running down through it. There was not a snowflake to be found around home, but out here, weaving out through the tall trees across the island to the lighthouse, the main trail still had two feet of packed snow on it.

The word buzzing over the VHF radio was there were thousands of harp seals around the bay. Ice conditions had improved slightly the past couple of days, allowing seal hunters to get out and harvest a few animals. Later that night, we got a call from Comfort Cove Coast Guard Radio informing us there was a hunter overdue. We spent most of the night spying out through the darkness and keeping in contact with the *Sir John Franklin* by radio. The ship carried out a search pattern through the many miles of dangerous ice and leads of open water. From time to time, we could see the ship's powerful spotlight shooting out through the fields of ice. With no radio or flares, it was like searching for a needle in a haystack. Finally, and luckily after countless hours of searching, at lunchtime on Tuesday, a Mr. Osmond from Ragged Point, Twillingate, was safely located and picked up. He was thirteen miles north of Long Point, Twillingate.

Then, just two days later, on Wednesday night, May 5, another group of hunters was reported missing from Lushes Bight. They were better prepared—they radioed and informed us they were trapped in rough Arctic ice with their eighteen-foot speedboat. They could see our main light flashing, but we could not see them. We reported this to Comfort Cove Coast Guard Radio, and within a few minutes, we received a phone call from the Search and Rescue office requesting all the details, including local weather conditions. The hunters shot off an emergency flare to indicate where they were located. We observed the distant flare and determined the hunters were north of us. However, in the pitch darkness, we could not judge if they were three miles or ten miles away. We relayed this information back to Search and Rescue headquarters, and approximately thirty minutes later, the large SAR Labrador helicopter buzzed past our lighthouse headed northward on a mission. Fortunately, the hunters had one last flare. They shot it off when the helicopter got close to them. Within minutes, the hunters were located and picked up safe and sound. They were exactly ten miles north of Surgeon's Cove Head Lighthouse. It was interesting to see the difference between the two recent rescues—the emergency flares and a radio certainly shortened the search time.

On May 12, I sighted hundreds of harp seals. It was a calm day with strings of loose ice, and I could see their shiny black heads popping up everywhere. That day I counted over twenty speedboats hunting the elusive seal north of the lighthouse. A few days later, we had a seafood treat for supper—fresh herring, seal, and lobster right out of the cold, crisp Atlantic.

On May 24, I celebrated another birthday out there. That day also marked eleven straight days of fog, drizzle, and zero visibility. I disliked being unable to see the beautiful wild ocean below, not to mention listening to the foghorn blast non-stop for days on end. Finally, I returned home on May 31 for a late birthday cake with Alice and my little baby boy, Dylan. My son was growing like a weed. I could see he was stronger and more alert, plus he had some bright new white teeth. I had missed him dearly.

Baby Dylan, Barry, and Alice visiting

On August 13, Alice and Dylan came to visit me at the lighthouse during my first and only shift with Lloyd. This was Dylan's first visit, and that day in the kitchen he took his very first steps. I am not sure if it was the bright, shiny floors or what, but he began walking there and loved it, giggling as he went. That was a thrill for me to experience! Later that month, the Canadian Coast Guard carpenters, Fred Masters and Bill Mathews, arrived at the station. They flew in on the CCG helicopter with a load of building materials, and in a few days they had built a lovely new patio onto the back of the dwelling.

On my days off in the harbour, I plugged away at building my cabin, nail by nail. I didn't use a power tool the whole time—just sweat and muscle.

On October 17, 1993, the *Sir Wilfred Grenfell* arrived and refilled our large, thirsty fuel tanks with diesel. This was always a major operation at that lighthouse. The ship had to wait for ideal wind and sea conditions, which was rare in the fall. The *Grenfell* would hook a couple of heavy lines onto the large eyebolts drilled into the nearby cliffs, then with the assistance of their small, fast rescue Zodiac, they would haul hundreds of feet of fuel hose into our high-risk gulch. There, we would winch the hose up to our wooden landing, and with help from three or four of their crew, we would drag the heavy fuel hose up to the fibreglass fuel tanks near the dwelling. Once everything was secured and in place, one guy would radio back to the ship, and pumping would commence. Thousands of gallons of diesel fuel would pump all the way out from the ship, across the cove, up the steep cliffs, and into our three tanks, topping up our supply for the furnace and Lister motors for the coming winter. This tricky operation was carried out twice a year, every year.

In November, I carried out my last shift changeover for the year with my own seventeen-foot Sunray speedboat. I was anxious to get home and was pounding my way back in the bay when I hit a hard wave. I guess I was trying to go too fast—my boat twisted slightly with the smack. The header under my feet that was fibreglassed into the stringers in my floor had broken off. Many people do not realize the ocean in the fall is much heavier and denser. I had seriously weakened the hull of my boat, so I had to throttle back and carefully limp home.

Later, on a chilly New Year's Day, 1994, I drove down to Valleypond on New World Island along with my nephew, Darryl, to meet Richard and Lydia Wells. They had hired a longliner to take them back to Exploits Island with their supplies for the long winter. I had just bought a used Moto-Ski Spirit twelve-horsepower snowmobile to use on the island. We removed it from my pickup and tossed it onto the deck of the longliner. Richard removed it a couple of hours later at his wharf in the harbour.

By January 19, the Canadian Coast Guard helicopter was transporting me back to the lighthouse. We soon discovered our Lister diesels were not running well. Two motors had shut down. We reported our concerns to the Marine Aids Office again. A few days later, I skied into the harbour and rode my Moto-Ski Spirit back to the light. On my very first ride out, I broke off the right ski! The next day, I dragged the machine into the spare basement workshop and bolted the ski back together. Five days later, I broke a boogie spring—another visit to the repair shop. Repairing my Spirit or Arch's Elan was a regular occurrence. The trail was rough this month, and we did not take it easy on the machines. All we needed was half an inch of snow or wet grass.

On January 28, the *Sir Humphrey Gilbert* escorted the first paper boat into Botwood through seven- to eight-tenths coverage in ice. I had my old hockey skates at my cabin, and on January 30, I laced them up and went for a wonderful skate around the Exploits harbour. The ice conditions were excellent—not a soul around, just me on a clean sheet of ice from

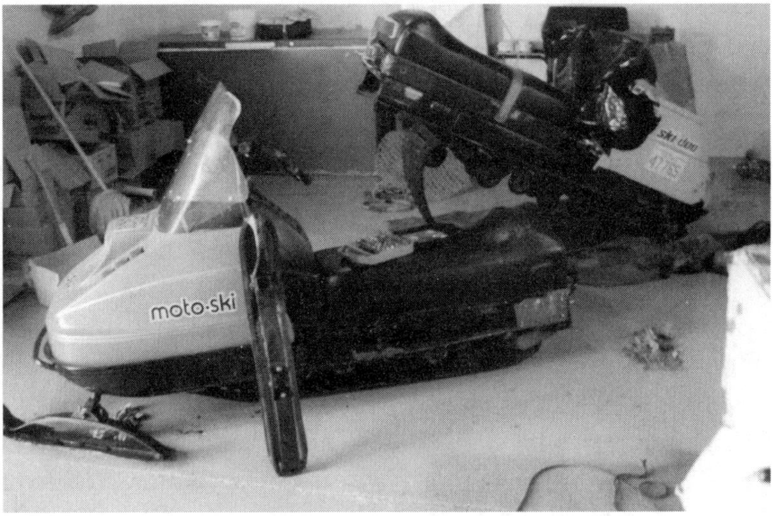

Moto-Ski and Elan in basement for repairs

Garden Cove to Lower Harbour. I whizzed into every cove and nook, smiling all the way. Richard told me later it made him feel good to see me out skating around. It reminded him of years gone by. He had not seen anybody skating in the harbour in decades.

By now our third and final Lister motor was also not running properly and would not carry the required power load. The motors were overdue for a tune-up, and we had to shut this motor down as well. This was a rare situation and a serious one. With no generated power, we would have no lights or heat and be forced to abandon the lighthouse. We were down to our last backup, which meant Arch Budgell and I had to start up the old HA unit, which was located in the foghorn building. It had to be cranked over by hand to get it started, but thankfully the old beast fired up and we kept the light shining. This generator had no air-cooling system, which meant we had to keep the doors and windows open to the winter weather. Finally, on Friday, February 4, 1994, two technicians arrived from St. John's by helicopter. In a couple of days, they had our Listers running like new.

On my winter shift, I kept busy painting the interior of the large dwelling. On the days off during my shift, I motored around in the woods cutting a bit of firewood. I hauled out five loads and dropped them off at cabins around the harbour. I enjoyed this, especially with my Moto-Ski now running well. A few days later, the regular snowmobilers started travelling over the bay ice, arriving in Exploits harbour and going out to visit the lighthouse.

On February 15, we had a vicious snowstorm—winds seventy to ninety mph from the north-northeast along with twenty-seven inches of snow. The schools in Lewisporte were closed for three days. The winds at the head were blowing so strongly over our dwelling that a window shattered in Arch's bedroom and every shard of glass got sucked outdoors! We tried unsuccessfully for two days to snowmobile to the top of the hill from the lighthouse. There was just too much new snow. On the third day, I managed to cross-country ski in to my cabin and get my chainsaw. Several trees had blown down across the trail. I also dropped in and checked on Richard and Lydia.

That same day, Captain Chafe on the Canadian Coast Guard *Sir John Franklin* gave us some marine charts and had them dropped off to us by helicopter. We mounted them on a large piece of plywood and placed it on the wall next to our CCG radio and phone. Captain Chafe had been calling us occasionally on the radio, inquiring about the local ice conditions, for several winters.

On March 30, the large helicopter 305, piloted by Kenny Steele, picked me up in Porterville and dropped me off on the head, where I met with relief lightkeeper Eric Dove. Eric was filling in for Arch for a few days. On April 3, Easter Sunday, the ice had broken up three-quarters of the way around the island, leaving a small ice bridge leading to the island. That day we were invited to Richard's for a nice cooked Sunday dinner and a visit. Sunday was always a day of rest for Rich and Lydia.

By April 6, the last brave snowmobilers, the Browns, visited Exploits harbour. Over the next couple of days, a big sea made, and along with strong winds, it broke up the remaining pack ice that had surrounded our island. The ice route was cut off for another season.

On Tuesday, April 12, the snow was hard-packed and you could go anywhere on snowmobile. Arch and I went exploring the harbour on our machines. We found an old grown-over trail leading out to Long Point. It took us two hours to navigate and beat through the woods along the northern side of Peyton's Pond to get up on the barrens. It was exciting new territory for us. The next day, I cut a rough trail and rode my Moto-Ski Spirit right up to the top of Man of War Hill (also called Flagstaff Hill). There was not a snowflake up on that windswept rock, but what a thrill—the best view on Exploits Island! I could see for miles back into the bay. I could almost see home.

I soon returned to the lighthouse and told Arch where I had gone on my sled, and he wanted to go up there as well. So, I grabbed my camera, and we both rode up to the highest

Barry Porter and Arch Budgell on top of Flagstaff Hill

point on the island. We enjoyed the view at 553 feet above sea level and captured a photo to prove it. Ours were the first-ever snowmobiles up there. I returned to the summit a few days later and chiselled my name into a rock there. A Mr. Bill Party had carved his name into the rock way back in 1930. I often wondered what this man had been doing up there back then.

Only a couple of days later, my darn motor seized up on my snowmobile while crossing the island, so Arch had to tow me out with a piece of crazy carpet tied under my track. Later, I removed the motor and took it ashore in a cardboard box.

On April 25, 1994, my father had a medical crisis. He discovered he had cancer of the kidney and required immediate surgery. I was stressed on the island worrying what was going on with my dear father. Stuck on an isolated island is a difficult place to be during a serious family issue. Thankfully, my supervisor, Randy Dawe, arranged for a relief lightkeeper to replace me and flew me home, shortening my shift by a few days. Father had his kidney removed the day I flew in. Now at ninety-one years old, he is still cancer-free.

Later during my June shift at the lighthouse, I decided to make a quick visit home in my speedboat. Arch, Lloyd, and I would make the rare visit home during the summer season when conditions and timing lined up. June 3 was my day off and the forecast was good, so I left early and walked across the island. I jumped aboard my speedboat and cruised in the bay. After seeing my wife, Alice, and my sweet baby boy, Dylan, I was preparing to leave again when I noticed the wind had chopped in from the northeast. I finished packing up and began my twenty-mile trip out the bay. It was going to be rough—this wind was the worst kind for heading out the bay.

When I got near Cabbage Harbour Light on Thwart Island, the weather deteriorated. The winds increased to thirty to forty mph, the waves got choppier, and it started to snow—yes, snow on June 3! This was not in the forecast. Visibility was reduced to 100–200 feet, so I had to soak along near the western shoreline. At this speed, it took forever to get to High Grego, then Little Grego, and finally I reached Muddy Hole Point. The snow was quickly building up, inch by inch. I had my rubber clothes on and Floater jacket with my cap pulled down over my eyes, and I was peeping out just a quarter-inch above my windshield, but the driving snow was still stinging my eyes. It was no time to panic—but the worst was yet to come. I had to leave Muddy Hole Point and steam blindly into the driving wind for two and a half miles northeast across the Ships Run. To make matters worse, I also had to watch for the large swells roaring in on my port side, because one of those could easily swamp my boat.

I had VHF radio contact with Arch at the lighthouse from time to time, which made me feel better, but the conditions were rough. I tucked in behind Muddy Hole Point for a little shelter to regroup and double-check my fuel supply, hose connections, and ropes. Thankfully, my 115-horsepower Mariner was running perfectly, so I headed across. Visibility was down to 100 feet with heavy slop snow hitting my face and huge swells rolling in. Every minute, I had to turn my little seventeen-foot boat into the swells and ride it out, then straighten up again. I tried to keep a heading on my compass, but it was going around in circles.

I cruised on for a while, and the next thing I knew, I was back exactly where I had started. In all the cutting into the wild ocean swells and straightening up, I had completely turned around and did not realize it! I attempted to cross this rough body of sea again, though I could only go quarter-speed due to the poor visibility and sea conditions. I motored on but ended up making a complete circle again! By now I was getting cold and wet. I radioed Arch and told him what had happened and that I was making one last attempt to cross Ships Run. If I failed, I would go back along the shoreline and break into one of the small fishing cabins I had seen earlier. I also told him to call Alice with an update and tell her I loved her! I was starting to get scared. My mind flashed back to November 1977, when my friend Elliott Perry drowned in a similar storm only a few miles east of my location. I had to refocus and complete this voyage.

I checked my wristwatch to time myself, and off I went again, paying extra attention to my swinging compass. Soaking across the run, I ducked breaking swells and faced the blinding, freezing snow as I went. It seemed to take forever, but finally, after thirty tense minutes, I saw land through the thick snow. It was Exploits Island. What a relief! I got in by the Oven and Duck Island Tickle and gave my 115-horsepower some extra throttle to power through the remaining two miles to the harbour's mouth. Finally, I landed at Richard's wharf late in the afternoon. I was beat. I tied my boat on at Rich's wharf for the night—I would move it on another day. There were several inches of heavy snow in it by now. It had taken me over three hours to make my trip compared to the usual one-hour ride, and I had burned double the amount of fuel. It was quite the journey out the bay—it was the scariest solo boat ride I had ever taken in my life and one I'll never forget.

I slowly trudged through the six to eight inches of heavy June snow up to Richard and Lydia's house for a hot cup of tea. When I removed my baseball cap, four pounds of snow had moulded hard onto its peak. It felt good to enter their warm and comforting home. After getting warmed up and revitalized at Richard's, I still had a difficult walk across the island in slippery snow. I suited up again with wet rubber clothes, my knapsack, and radio, and walked on through the heavy snow. After a challenging ninety minutes, I reached the warmth of the basement entrance at the lighthouse. I was exhausted. I was late for my supper, but at least I had made it back safely. A little later during my cleanup, I noticed in the mirror that my eyes were bloodshot from the blinding snow hitting me. I had learned my lesson—that was my last trip to visit home in June month.

The next day, I missed a good friend's wedding in Twillingate. Alice stood in the wedding party and actually got the car stuck in the snow that morning.

The rest of the summer shift was routine. The *Grenfell* refuelled us again on July 17, and while I was painting the white clapboard siding the next day, I saw an iceberg flip over for the first time. After all these years of watching over a thousand icebergs float by, I had finally caught this rare event. On July 28, several visitors came out and stayed for the night. They included a few from Nova Scotia (Jim Taylor and crew), along with Don Manuel and Dave Eveleigh and family. They wanted to spend a night at a real lighthouse, so we made it happen. This was the only time we ever tried this. We spent a lovely night together with a big supper and telling stories.

On my days off, I drove to St. John's on August 11 and attended an important meeting concerning automation. That dreaded word was being whispered throughout the Coast Guard department again.

By October 1994, I was back keeping light on the head. On Monday, October 3, technician Gary Soper and welder Gord Lake were flown out to the lighthouse. Gary had some routine work to do, and Gord had a major job in replacing the steel catwalk and pipe railing around the top of the light tower. Being a former welder, I was interested in his project. It was also good to have the boys around to chat with and have a game of cards. Gord was interested in historic Exploits and the John Peyton–Beothuk connection. He was thrilled to be on the island.

By Friday, their work was winding down. It was a wet and windy day, which meant Gord could not do any welding on the light tower, so I took him for a scenic tour of the island. We walked to the harbour, and I took him down to see the graves of John and John Peyton Jr., who were buried in the same plot in 1829 and 1879, respectively. While there, Gord said a heartfelt prayer at their resting site.

I took him up to meet the famous mayor, Richard Wells. Gord's family roots also came from a small, resettled island in Placentia Bay, so he could relate to Exploits and Richard's peaceful way of life. I sat back and enjoyed my cup of tea in his kitchen while I listened to Gord and Richard tell their island stories. Each story they told seemed to get a little more far-fetched. Gord proudly spoke about his family history on their island going back over a couple of hundred years. After listening patiently, old Richard shot back and told my friend about his ancestors fighting in the Battle of Hastings in East Sussex, England, way back in 1066. Upon hearing that wicked story, poor Gord was flabbergasted and almost fell on the floor. Richard had won! We soon said our goodbyes and hiked back to the lighthouse.

One thing I found myself doing on most of my hikes across Exploits Island or Bacalhao Island was singing, humming, or whistling a traditional Newfoundland song. It was called "Pad's Song" by Pat Byrne. I had heard him sing it at a folk festival somewhere along with his brother, Joe, and Baxter Wareham. It's from the album *Towards the Sunset*. For some strange reason, that song would get stuck in my head, and I found great enjoyment and pleasure in it.

Later in my shift, the *Sir Wilfred Grenfell* was anchored just outside Exploits harbour waiting for ideal conditions to refuel our lighthouse. On October 23, the wind and seas allowed the ship to pump our fuel tanks full. Then, approximately four hours later, during my routine station inspection, I discovered one of our large fuel tanks was leaking a small amount of fuel! This was a serious problem. Luckily, we had a surplus of empty forty-five-gallon drums at the station.

We had to remove most of the fuel from that tank before we had a major diesel spill on our hands. Arch and I spent hours in the cold and darkness, right up to midnight, pumping the fuel out of the large tank and into individual drums. Disaster averted!

Richard Wells, Exploits Island

While working at the Surgeon's Cove Head Lighthouse, I had the privilege to spend a lot of time in Richard Wells's company. Richard was known as the mayor of Exploits Island. Whether sitting in his kitchen having a chat over a cup of his strong tea or out in speedboat with him checking his bait net or in the woods helping cut a load of firewood, it was always an enjoyable time.

Richard Wells of Exploits Island assisted us lightkeepers immensely over the years. We had a close connection with him. Many times in the fall, he would let us store our boxes of food and supplies in his stage for a couple of days during a shift changeover, when the seas were too rough to enter the gulch and winch up or even throw our boxes ashore under the lighthouse. There was an old telephone cable running from the lighthouse directly to an old-fashioned crank phone in Richard's house for years, and we were also connected via his CB and VHF radio. From time to time we would ask Richard to walk over to the government wharf in the middle of the night to check on an overdue boat or to pass along an important message to some boater. Richard would never question us when we asked. Nobody knows how many mariners he helped around Notre Dame Bay over the decades, so I feel I must devote a few pages of my book to the late, great Richard.

First, I will give you some background about this unique and kind man.

Richard's great-great-grandfather came over from Christchurch, England, in the early 1800s and settled on Culls Island. Between 1885 and 1890, Samuel Wells and his son William (Richard's father) moved to Swan Island, which is located three miles south of Exploits Island. Sylvia Wells gave birth to Richard on December 7, 1929, in the old Twillingate Hospital. The Wells family made a life on Swan Island along with another eight or nine families. Some of the family names were Jacobs, Dawe, and Cramm. They would buy most of their supplies in shops on Exploits Island. Richard told me he was only five years old when he started helping his father with the fish. This was the way of life on the edge of the wild Atlantic Ocean. By the time he was seven or eight, he was fishing full-time, hauling ropes, pots, and ripping oars, he said. Rich informed me they were paid $4 for a kettle of dried hard cod, and the day World War II was declared, the price of fish went up by twenty-five cents.

Fishing was survival on the coast of Newfoundland, and schooling came second. Richard would attend school from Christmas to May month, when there was no fishing taking place. He would often take his father's rowboat and paddle across to Exploits Island to visit friends and have some fun. Around 1946, Richard and his family packed up and left Swan Island, relocating to the larger centre of Exploits Island. He was self-taught, and when he did attend school, Richard took two grades a year to catch up to his schoolmates. The schoolteachers in Exploits were amazed by Richard's keen memory and said he was highly intelligent. Most of his school buddies quit school in grade seven or eight, but Rich continued attending up to grade ten. He did not write his final exams because he was busy fishing with his father.

In Exploits, he put down roots and said he was never moving again. Richard lived a happy life tucked into his cove on the western side of the harbour with his parents. His brain continued to soak up every old story he heard from the older men. He once told me a story from his Uncle Alex's great-grandfather. That man used to observe Shanawdithit every day on John Peyton's property. She was the last known living member of the Beothuk people. He told the story of her walking up on Lacey's Hill and spending hours there just looking out the harbour and up the bay. Richard also mentioned Shanawdithit preferred blubber on her bread instead of butter.

Another old story Rich shared with me was from 1881, when the British Admiralty was carrying out marine surveys of the bay for the navigational charts. One of Richard's relatives observed the sailors row in from their large vessel onto the beach on Swan Island and have their lunch. The crew were all dressed in their impressive uniforms as they had tea and biscuits on the rocks there. A few local children talked to the sailors and were given some English biscuits, which was a special treat for the kids. Richard said he could show me the exact rocks where, a century earlier, the British crew had their lunch.

Richard spent hours listening to the foreign news on his RCA Victor radio, and he read every article and every book he could get his hands on. At the post office he would read all the national and international news that came in by wireless telegraph. The postmaster and telegraph operator, James Winsor, would write all incoming news in a large book for the public to see. Richard also told me he would study the maps of Spain, Germany, and other countries from the *Family Herald* magazine and then draw them from memory.

A few years earlier, I had heard stories about Rich memorizing the daily World War II radio reports. In June of 1996, I met the famous Newfoundland artist Gerald (Gerry) Squires, who was staying at a cabin in Exploits harbour. Gerry had lived on Exploits Island in his youth. His parents were Salvation Army officers there during the 1940s. Gerry told me the story about Richard's keeping a tally of every Newfoundlander killed in World War II, daily, from 1939 to 1945. When the war was over, a radio program announced the total of Newfoundland soldiers killed, but the number did not match Richard's. He sent off a telegram, and sure enough, the radio announcer apologized and announced the correct number a couple of days later.

Richard and his sweetheart, Lydia, stood together and watched the community slowly dwindle—losing its post office, teachers, shops, and churches. Eventually, all the residents resettled to nearby communities like Lewisporte, Campbellton, and farther afield. The provincial government officials even visited Richard and Lydia and pressed them hard to resettle—or else. He told me they basically threatened them, but Richard was not resettling. The beautiful old churches, majestic houses, and fishing stages started to deteriorate and collapse. Richard witnessed it all but still refused to leave. He stayed put, becoming the island's caretaker and the unofficial mayor of Exploits Island. He and Lydia fished together, grew their own vegetables, and tended to their herd of rare Newfoundland sheep in their own little part of heaven. Only one other resident stayed year-round, that being Winston Butt, who lived a contented life in his two-storey house up in Butt's Cove. Winston finally left the island for the winter seasons in 1984.

The 1970s saw a completely different era in the rich history of Exploits. After years when the island was almost totally deserted, the occasional American draft dodger drifted into Exploits and made it their new home. The unpopular Vietnam War was raging, and young American men flocked to Canada to avoid being drafted—or, how the song goes, "called up to kill in a foreign land." These young men escaped to several provinces in Canada—British Columbia, Nova Scotia, and Newfoundland, to name a few.

Some found their way to Exploits Island, where they planned to "live off the land" in peace and harmony. Some of these draft dodgers (hippies, as some locals called them back then), were John Moore, Tony Evans, Diar and Kitty Drake, Tom Nato, and Max and Janette Wood. Janette actually had a baby—the only baby born on the island in the past fifty years. Fortunately, Joyce Budgell, a local nurse, was in the harbour at the time and assisted with the birth.

The Americans bought some of the old, abandoned houses in the harbour for cheap prices. They all tried their hand at fishing and farming, but living off the land during the harsh winters on Exploits Island was not for the faint of heart. These young folks were not used to cutting firewood for heat and carrying heavy buckets of water to drink. They found it difficult adjusting to life in Newfoundland. Richard told me stories of having to give some of them food because they were half-starved or provide firewood for the new settlers. He also told me of wealthy parents travelling up from the US to Gander, then hiring a small airplane to fly into the harbour to visit their loved ones.

There is a story of one of the draft dodgers telling his father in the United States that he was going farming on Exploits Island. The next thing, one of the CN coastal boats dropped off a huge 4x4 farm tractor at the government wharf. This machine was designed for the endless flat fields of Saskatchewan, not the small, limited gardens of Exploits. The powerful farm tractor was too wide to drive around the narrow pathway of the harbour. The young American farmer had to wait for the winter freeze-up before he could drive his new tractor across the harbour ice to his little garden. Needless to say, his oversized tractor and his dream of farming did not work out.

On Friday, May 15, 1992, Liberal MHA Graham Flight pulled up to Rich's wharf in his nice cabin cruiser. Graham was the Minister of Forestry and Agriculture in Premier Clyde Wells's Liberal government cabinet. Also, he was Richard's nephew. Accompanying him were several scientists and officials from the provincial Department of Agriculture. I happened to be visiting on my day off, giving Rich a hand at his wharf, when they arrived. They were there to inspect and observe Richard's herd of sheep. I had always heard they were a rare breed of Newfoundland sheep. The officials took blood samples, measurements, weighed and photographed them, and attached tags on the ears of Richard's beloved sheep. I listened as the government representatives asked Richard dozens of questions regarding his flock. One researcher wrote down every word that came out of Richard's mouth. Then one asked him about the sheep's diet. Richard calmly and carefully explained that his sheep ate hay, but he also slipped a scattered salt capelin or a young green fir bough into their diet, and his sheep enjoyed it. The guy pulled off his glasses and scratched his head in disbelief. They departed after a few hours. The sheep's blood samples were sent to the Nova Scotia Agricultural College in Truro for research. Many months later, Richard received official word that his sheep were indeed a rare Newfoundland breed. The original flock had been brought over from Christchurch, England, a couple of hundred years ago and had never been bred with an imported government ram. Eventually, the Newfoundland Department of Agriculture acquired five sheep and one ram from Richard and kept them at the "prison farm" in Salmonier Line. The provincial government maintained a small farm there until it closed a few years ago. The latest update I was able to acquire on

Richard and baby lamb

Richard's sheep was they are now being kept at Lester's Petting Farm in St. John's.

Richard saw it all over the years. For decades, many speedboats, sailboats, cabin cruisers, longliners, and even world-class yachts that visited the remote but beautiful Exploits Island also visited Richard, the "mayor." With the ongoing marine traffic around Notre Dame Bay, Richard became known around the province and around the world. Besides providing a lunch for these many visitors, Rich could tell some incredible story from the past or a bone-chilling ghost story. Richard was a renowned storyteller in a league of his own. All visitors were welcomed into his little home, and no doubt Lydia offered everyone a lunch along with a tasty cup of loose Red Rose tea from the white enamel kettle that was always steeping on their wood-fired kitchen range.

I remember visiting Richard and Lydia's for a big Easter Sunday dinner during my time at the lighthouse. It was April 1994, and I was asking about the hundreds of visitors they would get over the years. A few minutes later, he went to their parlour and returned with their guest books from 1980, which contained a remarkable 2,681 names signed in it for that year alone. Lydia said at times it was hard to get any work done due to so many visitors. She once set the table five times in one day for folks visiting their home and island.

One thing I enjoyed was delivering Richard and Lydia's Christmas mail to them. It all depended on our shift and the timing, but Richard asked me a couple of times to go to the little post office in Little Burnt Bay and pick up their mail before I returned to the lighthouse. I remember walking into the post office and the lady passing out this heavy, large, grey-coloured mail sack stuffed full of Christmas cards and small gifts. It probably weighed forty pounds! A day or two after arriving at the lighthouse, I would drop off this valued mailbag to Richard. I was curious about this sack of mail, so a few days later, when I was visiting, I asked Richard where the farthest Christmas card came from. Old Richard turned to me, scratched his head, and said a doctor from the Amazon rainforest in Brazil! Later, in 2008, he told me he received 120 Christmas cards that year. Richard would have small bottles of foreign rum or strange cigarettes mailed to him from all over the world. I knew when Richard was running low on his regular, much-loved tobacco because he would be smoking a cigarette with an odd smell to it. It could be a cigarette from the USA or a cigar from Germany.

Richard was the go-to guy for spare parts for outboard motors or snowmobiles, gasoline, supplies, or the use of his valuable mobile telephone. Often, when someone ran into trouble twenty miles out the bay, they went to Richard. God help you if you got stormbound and ran out of smokes! One thing Richard always had lots of was tobacco. He could roll you up a pack of tailor-made smokes real quick—but for a price. Old Richard loved his smokes. I used to tease him every time there was a new provincial budget and the price of cigarettes would increase. I'd say to him, "The price of smokes is going up again, Rich," and he would just laugh and reply, "They will never go up to the price they are worth," and then light up another cigarette.

Another love of his was meeting people. He was interested in who you were and where you came from regardless of your age. Rich was curious to know who your parents were. He knew the family tree of almost everyone in this bay. Every time I returned to work on the lighthouse after being away for four weeks, when I visited, he would have a dozen questions waiting to fire at me. He was always interested in what was happening in the bay. He would always ask about the Porters and about other people. My sweet grandmother, Sarah Elizabeth Porter, was originally a Ball from Stanhope, and her brother Stephen married a Lucy Wells from Exploits, so there was a family connection. Richard told me that, when growing up, whenever he and his father took the long motorboat ride into

Botwood, they would often stop in Porterville to visit Sarah and have a cup of tea and a good chat. One time during their visit, he was admiring the Porter brothers' sawmill. He was sizing up the belts, cables, and pulleys, when he accidentally fell onto the sharp sawblade. Luckily the blade was stopped in time, but it was a bad cut, and my nan bandaged up his hand. He proudly showed me the scar to prove it.

Richard in speedboat

I admired Richard's easy-going lifestyle. He enjoyed his quiet, happy life on Exploits. His life here was totally stress-free. He and Lydia fished lobsters, cod, and whatever species was in season. They grew their own vegetables, which they stored in their root cellar. They lived like most people lived in rural Newfoundland decades earlier. Richard and Lydia had no electricity or running water, but if you had never had these luxuries, then you did not miss them. They had no refrigeration, so all their food had to be fresh, smoked, dried, salted, canned, or bottled. That was never an issue, and I enjoyed many, many delicious cooked meals and hundreds of tasty lunches with these lovely folks. Before every lunch was served, no matter how much chatter was in his kitchen, Richard would suddenly shut it down and close his eyes for a heartfelt prayer of grace.

On the island, their modes of transportation were snowmobile and speedboat. Richard and Lydia each had their own speedboat and their own snowmobile and two mighty twelve-horsepower Elan Ski-Doos, and they took pride in each one of them.

Richard had a little generator that he ran in the daytime to charge up the batteries for his radios or small black and white TV. He refused to run the generator for lighting. An old Coleman lantern was their main lighting source. They also cut their own firewood for the long, cold winter months. Richard would pick out a wooded area across the island and cut select trees from his spot. He would cut all the crooked and dying trees first and carefully thin out the rest. No wood was wasted by Rich—he took all the firewood and all the large limbs. After he had carefully harvested all his firewood and left the area, the cutover he used would look as neat and tidy as a park. Back near his wood house, he often collected the majority of sawdust to burn or use elsewhere. Richard was "green" decades before it was cool to be green! He recycled and reused all his metal and glass containers for some useful purpose. All his life he collected driftwood he would come across while out fishing or steaming in the bay. He wasted nothing and always respected Mother Earth.

Richard enjoyed his AM radio and his CB, and later his VHF radio and the mobile phone. He kept in contact with hundreds around the bay and around the world. One late fall in the mid-1990s, a large cabin cruiser was tied up at the government wharf in Exploits harbour for a few nights. They were headed to White Bay for the winter but had some engine trouble, and while there, they also discovered their valuable VHF radio was not working properly. It was a cold, windy November month, and there very few boats around. Richard lent these strangers his only VHF radio to assist them on their long steam across the bay. At least if they ran into trouble they had a working radio to call for help. He then had to wait a couple of weeks before the radio got shipped back to him. Rich told me, "They needed it more than I needed it." God love him!

A couple of times over the years, my co-worker Arch Budgell and I tried to get some recognition from the Canadian Coast Guard for Richard's efforts helping boaters over the years, but we were always turned down.

I have many fond memories from my visits. One that sticks out is a cold winter's day when I was in the harbour and helping Richard cut a few large, heavy wharf sticks. He was planning to rebuild his wharf and stage, so he was cutting a few sticks across the island. We had cut and loaded several long sticks onto Rich's undersized wooden sleds. I did not think the twelve-horsepower Elan would move, but with Rich on the throttle and a helping push from me, with a puff of blue smoke, off we went.

We headed back to the harbour, and I sat on top of the heavy load. While Richard was towing this oversized load down over the long Farmers Hill, I realized the load was starting to push Rich—instead of him pulling the load. Sitting on the hefty sticks, I could feel the sled picking up speed. Just when it felt like the logs were going to pass Richard, old Rich glanced back with this puzzled look on his face and a smoke dangling from his lips. Then, suddenly, *boom*! We jackknifed and crashed. Sticks shot out through the alders, and we landed in the ditch upside down covered in snow. The wharf sticks were scattered all over and the sled and tow hitch were twisted up. A total mess. We had a great laugh about it, but then it took us another hour to get the sled straightened out and reloaded.

Richard's keen knowledge amazed me. One cold winter day, I dropped in on my little Moto-Ski Spirit and ended up having a general discussion about the wars and conflicts occurring in the world at the time. To my bewilderment, Richard listed over a dozen conflicts happening around the world. He also named the leaders involved and what the disputes were about, whether they were over land, religion, or other issues. He mentioned countries and territories I had never even heard of before. Another time I dropped in for a visit, on Thursday, September 23, 1993, during my shift off, I had my good friend Carl from Whitby, Ontario, with me. I knew he would enjoy meeting the legendary Richard Wells. At the time, the federal government, the United States, and the three big auto manufacturers were in negotiations about the new proposed free trade agreement. My buddy Carl had been working with GM for over thirty years in upper management and knew quite a bit about the free trade details. Richard and Carl had a lengthy discussion about the pros and cons of free trade. After we left Rich's and were cruising back into the bay in my speedboat, Carl said he could not believe how knowledgeable Richard was about the free trade talks. He was blown away.

Recognizing what an interesting treasure Richard was, I wrote a letter to CBC TV's *On the Road Again* program in Ottawa in the summer of 1996. I suggested they film a story on Richard and Lydia's life on Exploits Island. Sure enough, in late October, Malcolm Hamilton, the show's producer, flew down to Gander and hired Wally Snow to bring him out to research this interesting character. I made sure I was in the harbour to meet Malcolm when he showed up. He chased Richard around his yard and stage all afternoon recording everything with a little handheld video camera. I asked Malcolm if he thought he could do a story on him—he grinned and said they could shoot a full documentary on Richard.

Wayne Rostad interviewing Richard Wells

A year later, in October 1997, the show's host, Wayne Rostad, producer Malcolm, cameraman Keith Whalen, soundman Mike Champion, and lighting tech Tom Voisey loaded all their camera, lighting, sound equipment, and supplies aboard Kevin Manual's large cabin cruiser, the *Paula Denise*. The TV crew stayed at Wally's cabin and mine for the two-day shoot. During the filming, well-known entertainer Wayne Rostad turned fifty on Exploits, so we had a big kitchen party for him at Richard's home. There were accordions and guitars blasting, and some of the footage made it onto the show. Due to scheduling, the crew had to return to Ottawa to do production work. A few weeks later, Malcolm returned with cameraman Ty Evans from St. John's for another day of filming around the harbour. We had a ball during these two shoots, and the crew captured some excellent footage and a lovely story about Richard and his beloved island. The show aired on national TV during the first week of December in 1997.

This was not Richard's first time on TV or in print. Over the years, CBC TV's *Land & Sea* shot a couple of stories about Exploits Island and Richard, and several magazines and newspapers have written articles on him—the *Evening Telegram*, the *Pilot*, Air Canada's *enRoute* magazine, and more.

In fact, the first time I met Richard was late September of 1983, when we were standing on the concrete bridge between the two islands, and along with Richard was a writer and a photographer from the *National Geographic* magazine. I was working my first shift on the lighthouse, and I had just happened to bump into Richard while he was out showing these strangers around his island. The whole time Richard and I chatted, the photographer circled us and snapped photos. I bet he took thirty photos from every possible angle during those twenty minutes. A few years later, I asked Richard about that *National Geographic* article, and he informed me he had been contacted by the writer and the story was submitted, but it did not make the cut to be published.

Exploits Bridge, 1983

Over thirty-five years after resettlement, Richard and Lydia finally moved to their new winter home in nearby Campbellton, where three of Lydia's brothers also lived. Surgeon's Cove Head Lighthouse was de-staffed in September 2002, and I guess that pushed Richard to make the decision to leave his beloved island, if only for the few cold winter months. Every spring, as soon as the harbour ice melted and broke up, Richard and Lydia returned to their treasured homestead on the island and stayed right up till late fall.

A few years later, while I worked as the curator and manager at By the Bay Museum in Lewisporte, I interviewed and recorded Richard a couple of times for the museum's oral history collection. Even then, in his late seventies, he told me he was just as interested in what was happening in China and Russia as what was happening across the bay. That was the kind of gentleman Richard was.

Sadly, Richard Wells passed away on February 10, 2011. A true legend had passed. I cherished every visit I spent with him, and I'm grateful to call him my good friend.

Surgeon's Cove Head, Final Years

The year 1995 started off with an intense public meeting with the Canadian Coast Guard at the Brittany Inns in Lewisporte regarding the planned automation of Surgeon's Cove Head Lighthouse. The debate about unmanning lighthouses was front and centre again.

I was back on the lighthouse for the winter shift in February. These days, the CCG icebreaker *Sir John Franklin* was busy escorting ships in and out of the two main ports in this bay. Usually, to get from the port of Lewisporte over to Botwood, the icebreaker would travel northward out the main shipping route from Lewisporte to the ocean's edge near Black Island and cruise westward approximately nine miles, then enter the Ships Run near our lighthouse. The night of February 10, 1995, was snowy, and the foghorn blew for hours in the reduced visibility. Sometime during the night, the icebreaker left Lewisporte and headed for Botwood to meet up with a paper boat to escort it out through the ice-filled Notre Dame Bay. This time the *Franklin* took the unusual route of cutting westward, just south of Exploits Island, instead of its normal track of steaming outside the island. The icebreaker's captain probably took this odd route to save time and fuel because of the strong pressure on the tightly packed Arctic ice that filled the bay at the time.

A few hours after daylight, we were surprised when two snowmobilers knocked on our back door. They were Ross Winsor and Carlton Wheeler, our first official visitors for this winter season. They had travelled out from Embree. When we told them the icebreaker had crossed inside of the island a few hours before, the colour left their faces. Due to the fresh snowfall, they had unknowingly travelled over the newly cut icebreaker's channel. A close call—they could have easily ended up on the bottom!

On April 12, the largest icebreaker in the Canadian Coast Guard's national fleet, the powerful *Louis S. St-Laurent*, travelled past our lighthouse crushing the heavy packed ice in its path like cardboard. It had departed from the port of Botwood and was headed back to Nova Scotia. It was a huge, beautiful ship. Two days later, snowmobilers Jeff Manuel and Gary Winters from Lewisporte were the last two people to visit the lighthouse and Exploits Island for the winter. The fragile ice-bridge broke up that night, ending the snowmobile visits for the season.

An extra delight here on this isolated island was our occasional late-night visits to Richard and Lydia Wells's home in the harbour. We only did that when the bay was socked in tight with Arctic ice and there were no ships in the bay. We would finish our shift at 2200 hours (10:00 p.m.) and radio our wives telling them it had been a long day. We had been painting the horn house or basement and were going to bed early. After wishing our sweet wives a good night, we would quickly pile on our snowmobile gear and fire up our sleds, Arch's twelve-horsepower Elan and my twelve-horsepower Moto-Ski Spirit, and tear off across the island's trail into the harbour. For fun, it was always a race in and out with our throttles nipped. To add an extra challenge to this dark, twisting ride, my machine didn't have any working headlight or tail light—oh, and I also had no brakes!

Rich and Lydia were always happy to see us come for a late visit in the winter. After we arrived, we would switch Richard's VHF radio to channel 19 and monitor the CCG channel. We would then get into playing a game of darts or cards. Rich and I would usually be partners. Throwing darts in their dimly lit kitchen with a partially blind partner was always entertaining. It was always a great laugh, and a few drinks were had, but not too many. Of course, before we departed, we had to have one of Lydia's tasty lunches and a cup of their famous loose tea. We would then jump aboard our machines and flatten 'er back across the island—up the hills, across ponds, and twisting through the large fir tree growth. A scattered time, one of us would wipe out while trying to pass on the narrow trail or break off a boogie wheel spring.

By late April, the heavy Arctic ice pushed back into the northeast coast with a vengeance, trapping several boats and ships. Across the bay along the Cape John shore, there were four sealing longliners stuck in the heavy ice for over a week. They were the *Ocean Bellows*, *Kimberly Dianne*, *Row'n Roman*, and another one belonging to long-time sealer Mark Small. The Canadian Coast Guard icebreakers *Terry Fox* and *Sir John Franklin* spent several days assisting these small vessels. With the extreme ice pressure, these boats all experienced rudder or hull damage and were taking on water. Extra water pumps had to be dropped off to them by CCG helicopter to prevent them from sinking. This was a common occurrence during the dangerous seal hunting season on the northeast coast of Newfoundland. Also, during that same week, a large paper boat was stuck in the endless miles of packed ice. It finally arrived safely in Botwood after taking seven long days to travel the short distance from Long Point, Twillingate.

On May 4, my co-worker, Arch, got flown home because his father was ailing, and relief keeper Hardy Burry replaced him. At the end of my shift, the weather turned mild with rain and fog. We had zero visibility for days on end. The bay was still stuffed full of rough ice, and no helicopter was available due to poor visibility. By now the snow conditions were terrible. I could not go for a walk or a ski up the hill and definitely not across the island. I was losing out on my days off at home, but Hardy did not mind. It was funny—I was going stir-crazy being stuck here, but Hardy was smiling from ear to ear! Every extra day Hardy was stuck here at the lighthouse meant two extra days' pay for him. After five dreary days overdue, the ice conditions improved slightly, and Ford

Rideout was able to squeeze out through the pack ice with lightkeepers Lloyd Lilly and Carl Greening to complete a shift changeover.

Later, while doing some painting on the horn house during a regular Saturday shift on a calm, sunny June 24, I was observing the many boats cruising about. It was a beautiful afternoon. A couple of my hockey buddies called me on the VHF radio. They were out boating, going around the island in the new cabin cruiser they had just purchased. They told me to have a look down over the rocks because they were steaming close to the cliffs under my lighthouse. I took my binoculars, walked out to the edge of the cliffs, and looked down at my friends' boat. The foolish lads had their two wives' bras flying proudly high on their flagpole as they passed by the lighthouse!

At 7:30 p.m., I got an urgent call on the CCG radio from Karl Manuel in his new forty-two-foot cabin cruiser. He was in trouble—dead in the water. He had run out of fuel eight miles north of Surgeon's Cove Head. This was his maiden trip in his new boat! He had bought this beautiful vessel on the west coast and was steaming her back home to Lewisporte. Arch and I quickly jumped on it, making a couple of phone and radio calls. In no time, we arranged for a tow job and refuelling. Kerry Dalley, who was in his Cape Islander the *Taylor Belle*, which was tied up in Exploits harbour, steamed out to meet Karl and towed him to the nearest town of Fortune Harbour. There, our radio friend, Harold Hennifent, had a forty-five-gallon drum of fuel waiting on the community wharf for Karl's boat. Hours later, at 1:30 a.m., Karl radioed back to inform us he was safely tied up to the government wharf at Exploits harbour and again thanked us for our assistance.

In July 1995, I had the sad job of helping search for the Day brothers, who drowned near Browns Arm early Sunday morning on July 30. I was on my month off, and Gerald Hutchings and I helped organize and lead the gruelling ten-day search for these two young men. The community of Browns Arm was in shock. We were all grieving. Throughout the search, we had excellent support from the local towns and organizations. Assisting in this intensive search were the CCG *Hood*, a Search and Rescue helicopter, a Department of Fisheries and Oceans ship, a RCMP boat, the local Fisheries officer's speedboat, the Canadian Rangers, the Lewisporte Fire Department, Burton's longliner, and dozens of local men and several small speedboats.

By day two we had fifty men and several boats searching every inch of shoreline from Browns Arm all the way north to Little Burnt Bay. Every island, cove, and countless square miles of ocean and shoreline was walked and searched. This was carried out numerous times over the next ten days. It was a difficult time. I knew Danny and the Day family well, and Allan was an old buddy of mine. By day three, the RCMP dive team arrived. I towed Constable Phil Mathews and two other RCMP divers under water for three days straight. We carried out a detailed search pattern for miles with the sun blazing down on us. During this time, I had two black body bags sitting behind me in my speedboat. It felt weird, but we were on a mission.

On the third day of towing, I got sick from too much sun exposure and had to go home and go to bed. My cousin Truman took over towing the divers. Days later, on Sunday, August 13, Allan's body was discovered several miles out the bay on Black Island. Sadly, we didn't find Danny.

October 16 was a sad day for my family. My sweet lighthouse beagle, Gypsy, went to doggy heaven. She was almost fifteen years old. Her health had deteriorated for several months. The previous month at the lighthouse, I had built a sturdy wooden Cross and carved her name into it. It still stands today at her gravesite back on the farm.

Shifts came and went. By December, Arch and I were working through our final days on the Head and getting excited to return home for Christmas. Richard and Lydia Wells were in the bay for a week stocking up their winter supplies, so we took turns walking into the harbour and feeding their prized flock of Newfoundland sheep. On December 20, they returned to their island for the long winter months. By now we were one day overdue for our shift change, but there was no helicopter available. It was our Christmas shift to be off, and the weather forecast was calling for conditions to get worse.

The next day, Thursday, December 21, 1995, we received word again from St. John's that the helicopters were not flying due to poor weather. No changeover again that day! It was not looking good—we had strong northeast winds, and a big sea was building by the hour. We were getting anxious to get home, and Skipper Lloyd was also eager to get this shift change carried out. Lloyd contacted our reliable Ford Rideout to attempt our shift changeover. Sure enough, shortly after lunchtime, Ford's twenty-foot Sea Runner appeared in the cove with Lloyd and relief keeper Hardy Burry, who were ready for their Christmas shift.

Conditions were awful, with strong winds and salt spray mixed with scattered snow flurries. The rocks and cliffs were covered in snow and ice, and a big sea was washing into the cove. The whole cove area was feather white with swirling seas, foam, and backwash. It was like a giant flush bowl with seas twisting around and rising and falling fifteen to twenty feet. Getting two men and their supplies out of the boat and then getting Arch and me aboard was going to be extremely dangerous. It was freezing out—we were bundled up in heavy rubber clothes, gloves, and life jackets. We carefully climbed down to the edge of the slippery rocks where the sea was washing about. Ford stayed off a hundred feet, idling, observing the size and the timing of the ocean swells rolling across. He put out his grapnel this time to gain better control, something I hadn't seen him do before. When there was a slight break in the swells, he darted in to the steep, wet cliffs, enabling Lloyd to throw a box or two ashore. Arch, perched on the side of the rocks, caught them and then threw them back to me, and I placed them up and away from the occasional high swell that would wash up around our rubber boots.

Ford would then have to back off while holding the grapnel rope away from his propellers and wait it out again, putting his trust in his old reliable Yamaha motor. When he saw another break in the swells, he skilfully manoeuvred to the edge of the cliffs to get another box or a bucket ashore. This routine was repeated until all the boxes of supplies were unloaded. Slowly but surely, one lightkeeper at a time made the daring jump out of the moving boat onto the icy rocks. When Lloyd and Hardy landed on the cliffs, they had to scamper up over the rocks using their feet and two hands with the cold Atlantic swells nipping at their heels.

Finally, the time had come for Arch and I to leap back into Ford's speedboat. It was no place to screw up. You had to time your jump precisely, making the leap off the icy rocks when the boat was at its peak in the rising swell. If either of us timed our jumps wrong, we could land in the freezing ocean and probably get crushed between the boat and the cliffs. This stressful transfer took us over forty minutes to complete. In all my years as a lightkeeper, this was the most dangerous changeover I had ever made. When it was over, we still had a long ride back to Embree in the winter weather. Looking back, we should not

Big sea in the cove, taken from the boat, December 21, 1995

Most dangerous changeover, Ford Rideout's boat

have attempted this risky changeover, but because it was so close to Christmas, we had all put in an extra effort. I know one thing—I was a happy man when I stepped on solid ground at Ford's backyard. There to meet me were my dear wife, Alice, and my three-year-old boy, Dylan. Daddy had made it home for Christmas!

Winter in 1996 was a strange one. We had very little snow, mild temperatures, and hardly any ice in the bay. They called this climate pattern El Niño. On March 11, Arch flew ashore on holidays, and relief keeper John Mutford from Mutford's Cove on Twillingate Island replaced him. The next day, Canadian Coast Guard technicians Gary Soper and Dave St. Croix arrived by helicopter for a week's work at the lighthouse. They had to give our generating equipment a good tune-up and inspection.

It was good to see the boys again. At nighttime we would have our usual game of cards (Tricks) and enjoy a good laugh. Sunday was usually a more relaxed day on the lighthouse. That morning, my friend Rod Wells visited the light in his speedboat. There was little local or Arctic ice, so there were a few speedboats visiting the harbour all winter. When Rod left, he delivered Dave, Gary, and me to my cabin in the harbour. There, with their help, I nailed some roof trusses in place before we walked up and visited the only full-time residents on the island, Richard and Lydia Wells. Once there, many stories and laughs were shared during our afternoon visit, plus a few drinks of Richard's special moonshine. Before we left, since he had a couple of highly trained technicians in his company, Richard asked the boys to have a look at his small Yamaha generator. It had not been running properly. That request was a total disaster. The boys had to give up the repair job soon after it started, because by that time we had sipped a few too many drinks of Richard's powerful 'shine. Then we had the challenging long walk out across the island. We slipped, giggled, and slid some more on our way back to home base at the lighthouse. A fun day, for sure!

Later during my July shift of 1996, my parents steamed out from Porterville to Exploits in Father's old fibreglass boat. They set up and stayed at my cabin in the harbour for five days. It was nice to be able to walk in across the island on my day off and visit my parents. Father did some work on my cupboards and countertop, which were still in various stages of completion. That month, I built a new wharf along with my neighbour Gary Woolfrey. I had cut all the large wharf sticks during the previous two winters.

During my August month home, Alice gave birth to our second child, a beautiful baby girl. It was another proud day for me. We had a healthy boy and now a sweet little girl, whom I named after my dear grandmother Sarah Porter (Ball).

By January 14, 1997, all the lightkeepers on the northeast coast had gathered in Gander for several days of training. Every four or five years, we met for first aid training or other courses. A few days later, on January 22, our main contact person, Randy Dawe in the Marine Aids Office St. John's, retired after thirty-one years of service—a job well done dealing with all affairs of the many lightkeepers around the province.

On April 29, Arch and I snowmobiled up to the top of Flagstaff Hill again for the first time in three years. Snow conditions were excellent, and we were able to ride our way to the summit, and later we picked our way across the interior of the island to Farmers Hill and back onto the main trail.

By June 4, I was back on the light again. It was a rainy and foggy day mixed with strings of Arctic ice and sea. Due to rough seas, Ford Rideout had to drop Arch, me, and our monthly supplies off on Richard's wharf in the harbour. Then we had the ordeal of carrying all our boxes and bags nearly three miles out across the island to the lighthouse. We made two long cargo trips in the rain and then another couple of major hikes across the island the next day. It was challenging work when we had to land our monthly supplies back in the harbour.

Sir Wilfred Grenfell preparing to refuel light station

Land crew ashore refuelling the fuel tanks

Watching the Olympics or the NHL playoffs was always a treat when working my shifts. It helped break up the long nights. On June 7, 1997, my favourite team won their first Stanley Cup in over forty years. The next day after lunch, I took down the Canadian flag and hoisted up my red and white Detroit Red Wings sweater and flew it proudly for three or four hours. Another first! From a distance it would pass for the Canadian flag.

The next week, the *Sir Wilfred Grenfell* secured some lines ashore, dropped anchor under the cliffs, and refuelled our large fuel tanks again. After the job was completed, the mate asked about purchasing some local lobsters, so I jumped aboard their fast rescue craft and guided them in to the lobster pool in Embree. There they stocked up on dozens of lobsters for everyone aboard the ship. We left, and in no time they dropped me off again on the cliffs below the lighthouse. Side note: Arch and I didn't get a taste of the lobster!

In October 1997, the CBC TV show *On the Road Again* with Wayne Rostad flew into Gander to shoot a story about the great Richard Wells and his beloved island. Since I was the contact person for the show's producer, over the year we had many phone conversations. During these, Malcolm kept asking me more about my Porter family and the small community of Porterville. Then he asked me to send him a video of my town and a few of the residents. Later, during one of our phone calls, Malcolm informed me the crew was flying down to film a story on Richard, but they were also shooting a story about the "Porters of Porterville," and Wayne had written a song for our show. What a treat! My small community was unique. All the residents living in the community were Porters. Except for one resident, they were all my uncles, aunts, and cousins. Porterville was settled around the 1850s and was known as being an old farming and sawmill village. The Porter clan had a good reputation of being honest, independent, hard-working folks.

Wayne and Barry at the sign

On Wednesday, October 8, the *On the Road Again* crew and host Wayne spent many hours filming and capturing the story of my relatives. It was an exciting time in our small community to have a national TV show filming there. They filmed the residents working the sawmill, their farms, the community wharf, and our church and the kids. Wayne sang his song throughout the piece, and we finished filming with a large potluck dinner in my garage. We had cooked three turkeys and two hams with countless salads for the Porter clan and the film crew to enjoy. It was busy but also great fun. The two programs aired later on national TV in December 1997 and January 1998.

Lightkeeper group in Gander for training (October 1997)
Back L-R: Neil Wakely, Clayton Bowers, Carson Sturge, Tom Bragg, Jack May. Front L-R: Barry Porter, Stu Bragg, Arch Budgell, Stu Welshman, Lloyd Lilly.

On October 27, many of us lightkeepers were back in Gander again for more meetings about automation, retirement, and early departure programs. These meetings were always educational but also great times to meet our fellow lightkeepers, to share stories, and to unwind. After a full day of training, we would usually end up in somebody's hotel room for a few hours of laughs and drinks. Quite often, we ended up in lightkeeper Tom Bragg's hotel room for some fun. I remember counting thirty-four folks in his room one time! When you gather a few lightkeepers together, it is bound to be entertaining.

In early November, Alice phoned me at the light to let me know our son had tripped, fallen down Pop's basement stairs, and hit his head on the brick chimney, resulting in three stitches. I must admit Alice was finding it difficult the month I was working away out on the island. She was like a single mom working shift work with two young kids to raise. We had a great babysitter, Brenda Baker, but it was still hectic!

By December 1997, our large diesel fuel tanks were getting low again. We had experienced weeks of high wind and seas. We had strong northeast winds, fog, and a temperature of two degrees. The *Sir Wilfred Grenfell* had been tied up in Lewisporte for a week waiting for the weather and sea conditions to improve. On December 5, one tank was completely empty, and we had two days of fuel remaining in the other tank. This was a serious situation. If we ran out of fuel, the main light and foghorn would shut down. The fuel lines to the Lister motors and furnace would become airlocked, and with no heat, all the waterlines would freeze up. We were on the phone every day to our Marine Aids Office in St. John's, but Mother Nature was working against us. On Sunday, December 7, our visibility improved slightly, just enough for the workhorse Canadian Coast Guard 305 helicopter to airlift eight forty-five-gallon drums of fuel from Lewisporte to our station. Arch and I quickly pumped several drums of fresh fuel into the large tank. This emergency fuel drop kept the light shining on the Head. Finally, on Monday, the raging sea subsided enough to enable the fuel lines from the *Grenfell* to be brought ashore and hoisted up from the gulch. The hollow fuel tanks were replenished again—a great relief for all hands.

Then, on December 16, a large Christmas iceberg magically floated into Lower Harbour. That day, Richard Wells and I were down there in his boat collecting rocks for ballast in his wharf, and I was able to retrieve a few large chunks of 10,000-year-old ice for my Christmas drinks. On December 17, we did our shift changeover, and the next day I put up our Christmas lights at home, got myself a haircut, and started my wild Christmas shopping marathon. This was a regular tradition for me. I'd usually get home only days before Christmas and have a list of twenty or so names. I would fly through the stores in Central Newfoundland. Look out, a frantic lightkeeper has gifts to buy!

Lightkeeper Arch Budgell near Lower Harbour, Exploits

The following winter was another mild one. The local bays and harbours didn't freeze up, so snowmobilers were unable to visit. Only a few brave cabin owners entered the harbour by speedboat during the winter. Soon came spring, and the beautiful humpback whales and icebergs were in my backyard again. The scenery at my workplace was breathtaking on those calm days. On a sunny Wednesday, May 20, 1998, I was up on the ladder scraping and painting the old iron light tower and admiring the view around me. Several large humpback whales were gently soaking around the cliff just below me, and massive icebergs seemed to be everywhere. There must have been a bumper crop of icebergs that year. I took the time to count them, and I recorded 120 majestic bergs from my vantage point. On May 31, we had our annual visit from Bob Hicks, the owner of Gros Morne Adventure Tours. Bob operated a kayak company out of the national park but would make a couple of side trips each season to the Bay of Exploits with a crew of kayakers. He hiked across the island with his guests and paid us a visit. The tourists would always be thrilled to visit a real working lighthouse.

After much thought and debate with Alice, I applied for "care and nurturing leave." This was a small clause used by the Public Service Alliance of Canada union. It enabled a person to take a leave of absence without pay to care for children. It also meant the Canadian Coast Guard would keep my position at the lighthouse for when I returned to work. Alice had her hands full raising the kids while I was away, and I felt I was missing out on too much valuable time while my children were young. After being away for a shift, for the first couple of days back I felt like an uncle instead of their dad. That was difficult for me. We decided money was not everything, so we agreed to take a major cut in income and adjust our lifestyle. To have one parent with our children twenty-four-seven was worth it.

I know my co-workers, and probably also my supervisors in St. John's, thought I was nuts. I'm pretty sure no other lightkeeper had ever applied for this type of leave! After weeks and months of inquiring, my leave was finally approved.

On Wednesday, September 23, 1998, I departed Surgeon's Cove Head Lighthouse and returned to my home sweet home. At age forty-two, I began my new career working full-time at Mr. Mom duties. Sarah was two, and Dylan was six. I got totally involved, doing most of the shopping, cleaning, homework, potty training, and working as chief cook and bottlewasher! And there were extra activities like music, Brownies, hockey, library, swimming lessons, and volunteering at school. I did it all, day in and day out, not for months but for years. It was a big commitment, and I gave it my all. I had tried different careers in my life, and this was the hardest job I ever had—but also the most rewarding. The quality time I spent with my children and Alice was priceless. We were able to spend all summers camping around the province in our fifth wheel trailer. During these summers, I also began taking Dylan on our annual father-and-son bike runs on my motorcycle. I took him to remote locations around this grand island, where we camped out in my pup tent or rented a cabin. We visited places like Cape St. Mary's, L'Anse aux Meadows, Gaultois, Trepassey, Tilt Cove, and Lamaline. Great memories were made!

My family at Rose Blanche Lighthouse

During my new Mr. Mom duties, in January 2000, St. John's CBC journalist Jonathan Crowe contacted me and asked if he could visit us and film a segment. He was working on a new show called *Family Series*. The next week, he arrived with camera, lights, and action. He filmed us all over for a few days—at home, school, outdoors, in the grocery store, and at Alice's workplace. Two weeks later, a seven-and-a-half-minute film aired on the *Here and Now* supper news program. It told our unique family story, and it was well-received.

Most of my family and friends figured I would not last doing this Mr. Mom thing, but I did. I had meant to be away from the lighthouse for two or three years, but it went on for almost

Dylan at Ferryland Lighthouse

five years. In September 2002, I was all packed up on the day I was supposed to return to work on Surgeon's Cove Head, but the lightkeepers were suddenly removed. A Canadian Coast Guard work crew was flown out to begin installing modern automation equipment. Sadly, Surgeon's Cove Head Lighthouse, as it had been known, was finished.

The next year, I was transferred back to Long Point Lighthouse in Twillingate.

6 My Lighthouse Beagle and Other Stories

When I obtained my position of lightkeeper at beautiful Long Point, Twillingate, I owned a loving beagle named Gypsy. After a few months of taking the long daily commute to and from Twillingate, I moved into the huge old lighthouse. The century-old dwelling was built for two lightkeepers and their families, so there was lots of room for just me and my lighthouse beagle. This would be my unique home for the next four years. Gypsy and I had a great time, and we really bonded there. She was with me practically twenty-four hours a day, seven days a week—a lightkeeper and his trusty dog. While living there, I soaked up some of the most beautiful sunsets one could see in this country and weathered out many vicious Atlantic storms and countless days choked with fog.

Gypsy at Long Point

Growing up, our family always had a dog around the home, mostly "crackies." Gypsy was the first dog I truly owned myself, and she was also my first female dog. I chose not to have her spayed at first and carefully bred her twice, once in April of 1983, and again in May 1985. Gypsy gave birth to her second litter in the spare living room at Long Point Lighthouse. There were lighthouse puppies scampering around at the station for a short time. That was a neat experience—I wanted to keep all the pups, but I couldn't, so I found good homes for them. One sweet puppy named Snoopy went to my sister.

We met thousands of tourists while working and living there perched above the wild Atlantic Ocean. The visitors loved the scenery, and the friendly lighthouse beagle only added to the attraction. During the second summer at the lighthouse, a part of a commercial was filmed at Long Point for the provincial Department of Tourism. A snippet of my two university summer students and Gypsy running up a trail made it onto the TV ad.

As the summer of 1987 rolled around, I was finally going to take a proper holiday. This was after working for almost three years at this land station, which required me to work an eight-hour shift every day of the year with only minimal time off for holidays. That summer I took seven weeks off to take part in my "dream holiday," which was a motorcycle trip across North America. On Sunday, May 31, I pulled out of my driveway and left to drive all the way to sunny Porterville, California, with my girlfriend, Alice. My ride of choice was my new Gold Wing motorcycle, which I had bought the previous summer. I left Gypsy in the care of my parents in Porterville. She would be good company for them. Off we went on this wild adventure of a lifetime!

We headed west to Ontario, then south into the United States, and slowly swung westward through the States. On June 18, 1987, we finally reached the Pacific Ocean at Long Beach, California. Two and a half weeks had passed since we left home, and we had approximately 10,000 kilometres under our butts. I slipped into a phone booth and phoned my parents to check in on them and Gypsy. That was when my mother told me the bad news—my beagle was not well! Father had been out in boat with Gypsy a few days earlier. Gypsy had been jumping in and out of the boat that day and somehow injured her back. She had been in terrible pain, so they took her to see her veterinarian, Dr. Michael Bland in Grand Falls. He gave her a needle and some meds. Gypsy was resting in the basement in her bed the day I had phoned. This was bad news to hear when I was on the opposite side of North America! Her condition quickly got worse. She lost all feeling and movement in her hind legs. I would phone home every day checking on Gypsy's condition. It was terrible for me. I felt so useless. My parents and the doctor wanted to put her to sleep, but I refused to give up on my lighthouse buddy. Dr. Bland said to my mother, it was a long shot, but she could have major back surgery performed in Guelph, Ontario, at the University for Veterinarians. I was far away and upset, but I did not want to lose my beloved dog, so I decided I would take him up on it. With the help of my family, Gypsy was put in a kennel, taken to Gander Airport, and flown out to Toronto Pearson International Airport. There she was couriered to the animal hospital in Guelph by Blue Bird Taxi Company.

Due to this medical crisis, we shortened our bike tour through the United States by a few days and headed north back into friendly Canada. During all this driving, I made daily phone calls from hotel rooms, phone booths, and gas stations all over the country. (Those were the days before cellphones.) I remember this one day in particular, June 26, I phoned from Jasper National Park in Alberta and had a serious phone conversation with the veterinarian in Guelph. This was just after Gypsy had been examined by their medical team. The doctor informed me things did not look good for her—too much time had passed without surgery, they said, and Gypsy would live a very poor life, and maybe I should reconsider and put her down. But I refused. I was not giving up on my beagle. I instructed them to perform the back surgery, and I would be there in a few days. I just could not put my dear dog asleep without seeing her, and I was willing to take care of her the best I could.

Mile by mile, day by day, we were getting closer, and we stopped to overnight with my old Newfoundland friends who were scattered throughout Canada. We pitched in Edmonton, Saskatoon, and Winnipeg. We were cruising major miles every day on the Gold Wing, but Canada is such an enormous country, and it was difficult to make up much time when you have thousands of miles in front of you every day.

Finally, on Thursday, July 2, we arrived at the University of Guelph, Veterinary College / Animal Hospital. What a facility! It was huge, bigger than our Health Sciences Centre in St. John's. The facility dealt with everything from a budgie bird to a cow. It was an amazing place to see first-hand. I will never forget my first meeting with my beloved beagle since we departed on our trip. First, we met with her doctor, Dr. Walt Engwerson. He explained the back surgery he had performed on her and the poor prognosis. Shortly after, they brought Gypsy into our waiting room. The poor thing must have been traumatized—she'd had her back injury, then she was put in a cold plastic crate and flown to Ontario. There was not a familiar face to be seen, and then she'd had a major operation. All this drama with no Barry around, and suddenly I appeared! Gypsy was crying and whimpering as she strained to pull herself across the floor using only her front legs. She wanted to be with me. Her two back legs dragged behind her like limp rubber gloves, and urine ran out from under her. I will never forget that moment. Her back was three-quarters shaved, and she had a blood-covered incision about eight inches long stitched along the top of her back. I was shocked but also glad to see my dog. (I still tear up typing this thirty-five years later). But hey, she was alive, and I was there to help her!

Alice and I stayed with our friends in Whitby, and we drove out to Guelph to visit Gypsy every day. We met with Gypsy's doctor and received advice on her post-surgery care. After a couple of days' rest, we continued our bike trip back to Newfoundland. On July 8, we arrived home, some 22,900 kilometres, twenty states, and nine provinces later. What a ride!

Gypsy shortly after back surgery

On July 10, after several more days in hospital, Gypsy was flown home. She still had no feeling in her hind legs and very little bladder or bowel control. During her first checkup, I saw Dr. Bland prick her back paws with a sharp needle—no reaction, no reflex. It was not looking good, but Gypsy was only seven years old, and I was determined she was going to get a few more quality years if I could help it. I was in an ideal position at the lighthouse, where I worked and lived with my dog twenty-four hours a day. I could give her the best possible care. The doctors and staff at Guelph had been excellent, professional, and always encouraging. Over the phone, they instructed me on the different physio exercises Gypsy would require and informed me that swimming was excellent therapy for her. They also kindly told me they had never seen a dog recover from this type of back injury, especially considering the surgery had not been performed in the first couple of days after the disc had slipped. They wished me good luck. The medical cost was never an issue with them. They instructed me to pay whenever I could, which was kind of them. Within a year, I had the $2,500 bill paid off.

I began my mission to bring my beagle back to having a quality life at Long Point Lighthouse. She was not mobile, so I kept her in her basket and kept changing her blankets when they became dirty. On warm, sunny days I would place her outdoors in the sun outside my office. Well, the tourists would walk every inch of the lighthouse grounds, and most would see Gypsy and fall in love with her. They all wanted to know what had happened to her. It was funny that there were icebergs and humpback whales soaking by just offshore, but the tourists were more interested in my lighthouse beagle. She had thousands of photos taken of her in July and August that summer, and I think Gypsy really liked being the centre of attention. Those darn beagles are like that!

Since the best physio was swimming, I first converted a broken deep fridge into a swimming/wading pool for her. That was a total disaster. Her sharp claws cut through the plastic liner the first minute she was in it, so I scrapped that idea. The best physio workout for Gypsy was for me to get into a pond with her and swim behind her while holding her hind legs. I would stand behind her while moving them back and forth. She would automatically do the dog paddle with her front paws as I held her from behind and gently pushed her along. I continued this workout for the remainder of the summer and well into September until the pond water got too cold for me. During this period, I also welded up a K9 cart or wheelchair for her. That helped her to stay mobile in the early stages by pulling herself forward with her front legs.

I carried out the essential physio exercise on her back legs about five or six times a day, every day, for months. This would involve flexing and squeezing her toes, flexing her ankles back and forth, and moving her rubbery legs and her hips. This would take fifteen to twenty minutes for every session. I even had to squeeze her belly, and bladder, to make her pee. I had to empty her bladder to prevent her from getting water infections. It was a stressful time for me. I continued this personal care routine on Gypsy at the lighthouse.

After a couple of months into my mission, I was beginning to feel discouraged. Gypsy had just recovered from a water infection with meds, and now I was dealing with several open sores on her hind paws from where she had dragged them in her wheelchair. Her legs were still like soft rubber. It was pitiful. I was not seeing any progress for all my efforts—but she would look at me with those loving eyes, and I would push on. I would take her swimming in the pond behind the Legion in Twillingate—called Scratch Ass Pond. Then, one evening after work in late August, during our routine swim, I felt something. Gypsy was doing her usual dog paddle with her front paws, when suddenly I felt her right hind leg kick back at me! I could not believe it. A signal to kick had reached from her brain to her hind legs. I was so excited, I danced with joy and gave her a big kiss. Maybe, just maybe, my hard work and determination were paying off. This inspired me to continue in hope.

I pressed on for months through the occasional water infection, pulled muscles, and regular trips to Grand Falls to see Dr. Bland. Over time, Gypsy developed a little muscle mass in her hind legs, and her front legs really developed. She grew stronger and healthier. After about ten months into her physio routine, it appeared she had recovered as much as she possibly could. I decided I would slowly reduce the routine. Her bladder had now recovered, and her bowels returned to sixty per cent. I always had to time her meals and her bowel movements. She could even wag her tail again, something she could not do for months. She was what I called "front-wheel drive." She could walk well, but when she tried to run, her hind legs could not keep up with her front legs—they were out of sync. She would have trouble climbing up steps, but other than that, she was fine. Mission accomplished. Only my girlfriend (now my wife), Alice, and my wonderful veterinarian, Dr. Michael Bland, knew the time and effort I put in with my much-loved beagle. Compared to the first time I had seen her at the hospital in Guelph, I was overjoyed with the results. It was quite the undertaking, but worth it. Gypsy was my lighthouse beagle.

For years later, whenever Dr. Bland and I would meet, he would mention Gypsy and give me a big smile. I am proud to say Gypsy lived another seven happy years with me and Alice. I transferred to Bacalhao Island Lighthouse for four years, and Gypsy went out there with me for several shifts. She enjoyed lighthouse living. Amazingly, she managed to navigate over the rocks and the rough terrain. She would often join me when I went berry picking down over the islands or out in speedboat to try for a fish. Gypsy even spent some time with me later when I started work at Surgeon's Cove Head Lighthouse on Exploits Island.

Gypsy had lived a great and unique life and was my "lighthouse beagle" on three different lighthouses in Notre Dame Bay. My beloved Gypsy went to doggy heaven on October 16, 1995. I buried her in the back corner of our farmland, under a huge old pine tree, and placed a nice wooden Cross there.

A year after she passed, my neighbour Hubert told me that Gypsy would slowly walk up the road to the government wharf around the end of my shift. He said that, a day or two before I was due to be flown home, he would see Gypsy strutting up the road, and then, after waiting there for a while, she would slowly return home. Hubert often watched her, because it was rare for Gypsy to leave our yard after she got older. For some reason, she knew when my twenty-eight-day shift was ending. Neither Alice nor I knew that she would take this walk up the road and wait for me!

Radio Communications

Radio communication was an important part of our job and also a way of life on the lighthouses. It might be talking with the Canadian Coast Guard Radio Station, CCG helicopters, CCG ships, and other marine traffic—it was all part of our daily routine. And of course talking to the other lighthouses in Notre Dame Bay! Keeping radio communications with our family and friends was also an essential part of our well-being and mental health. The VHF radio, mobile telephone, and antenna were supplied by the Canadian Coast Guard. Most lightkeepers also had their own personal CB, VHF, or portable radios at the lighthouses. When I first became a keeper of the light, the CB radio was the main piece of equipment we used to communicate. Later, VHF became our radio of choice.

The lighthouses had a daily weather report schedule with Comfort Cove Coast Guard Radio station using the VHF radio. Every morning, the radio operator would call the lighthouses in Notre Dame Bay to request our local weather and ice conditions. This important radio station was located on the top of Loon Bay Hill and began operation in January 1967. It replaced the old radio station that was in Twillingate and had been managed by Canadian National Telegraph Company (CNT).

The Coast Guard ships would occasionally make radio contact with us requesting local weather, wind, sea, or ice conditions. Frequently, our Coast Guard helicopters would radio us to request weather conditions, changeover information, or check the jet fuel inventory on station. There were usually a dozen or more bright yellow forty-five-gallon drums of helicopter fuel stored on the edge of the helicopter pads to be used for a backup supply for the whirlybirds. The local fishermen and hunters also contacted us looking for weather and ice conditions in the area. Recreational boaters radioed us regularly to check on the conditions at the lighthouses, because quite often they were different from the conditions in their safe harbours in the bay. Sometimes we would have to give directions to amateur or lost boaters who were not sure of the correct route. I have seen it all.

Nighttime was when the CB or VHF radios really came alive. There was a huge radio community along the coast of Notre Dame Bay. I did not realize how many radio owners and operators were around until I went to work at the lighthouses. Thousands of residents had radios mounted up under the cupboards in their kitchen, cabin, or shed so they could make contact with their fishing and hunting buddies, or maybe just give a shout out to their friends out there in radio land, while others tuned in to listen to the nightly radio chatter taking place. It was a part of their nightly entertainment. We lightkeepers had friends and radio acquaintances who would contact us almost every night for a chat, maybe to get updates on the sea or ice conditions, or it could be about seals, birds, marine traffic, or anything. There were folks I had regular radio contact with for years whom I never actually laid eyes on in my entire life—strictly friends through the radio airwaves. I would talk to some for a few years and have a picture in my mind of how they looked, going only by the sound of their voices. Then I might finally meet them somewhere, and they would look totally different from what I had imagined!

I spoke to relief keeper Dave Fudge at Cape John Gull Island Lighthouse for many years. He was from Ming's Bight, but I had never seen the man, just enjoyed our many chats on the VHF radio. On a calm but chilly Tuesday, December 29, 1998, Wally Snow, Bill Walsh, and I cruised out the bay to Exploits Island. We did a late winterizing job at our cabins and then decided to visit our friends Richard and Lydia Wells. As I was removing my winter boots in their porch, I could hear this familiar voice coming from the kitchen. I recognized his tone and mannerisms—it was Dave Fudge! I didn't know, but he was working the Christmas shift on Surgeon's Cove Head and happened to be in the harbour visiting Rich. After listening to him for ten years, it was a real treat to finally meet the man face to face, but he was not at all as I had pictured him. We enjoyed a great chat over a cup of tea, and we never met again.

These regular calls over the radio were often our entertainment during the long winter season. The main VHF radio at the station always had the volume button cranked up in case an emergency call came in. After the supper dishes were all cleaned up and tucked away, the regular calls would start blasting in on the radio. Many of these folks on the radio were entertainers, storytellers, and comedians. They also knew they had an audience out there listening to them, which made them a bit wittier and maybe enhanced their stories that much more. Most radio operators also had their own unique style and mannerism when talking on the radio. Some had certain channels they would use so listeners knew where to find them. Topics ranged from how many fish "Jarge" caught today to the latest political event. I even heard grown men talk about characters like Victor and Nikki on the afternoon TV soap operas.

During the wicked stormy weather or the long, boring nights, the radios were greatly appreciated. Certain amateur radio operators stood out over others. Fellow lightkeeper Boyce Gray was one of them. He was from Shoe Cove and was stationed over at the famous Gull Island Lighthouse on a rock 525 feet above sea level off Cape John. It was the highest lighthouse in Atlantic Canada. Boyce was always funny, entertaining, and certainly a colourful character. The stories and jokes this guy came up with were endless. If I was having a lonely day on the light, a chat with Boyce was all the medicine I needed—he would always brighten my mood. I would be chatting with him on the radio, and before you knew it, you had killed an hour. I used to say to Boyce, if he had a good manager, he would be performing comedy in Las Vegas. He was my Dr. Phil and my Robin Williams, so, Skipper Boyce, I thank you!

There were many radio buffs all around this large bay, on Change Islands, Fortune Harbour, Twillingate, and all around the circle. They had some great radio "call names" as well—the Midnight Rambler (Scott Nippard from Embree), the Young Puffin (Glen Hurley from Change Islands), the White Cane (Doug Roberts from Wild Cove, Twillingate), the Black Cat (Millicent Farthing from Herring Neck), Exploits Radio (Richard Wells from Exploits Island), Mary J (Harold Hennifent from Fortune Harbour), and Jordon B (Wally Snow from Embree), to name a few. It was amazing how many people radioed the light stations and the large numbers of folks who were content to just sit back and listen to us shoot the breeze.

The most important contact was with home. Our girlfriends and wives were holding down the fort for the month we were away. They did not have it easy while keeping everything afloat with kids, work schedules, the house, and snow in the winter. They were essentially single parents for half of the year. God love our better halves! They tolerated the comings and goings of a lightkeeper's life in rural Newfoundland. That daily radio call from my wife, Alice, was priceless. Just to hear her sweet voice come from that cheap speaker in the radio helped me get through many long shifts on the islands.

In the beginning, we communicated through regular CB radios when I went to Bacalhao Island. That was not so successful, so I upgraded to a sideband CB radio and a higher antenna. That made a slight improvement, though most of our conversations were noisy and had dropouts. Over time, I experimented with improved antennas and cables with the help of my friendly electronic technician Bern Day, who lived nearby. The real problem boiled down to the fact that my antenna in Porterville was too far away from my other antenna on Bacalhao Island—they were approximately forty-one miles apart. The process was trial and error and took years to work through.

Finally, I upgraded my radio system again. This time I moved to the more powerful marine VHF radios along with power inverters and new antennas. More than $1,000 later, I was set up again. Alice and I would pick a certain time and call each other on this new radio set-up and it worked! I was incredibly pleased to be able to talk to home with no static blasting in. We used this VHF system for several months, but in the back of my mind, I still knew half of Notre Dame Bay was listening to my personal conversations with my wife. Besides the scanners tuning in, I could almost hear the hundreds of radios clicking over to channel 60 at 10:30 p.m. because that was when lightkeeper Porter talked to his wife. Each keeper had his own favourite channel and time for that important connection home, and many eavesdropped.

Our Canadian Coast Guard mobile phone was often noisy or out of order and expensive to use. There was no privacy on these radios, and it was difficult to talk personal business on the islands. Alice and I were married in 1990, so the next year we decided it was time to try to start a family. Due to the shift life, we had a limited window to "work with," but by early January of 1992, as they say, Alice had a bun in the oven. I was away on the island when she discovered she was pregnant. So, earlier, we had devised a plan in case she had to inform me of any "positive" baby test. Due to the fact so many people were listening to us, we used a code—"puppies" being the key word. On January 26, Saturday night, Alice snuck the code word into our conversation without half of Notre Dame Bay learning our secret. We had experienced so many great things and travels together, and now were about to start a new chapter in our life. We were becoming parents.

The lack of privacy started to bother me more and more as I used my radio for those important home-connection chats. I was okay with people listening to us in general, but I knew this old guy just down the road from me in Porterville was glued to the channel I used every night I talked to Alice. His radio name was The Blue Spud. A fine old fellow, but he would repeat half of my conversations to his friends! Over time, I looked into getting a private channel installed into my two radios. After many phone calls and research, I drove two hours to see a radio technician out in Wesleyville, down around the Loop. This guy really knew his electronics, so I left my radios with him. He installed a scrambler in each of my two VHF radios. This chip scrambled my outgoing radio signal and unscrambled it in my radio on the opposite end. It was similar to a radio system used by fishermen at the limited yet lucrative tuna fishery that was taking place off the Virgin Rocks east of Newfoundland. From then on, anybody listening to Alice and me on channel 60 would only hear a mumbled, jumbled sound. Perfect!

A week later, I drove out to Wesleyville to pick up my new private radio systems. It was expensive—it cost me over $600—but I did not care. It was going to be worth it. I was finally going to have privacy while talking to my dear wife, Alice. During the four-hour drive, I was smiling from ear to ear just thinking that the old Blue Spud was not going to eavesdrop on our nightly chats anymore. I could not wait to hook up my radios and check out my new private channel on my VHFs.

Call it irony, if you like, but a day before I was scheduled to return to my shift at the lighthouse with my new and improved "private" radios, my dear old neighbour down the road passed away suddenly from a heart attack.

Automation

> "The automatic transfer of one unit of a complex industrial assembly to a succession of machines."
>
> — *Funk & Wagnalls Dictionary*

Automation and de-staffing were always dreaded words for us lightkeepers around the island. Replacing lightkeepers with modern automated equipment was taking place in lighthouses all around the world for decades. Lighthouse automation began in Canada back in 1970 with Prime Minister Pierre Elliott Trudeau's Liberal government. Between 1970 and 1996, 264 lighthouses were automated in Canada.

When I started my first shift as a lightkeeper way back in 1983, my co-worker, Calvin Moore, told me, "Do not expect a career here, because the lighthouses could be automated any day!" That possibility, which at times felt like a threat, dangled over my head and the heads of all my lightkeeper brothers throughout my career with the Canadian Coast Guard, whether it was during our union contract negotiations, or when requesting renovations and improvements to the dwelling, or ordering supplies. Automation and lack of job security were always lurking around the corner and always in the back of my mind when I was taking out a loan to buy a new truck or doing major renovations to our home. The senior lightkeepers were not quite as concerned because most of them had enough years with the Canadian Coast Guard. They hoped to qualify for a pension or some type of "package." For years, I was the youngest lightkeeper in the NL Coast Guard region, so I was always aware and genuinely concerned about automation—not to mention the fact I disagreed with the principal of it.

Some bureaucrats in Ottawa, sitting in their fancy offices a thousand miles from any salt water, were making decisions regarding the safety around our dangerous coastline waters. Of course, I wanted to keep my job, but I also felt that a computer chip, or a solar panel bolted onto a cliff, could not provide the same service as a salt-blooded lightkeeper perched out there with a radio and a set of binoculars.

Over the years, technology improved for the marine users with global positioning systems (GPS), radars, loran C, and cellphone and VHF radio coverage. Unfortunately, there were still areas in this bay with no radio or cell service. To add to this issue, many of the smaller-boat operators did not have the modern equipment or did not know how to operate it properly. Having said that, I have also seen large ships, with the most modern equipment available, get in trouble and make major errors in this large bay. In January 1985, the freighter *Manolis L*, loaded with paper products and topped up with tons of fuel, struck a rock and sank behind Bacalhao Island. It created an environmental nightmare in the Change Islands area for years. Later, on October 24, 1996, my father and I, along with my young son, witnessed a large paper ship loaded with Abitibi Bowater paper get lost in the fog. It cruised out the main shipping run from the port of Botwood and attempted to navigate into a small harbour called Great Muddy Hole, just south of Muddy Hole Point (approximately one mile off course). Due to poor visibility, the crew had mistaken this cove for the main route leading out to the wide Atlantic Ocean. Sitting there in my speedboat, I could not believe what I was seeing, but luckily someone on the ship's bridge finally realized they were headed in the wrong direction. The crew hastily stopped the huge ship before it hit the jagged rocks and slowly reversed it out of this dead-end cove. Certain disaster averted!

I had seen our modern equipment and their backup systems fail many times at the different lighthouses I worked on. For example, one day the important "backup" bulbs for our main light in the tower would not power up. Next to the main bulb, there was a spare bulb that was spring-loaded and designed to rotate in place when the main bulb burned out. Also, sometimes the automatic fog detector would not register the reduced visibility in fog or snow and failed to warn mariners. This would occasionally happen when the videograph window became covered in freezing glitter or heavy salt spray. The fog detector was called a videograph. It shot a strobe light two miles out across the ocean through a small window in the fog alarm building. If the light bounced back, it meant there was reduced visibility caused by fog, snow, or heavy rain. This would engage the foghorn to blow. Under ideal conditions and in a perfect world, this technology would perform precisely as designed. However, when this equipment is installed in a harsh environment where it is exposed to extreme temperature changes, salt spray, corrosion, high winds, freezing rain, and even seagull droppings or a spider's web, the working performance of these important aids to navigation is negatively impacted.

On several occasions, I had to climb up in the light tower and manually replace burned-out bulbs in the main light or scrape freezing ice off the videograph window to enable them to work. A real, living lightkeeper, not a computer, would have to be there to perform these jobs. We lightkeepers—"lifekeepers"—were the backup to the backup system.

Another reason I disagreed with the automation and de-staffing of the lighthouses was that we were providing an important service. We radioed existing weather, sea, and ice conditions to the local fishermen, hunters, and recreational boaters in the area almost every day. We had also assisted the Canadian Coast Guard ships or the Search and Rescue helicopter on several rescues in the area throughout the years. And there was no way to determine how many accidents we prevented by informing boaters of the rough sea or wind conditions right there around the lighthouse. I felt, in those cases, we lightkeepers were justifying our existence out on these weather-beaten lighthouses.

During the winter of 1985, I had my first dealings with the feared automation and cuts debate. At that time there were fifty-six manned lighthouses in Newfoundland. A federal committee studying the lighthouses in the province asked me about the importance of Long Point Lighthouse. I wrote a long letter explaining the significance of this particular light station and gave great detail describing the amount of marine traffic around this historic station and how valuable this old lighthouse was to the local marine operators and the local tourism industry. I sweetened up my letter the best I could, trying my best to keep a lightkeeper on Long Point. Mercifully, Long Point Lighthouse was spared during that series of lighthouse de-staffing.

That phase saw several lighthouses around the province become unmanned over the next few years. The nearest lighthouse and lightkeeper affected in this area was John Sheppard at Burnt Point Lighthouse on Fogo island. It was de-staffed and the dwelling completely removed from the site, leaving only an aluminum structure with an automated light and solar panel overlooking the cold Atlantic waters.

By 1994, the cod moratorium was well-established in Newfoundland, and the lighthouse-automation discussion was spreading again. On June 29, 1994, I attended a meeting at a hotel in Gander with Mr. Randy Dawe and Mr. Ray Browne regarding the de-staffing of Surgeon's Cove Head Lighthouse and others. The big shots in Ottawa meant business, but this time I decided I was going to try to fight the process, and hopefully I could prevent the shutdown of this popular lighthouse on Exploits Island or at least delay the automation plans. I informed my co-workers (Lloyd, Arch, and Carl) what I was planning to do, and a couple of days later, I started on my mission. I printed up several petitions protesting the de-staffing of Surgeon's Cove Head Lighthouse on scenic Exploits Island. On July 2 and 3, I drove hundreds of miles to drop off pages of petitions to key communities in Notre Dame Bay. I delivered my petitions to the local drugstores and shops in Summerford, Virgin Arm, Twillingate, Springdale, King's Point, Roberts Arm, and Triton. I also set up a table with the petition in the local Lewisporte Mall collecting signatures. About a week later, I went around and collected dozens of sheets containing names of concerned residents. Amazingly, in six or seven short days, I had collected almost 2,000 names—a strong message of support for Surgeon's Cove Head Lighthouse!

Later, on August 11, 1994, I attended another meeting at the southside base in St. John's with Mr. Randy Dawe, Mr. J. Thomas (Commissioner of Coast Guard), Mr. Ray Browne, Mr. Lorne Humphries (Director General), and a representative from my union. They informed me the Canadian Coast Guard was planning to conduct public consultation meetings in thirty-two communities in Newfoundland to discuss the de-staffing of all the lighthouses.

Finally, on a chilly night in early January of 1995, the Canadian Coast Guard held its consultation meeting in Lewisporte at the Terry Fox Room in the Brittany Inns. They were chaired by Mr. Michael Clements. The room was packed. It was by far the largest turnout at any of their meetings across the province. Eighty-one people registered, and others came in later, pushing the attendance up to 100. It was a great show of support for our beloved and respected lighthouse. Favourable formal presentations were given by the local yacht club, the Rod and Gun Club, Lewisporte Town Council, the Chamber of Commerce, the Canadian Wildlife Services, the Lewisporte and Area Development Association, our local MHA, Melvin Penney (with my petition in hand), MHA Neil Winsor, and other concerned residents. The meetings became heated at times during the three-hour session, but it was an excellent debate.

Later that year, MHAs Melvin Penney, Neil Winsor, and Walter Carter spoke in great detail in the House of Assembly about the importance of staffed lighthouses. Soon after, Melvin Penney went to Parliament Hill in Ottawa along with our federal MP, George Baker, and met with Robert King, Director General of Marine Navigational Services. While there, Melvin voiced his concerns and presented my petition to Doug Young, the Minister of Transport in Ottawa.

A few more lighthouses were de-staffed during this time, but fortunately, Surgeon's Cove Head Lighthouse was spared the Ottawa automation machine for another few years.

From our local newspaper in Lewisporte, the *Pilot*, October 14, 1998: Premier Brian Tobin said he has "received assurances from federal Fisheries Minister David Anderson that DFO will not proceed with plans to de-staff and decommission further lighthouses in NL."

The lighthouses in this bay shone brightly for another few years, until December 2001, when Bacalhao Island and Cape John Gull Island lighthouses were de-staffed. Then, sadly, on September 18, 2002, the lightkeepers on Surgeon's Cove Head, Exploits Island, were flown home for the last time. No lightkeeper stood watch over the ocean there for the first time since 1911.

In October 2011, a report called *Seeing the Light: Report on Staffed Lighthouses in Newfoundland and Labrador and British Columbia* was published by the Standing Senate Committee on Fisheries and Oceans chaired by Senator Fabian Manning.

Below are a few highlights from the report:

> The Committee heard that the Coast Guard engaged in a strategy to downplay the role and capabilities of staffed lightstations to support the de-staffing effort, and that lightkeepers, for their part, had sought to enhance the services they voluntarily provide.
>
> The Committee can only conclude that staffed lightstations and lightkeepers play a key role in public safety, and that any cost savings realized from de-staffing lighthouses will come at a very high price—that is the risk of loss of life. For this reason, the Committee cannot support the Coast Guard's 2009 de-staffing plan.
>
> Lightkeepers perform a variety of important tasks at very modest cost. They are held in very high regard on both coasts. Regrettably, they appear to be unappreciated by their employer, which prompted some discussion at

> our meetings as to whether or not the administration of lighthouses in Canada might be transferred to another government department or agency (e.g., Department of National Defence, Parks Canada, Public Safety Canada, Transport Canada). However, the public does not look at public services within the context of the particular mandates of departments or agencies. In our view, the focus should be on the value of the services that lightkeepers provide, not mandates. Staffed lighthouses should be seen as an opportunity, not a liability.
>
> The Committee recommends that the Canadian Coast Guard halt its current de-staffing plan, and that de-staffing, continued staffing, or restaffing be determined on a lightstation-by-lightstation basis through appropriate guidelines and thorough consultations. Until this is completed, current lightkeeper staff levels should be maintained in the Pacific Region and in the Newfoundland and Labrador Region.

Currently there are twenty-three manned lighthouses remaining in Newfoundland, and the only staffed lighthouse left in Notre Dame Bay is Long Point on Twillingate Island.

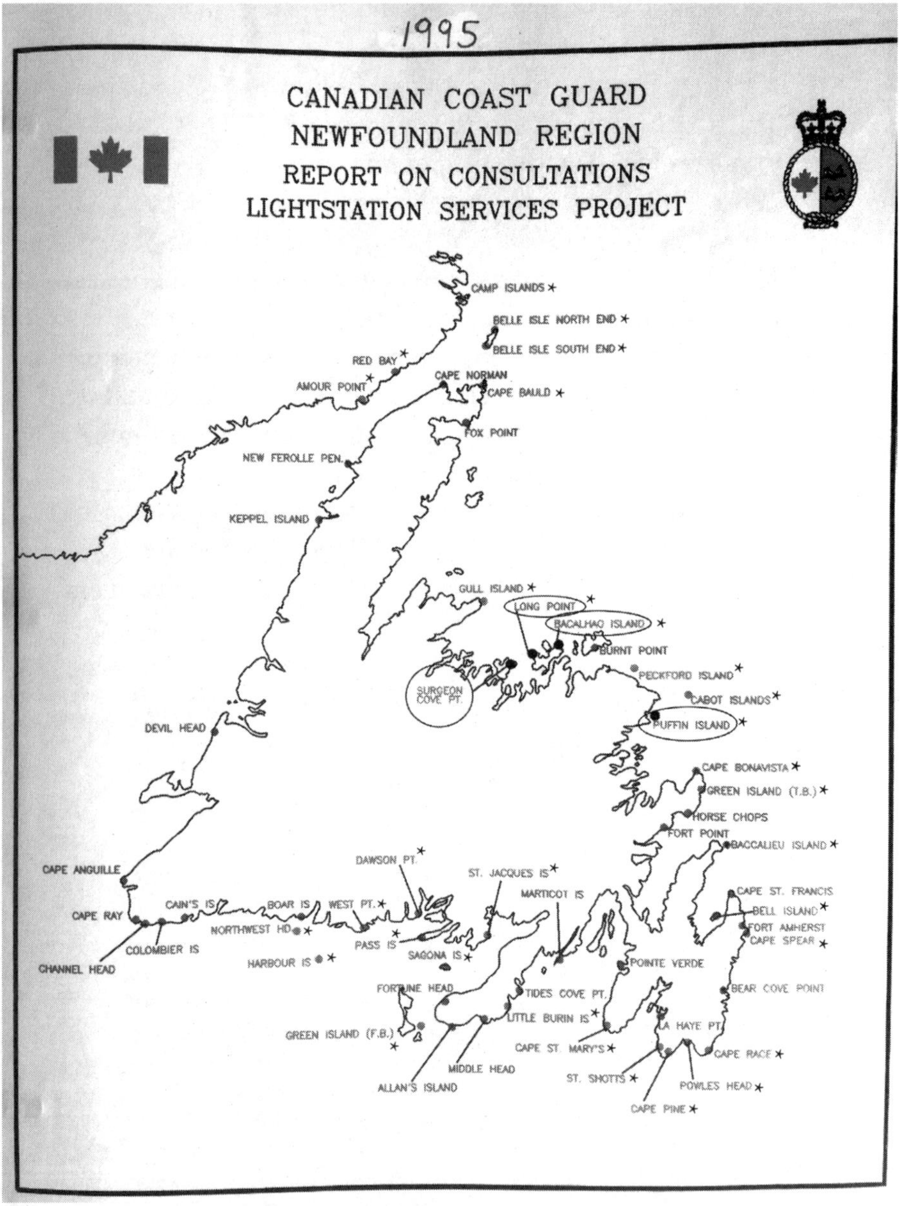

Asterisks (*) indicate lighthouses that were staffed.
Circles indicate lighthouses that Barry Porter manned.

Ghost Stories

Lighthouses have been connected to ghost stories for centuries, maybe because of their lonely, isolated locations or just the eerie image of an old house engulfed by fog banks and howling wind. It is the ideal setting for the supernaturally creepy world. I have two stories of my own related to this Twilight Zone.

My first summer working at Long Point Lighthouse had been a great one. Thousands of tourists visited the site, and I had two excellent university students working with me. By late November 1984, it was just my beagle, Gypsy, and me. I was seeing the harshest weather I had ever witnessed in my life. The vicious winds on the hill were unending with horizontal rain mixed with endless days of fog. During these terrible storms, the old dwelling always had a few odd sounds from whistles, creaks, cracks, thumps, and doors moving. For days my visibility would be practically zero, and the powerful old foghorn was blasting non-stop. It felt eerie to work and live there perched over 300 feet above the seas and unable to see a thing through the clouds of fog.

My wristwatch showed midnight as I started out on my station inspection. A terrible fall storm had been battering Long Point for several days. It was cold, wet, and ugly outside, and I was working my Friday night shift. By Saturday morning, I would be off shift and would return to my home in Porterville for a day to escape this hypnotizing weather. I slowly climbed up the 100-year-old oak stairs leading to the top of the lonely concrete tower. The main light was glowing, slicing out through the thick fog but failing to penetrate beyond a few hundred yards. Everything appeared to be working fine. With foggy conditions like this, the main light was next to useless — my foghorn was the main aid for marine traffic. I noticed as I was descending the staircase in the light tower that the foghorn had stopped. This meant visibility must have improved to at least two miles, because the videograph shut off automatically at that range. I was hoping the weather had started to improve. I clambered down the stairway to go check the equipment in the fog alarm building.

Thankfully, the light tower and dwelling was connected to the fog alarm building by what we called the tunnel. The tunnel was a narrow clapboard hallway stretching over 100 feet long. The interior was bare, rough wooden walls with the studs showing and a flat roof. The floor was also wooden, made well-worn and shiny by generations of lightkeepers walking to and from the foghorn along with its weekly mop-overs. It looked like a solitary one-lane bowling alley, except this one was sloping downhill. This tunnel had six heavy iron eyebolts with cables attached and anchored into the bedrock outside. The purpose of this apparatus was to prevent the tunnel from blowing away! That is an indication of how strong the winds were there.

Long Point's spooky light tower staircase, with Dylan and Sarah

As I walked down that cold, poorly lit tunnel, I could hear gales of wind swirling outside, and the old tunnel was actually vibrating. It was a bit scary with only three forty-watt light bulbs illuminating the chilly walkway. I stopped halfway down the tunnel to peek out through the tiny window to check the visibility, but it was covered in dried salt spray. I could not see a thing. I slowly opened the heavy wooden door and entered the fog alarm building. The warmth of the heaters hit me in the face as I reached out to flick on the lights. Nothing happened. Strange. Another flick, but still no lights. Maybe the switch had finally worn out—considering almost everything in the lighthouse was old and weather-beaten. Since I was in the building, I walked over to inspect the huge compressor that powered the foghorn.

By 1984, most lighthouses had an electronic foghorn, but Long Point still had the old-fashioned air horn—a powerful one at that, with a huge motor and large air tank and a matching set-up next to it as backup. It had an audible range of ten miles. Pretty impressive. The only lighting in the room was a beam coming in from the flash of main light from the light tower. It partially lit up the room with its five-second rotation cycle. I stood there for a bit observing the scene playing out in front of me. I thought I heard something a little different than expected, but I was not sure. Slowly, I turned around and walked toward the exit, when I heard the sound again. What the heck was that? I was alone standing in a 100-year-old building engulfed in a northeast gale. I held my breath and listened—but nothing. Then, suddenly, I heard it again! I had never heard this sound before.

I walked back over to the compressors again. I had to figure this out. Straining to pinpoint the source, the more I listened, the spookier this environment began to feel inside my head. The sound would occur every few minutes. I listened carefully, and when I heard it again, it sounded like a voice. Cold shivers shot through me in a wave. It happened again—I heard, "Let me out!"

I booted it to the exit door and out of the fog alarm building. Slamming the door shut, I tried to catch my breath while standing out in the tunnel again. I thought to myself, What the heck am I hearing? Is this place haunted? The previous lightkeeper had never mentioned any ghost to me. Mind you, I was the first lightkeeper to live in the old dwelling since the 1970s. I crept back into the fog alarm building but stayed next to the door. Sure enough, I heard again, "Let me out!" With that, I raced up through the tunnel. Olympic gold medallist Jonathan Bailey wouldn't have caught me in that 100-foot sprint.

After settling down in my comfy chair in my office back in the dwelling, I started wondering what was going on down there. I had only been working here at this old lighthouse for a few months, and I wanted to stay there. But I also knew if I was going to work there and keep my government job, I had to find out what this strange noise was and where it was coming from. After sitting in my office for about thirty minutes, I got up my nerve and decided to investigate the mysterious sound again. This time I grabbed a flashlight and a hammer, and with my beagle by my side, we descended into the narrow tunnel again. By now it was pushing past 1:00 a.m., well into the witching hour. If there was a ghost, I was about to find out. Visibility was holding at two to three miles, but a gale of northeasterlies was still battering the station. I gently opened the fog alarm building door, stepped inside, and flicked the switch, but there was still no power or lights. I felt braver this time with my flashlight shining and my trusty dog, Gypsy, by my side. I carefully inched over to the large green compressor again straining to hear anything. Standing there, I heard the sound again. This time, I stood my ground and tuned in. I held my breath and listened. Then I heard it again. I finally narrowed it down to where this was coming from.

Ah! I had figured it out. The compressor was pumped to the maximum, bursting with air, ready to blast whenever the fog bank rolled back in. The rubber belts on the compressor motor would occasionally squeak from the buildup of pressure in its large air tank along with the strong gusts of wind hitting the building. This emitted an awful sound that echoed through the square room. This room had terrible acoustics on a good day, let alone after midnight during a storm. Maybe it was my imagination, or maybe it was the "lighthouse spirits" testing the new guy on the hill.

Well, I guess I passed. I faced up to the issue, and I had solved the mystery of the fog alarm building. It had sure spooked me on that stormy November night at Long Point Lighthouse. I stayed there and enjoyed another four years at the beautiful old lighthouse with no other ghostly activity.

Long before I began work at Exploits Island Lighthouse, I had heard stories and rumours about this "Seeme" (pronounced *see me*) character. In the late 1970s, during visits to the island to friends' cabins, I had heard rumblings about a ghost out there, but I didn't pay much attention to them—not until a cold, windy day in March 1992 when the helicopter dropped me off on the pad at Surgeon's Cove Head Lighthouse. I was about to start my new position on Exploits Island. I had some experience by now—I had been keeper of the light for four years on Long Point, Twillingate, and another four years on Bacalhao Island. Obtaining work at this fine lighthouse on Exploits Island had been my desire for a few years. On Wednesday, March 11, I had finally achieved my goal.

Exploits Island was overflowing with rich, interesting history. It had been a booming fishing and trading community for over a century. Hundreds of people had made Exploits their home. It was also the home of questionable characters like John Peyton Sr. and Jr. in the late 1700s and early 1800s. For a few years, it was also home to Shanawdithit, the last of the Beothuk. Sadly, life on this island gradually dwindled, and resettlement finally shut it down in the mid-1960s, leaving only old houses, wharves, and churches to decay and crumble to the ground. Graveyards were slowly overgrown, inch by inch, but the rich stories and vivid memories remain.

My new work partner at Surgeon's Cove Head Lighthouse was Arch Budgell from Campbellton, who actually grew up on Exploits Island. That Wednesday I unpacked all my gear and moved into my very own bedroom. I stored away my monthly food supplies and made myself at home. Arch had decided he would finish working today's shift. At 2200 hours (10:00 p.m.), Arch went outdoors, checked the diesel generator and main light, then signed off for the evening. I was excited to continue my career at this important lighthouse. My first official shift was scheduled to start in a few hours, Thursday, March 12, 0200 hours (2:00 a.m.). It had been a long, busy day—changeovers were always that way. Arch decided to call it quits and went to bed around ten thirty. I grabbed a light blanket, dimmed the lights, and lay on the sofa in the living room to catch a little nap before I started my watch. I set the alarm clock for two o'clock and placed it on the floor next to me. It was just for a backup—after years of working this same shift, my internal clock always woke me before 2:00 a.m. It was never an issue. The sofa was comfy, and in a short time, I drifted off.

I slept like a log, but I was also having many crazy dreams. Then it felt like it was time for me to get up and go to work, but for some strange reason I couldn't get up—I could not move. It was like I was stuck or pinned down. I could not lift my body up off the sofa. It was weird because I was still asleep, but I was also aware of what was happening around me. Suddenly, I broke free and jumped up. Wow! I was all out of sorts and confused by what I had just experienced. I looked at the alarm clock. Strangely, it had stopped only minutes before two o'clock. Standing in the middle of the living room, trying to get my brain working, I looked at my wristwatch. It read 3:00 a.m. I had overslept a full hour! How was this possible?

I raced over to the large window in the living room and slid the window open. I poked my head out into the frosty air and looked in toward Upper Black Island and the shipping route leading into Botwood. It was a cold, clear night with a bright moon shining over the packed ice floes. I scanned the horizon along Muddy Hole Point and Northern Harbour following along the shoreline. I was relieved to see no ships were in trouble, but I felt terrible because I had overslept. With my head still protruding out through the window, I glanced farther out to the north toward the main light. To my shock, the light was out—black as your boot! Even the backup emergency light was not working. Not good. I could not believe what I was seeing. Was this still a dream? The main light rarely failed. I snatched a flashlight and raced down the basement stairs, threw on my jacket and boots, and headed out across the snow to the old iron light tower. I opened the heavy door and flew up the narrow staircase to the landing where the huge brass main light was located. The main light had a spring-loaded system with a bulb powered up and a spare bulb next to it. If the main bulb failed, the spare bulb would switch into contact and light up. If that failed, the smaller, emergency light had a sensor on it and was programmed to turn on. None of these systems had worked. I was shocked—the main light had gone out on my very first shift! I promptly flicked a few switches and got the new bulb to light. Thankfully, there was no shipping in the ice-packed bay that night. Nobody except for maybe a few seagulls or rabbits noticed the main light was out. I dared not even blink for the rest of the night, frightened to death I would fall into a deep daze again.

Later that morning, Arch got up and had his breakfast, and I never said a word about the bizarre night I had just punched. Soon he headed off into the harbour for a few hours on his faithful snowmobile. The whole day, I was still spinning about what had happened to me. Reliving it in my mind as I cooked supper for both of us, I felt embarrassed that I had overslept. Finally, I could not keep it inside me any longer. In the middle of our supper, I felt I had to spill the beans. I told Arch the whole story of what had happened during the night, and surprisingly, he did not flinch. He just chuckled and said, "Oh, that's just Seeme up to her old tricks again."

Many months later, I told the story to Richard Wells, who lived in the harbour. Richard filled me in on the story behind Seeme. Her real name was Lavita Seymour, and she lived with lightkeeper Gus Jefferies and his family on Surgeon's Cove

Head after her husband had passed away. The Jefferies' youngest daughter could not pronounce Seymour, so she called their live-in guest Seeme. Richard said Seeme had passed years ago, on New Year's Eve, in her bed at the lighthouse. Her bedroom was the same room that I had moved into that day! Welcome to Surgeon's Cove Head Lighthouse.

Seeme's cross-flagpole outside my bedroom window

To add to this strange event, in August of 1993, the Canadian Coast Guard carpenters came to the station and built an extension on our back bridge. They also poured a large concrete block on which they erected a steel flagpole only a few feet from the dwelling. Near the top of this pole were two metal arms extending out to accommodate the Canadian flag and the provincial flag. As luck would have it, this was positioned perfectly so that, in the night, when the main light rotated, every flash hit the top of the flagpole. It lit up like a large white Cross, and it was only visible when looking out my bedroom window.

Several years later, I told this story to two different lightkeepers, separately, and they both said the same thing had happened to them a few years earlier as well. They both confided in me that they had never, ever told a soul. Spooky!

What I experienced that night while asleep on the sofa is called the Old Hag. It was the only time I ever experienced it.

Off-Duty Rescues

Lightkeepers have been saving lives and preventing marine accidents in Newfoundland since 1813. That's when the first lighthouse was constructed at Fort Amherst, St. John's. In the early 1990s, during discussions with the federal government over contract negotiations, our national union (the Public Service Alliance of Canada) called us "lifekeepers." They even printed up stickers and distributed them across the country. Throughout my years working for the Canadian Coast Guard, I had been involved in several rescues at various levels of urgency. Oddly enough, it was during my days off (lieu days) from the lighthouse when I was directly "hands-on" with some life-or-death rescues, which involved mariners going under water and nearly drowning. Most folks have never been involved in real life-saving incidents in their entire lives. For some reason, I was in the right place for five separate stress-filled rescues involving more than a dozen lives. These stories still give me goosebumps years later as I write about them for the very first time.

It may be simply good timing, or due in part to my keen sense of sight and awareness, or an unknown force. After years working at the lighthouse, my eyes had become trained to automatically scan the shoreline or horizon looking for anything out of the ordinary. It may be a broken-down speedboat, smoke, whales, or any number of things. Once, from Long Point Lighthouse, I reported a forest fire starting up miles away up in Green Bay. Another time I spotted a large shipping container floating fourteen to fifteen miles northeast of Long

Lifekeepers sticker

Point. I reported that one to the authorities because it was a hazard to shipping. Days later, I was told by Comfort Cove Coast Guard Radio it had fallen off a freighter two or three days earlier during a severe storm up north. I still have a set of binoculars sitting on the window ledge at my home overlooking the bay, and another set of binoculars at my cabin overlooking the pond—just in case a rescue might be required. Recently, I spotted an empty fourteen-foot aluminum boat floating adrift approximately one mile east down across Indian Arm Pond. I promptly jumped aboard my own aluminum boat and towed it back to the safety of my dock.

Sunday, August 16, 1992, was changeover day. I had been off, and I was scheduled to return to work at Surgeon's Cove Head Lighthouse. It was a sunny day with the usual moderate to strong southwest winds. I had launched my seventeen-foot Sunray speedboat and tied it up at the Porterville government wharf. It was gassed up and ready to head out to Exploits Island. I was eating an early lunch when I looked out through my dining room window and noticed two speedboats steaming up along the Southern Passage of Thwart Island. They looked like the boats from the mussel farm down in St. John's harbour. The fishermen appeared to be headed up across the run to the community of Point of Bay. There, they would land at the wharf and have trayloads of freshly picked mussels put on a waiting truck. It was windy, and I knew the two boats were having a hard punch into the southwest winds this Sunday morning. There were always strong tides and currents in that area around the southern tip of the island, and the wind did not help.

Minutes later, I decided to look out at them again, this time with my powerful binoculars. To my surprise, this time I saw only one boat, and that one was sitting dangerously low in the choppy waters. Something was wrong. I raced up to the nearby wharf along with my brother-in-law, Gord Rowbottom, and jumped into my boat. We headed across the harbour toward the overloaded boat as fast as we could. With a new 115-horsepower Mariner on my boat, it only took minutes to travel that one mile. My boat was speedy, capable of doing fifty-three mph in ideal conditions.

As I motored up to the heavily burdened boat, I looked back to the east to see a gas tank and two paddles floating away in the distance—but no second boat. Now there were four fishermen aboard an overloaded speedboat. The gunnels of this boat were mere inches above the rough waters, and I could see it splashing in over its bow. This boat was in danger of sinking. I carefully inched up to the side of the boat, enabling two shaken fishermen to jump aboard my boat with some of their gear. One of the men was partially wet. This exchange seemed to lighten their overloaded boat enough to stop the water from splashing in over its bow.

They were now out of immediate danger, but I accompanied them over to Point of Bay's wharf approximately three miles away. Once there and out of danger, they explained to me they had loaded both of their open speedboats to the limit with fresh mussels and spread tarps over their valuable cargo. They then headed to Point of Bay, where the mussels would be trucked to the plant in Fortune Harbour for processing. There was no issue until they got halfway up along Thwart Island and hit the strong southwest winds. In this area you could experience rough water from the strong southwest wind that blew right out the bay from Botwood. This built up a large chop in the water combined with the strong tides running down the sides of Thwart Island. The fishermen were standing at the back of their boats and could not see the water splashing in over the bow due to the large fish trays stacked in front of them. They were unaware they were taking on water until it was too late. Their boat slowly filled up and began to sink. They barely had enough time to jump aboard the other boat that, luckily, was closely following behind them. The boat sank with a full load of mussels and all their gear. The four men were still in some shock but thanked me for getting them out of their dangerous predicament. They knew it could have been so much worse.

SS *Beagle*, my boat I used in this rescue and on many changeovers

By now it was time for me to get to work at the lighthouse. As I pulled away in my speedboat, the men shouted out to me, if I ever wanted a meal of mussels, drop by the mussel farm. I gently pushed my throttle forward and cut across the choppy waters toward Porterville's wharf. I finished packing up my boat, kissed Alice goodbye, and cruised twenty-three miles out into the bay to historic Exploits Island and took up official duties. All in a day's work.

Friday, August 9, 1996, was a quiet night in Porterville. We were relaxing at home enjoying my days off and waiting for our new baby to arrive. My wife, Alice, was big time pregnant, bursting at the seams, and that day was her due date. Our good friends Jimmy and Karen White had dropped over that night to see how mommy-to-be Alice was doing. Suddenly, at 10:00 p.m., the phone rang, and it was Jeff Lush calling from Comfort Cove Coast Guard Radio station. I knew him through work, but it was strange for him to phone me at home. He said he had received a concerning phone call a few minutes earlier from a boater reporting they were broken down off Wiseman's Head, and then the phone call cut off.

I told Jeff I'd have a look around the harbour. My company was just leaving, so I jumped into my truck and drove to a couple of lookout locations where I could get a partial view of our bay. Everything appeared normal from my vantage points—just a black, windy night. I phoned Jeff back and told him I could not see anything out of the ordinary. He thanked me and said good night. About forty-five minutes later, he phoned me again. Jeff was very concerned—I could hear it in his voice. At the radio station, these well-trained radio operators handled emergency calls all the time. Jeff told me that for some reason he had a bad feeling about this phone call. By now it was getting late, but I told him not to worry. As a lightkeeper, I would definitely check it out. Unbeknownst to me, Jeff had also contacted the Search and

Rescue Marine Distress Centre in St. John's and had them on standby. I phoned my brother next door and explained the situation. He was finishing up a game of cards with his buddy Ford and his wife but was willing to help. Excellent! At the time, my seventeen-foot boat, SS *Beagle*, was parked inside my garage, so to save time we took Dennis's boat, which was moored off at the government wharf. Ford came along with us as well because we didn't know what we were going to see in our search.

We had warm southwest winds that night which were gusting up to twenty-five to thirty mph. It was an extremely dark night, not a star or moon in sight, so we took our time as we motored up along the shoreline toward Wiseman's Head. This was approximately two and a half miles southwest of Porterville. The shoreline was familiar territory, but it looked different in the gloom. I brought along my powerful spotlight, which lit up the night quite well. We continued along, flashing the spotlight occasionally, but no boat was to be seen, just rocks and spruce trees. We hugged the shoreline to get a break from the strong winds, and we were starting to wonder if Jeff had received a prank phone call. As we rounded the rocks at Wiseman's Cove Head, the wind hit us in the face again. We continued just a little farther around the headland when, suddenly, my spotlight picked up something. Mystery solved—Jeff Lush's bad feeling had been very much correct. What we saw in my beam of light shocked us at first. A large cabin cruiser, twenty-eight to thirty feet in length, was dead in the water, bobbing up and down, attached to a single piece of rope stretched to its limit. I could see several scared faces looking back at us from the cabin windows and from the back deck—seven people in total, including a couple of frightened children along with a few dogs.

The cruiser had lost all power and was drifting toward the jagged cliffs off the old World War II coastal gun battery at Wiseman's. They had thrown the anchor out, and it hooked in the bottom only a hundred feet from certain disaster. Occasionally the anchor would drag a couple of feet and hook into the bottom again. It was a scary situation to be in with this strong southwest wind chopping down the bay. To add to their discomfort, they had no lights or any power. The boat was riding out the rough waters for now, but if the anchor failed, it could have been smashed into splinters in minutes.

Cellphone service in this area was terrible, and they had no VHF radio service, but they knew they had made partial contact with the Coast Guard radio station at Comfort Cove. All they could do was hope the anchor held in place and that help was on its way. They were relieved when we appeared out of the dark. The cruiser was out from the town of Comfort Cove and operated by Judd Ginn. I knew Judd from years ago.

We discussed the best way to carry out this rescue. Using the only light we had, Dennis and I secured a heavy line from the cabin cruiser to the stern of our boat. Dennis carefully powered up his motor to take the heavy strain off their anchor line. This was dangerous work in the darkness and choppy waters. Judd and his buddy climbed up to their bow and unhooked their anchor from bottom, and we took over control of the powerless cabin cruiser.

I could sense the relief from everyone aboard the stranded vessel as well as our boat. We powered up and towed the heavy cruiser, putting its stern into the wind, then slowly headed back to safer waters. It was a hard tow for Dennis's small, eighteen-foot wooden boat, one he had proudly built by himself a few winters earlier. From time to time, the strong wind would catch the cabin cruiser and drive it sideways on us, but my brother's thirty-horsepower Yamaha sputtered and strained through this difficult tow rescue in fine Coast Guard style.

About an hour later, we had the cabin cruiser safely tied up to the wharf in Porterville. Judd thanked us, and we parted ways. I returned home, phoned Jeff back at the Comfort Cove Coast Guard Radio station, and relayed the good news to him. He was quite relieved. A little later, I received a phone call from the Search and Rescue Centre in St. John's requesting all the details of the incident. It all worked out well. My friend Jeff had made the right decision on the mystery phone call, and we rescued the boaters from certain disaster.

It was well past 2:00 a.m. when I settled down in our bed next to my very pregnant wife. I was proud that we had delivered the stranded boat and its crew safely to Porterville's wharf. Just over a day later, Alice proudly delivered a beautiful baby girl, Sarah. Life is good!

On Friday, September 3, 1999, Alice, our kids, and I were camping in Notre Dame Provincial Park for the Labour Day weekend. We went up a couple of days before the weekend since the weather was fine. We were in Campsite 46, and Nan and Pop were next door in 47. Our kids were enjoying their company as well as the excellent weather and the relaxing park lifestyle. Today was another warm day, so around 11:00 a.m., I took Dylan and Sarah down to the swimming area again for more fun in the pond. I sat back watching my kids enjoy the beach. Several children were playing in the water, splashing and swimming.

Out of nowhere, the wind suddenly chopped in from the northeast and increased to twenty-five to thirty mph. With this unexpected surge, it blew two older kids who were floating on air mattresses right in on the sandy shore. It began to cool down, but most of the kids did not seem to mind. As I was monitoring my own children on the sandy beach, I noticed a lone young boy swimming out toward the island. The distant island was always a popular swim destination. I'd swum out to it many times while camping there as a kid and in later years. It was sort of a local challenge, a test of one's swimming abilities. It was only approximately a quarter-mile from shore—an exciting swim depending on one's fitness and skill.

There were a dozen or so children at the beach playing along the water's edge, and this one boy was battling his way to the island. It appeared as if nobody else was watching this swimmer out there. With the increase in wind and the roiling waters, it made for a much more challenging swim for the young boy. From the corner of my keen lightkeeper's eye, I watched him swim to the island. I could see he was having a difficult swim. At the same time, I took note of the exact location of the park's emergency fourteen-foot aluminum boat, the paddles, rope, and life ring. After much effort, the young lad finally reached the island. I thought he would get a good rest before attempting to swim back to the beach. Well, the rascal rested for no more than one minute, then he entered the rough water again. I knew this could be a problem, so I arranged for one of the mothers nearby to watch my two children for me just in case.

The boy swam about forty feet, and then he suddenly stopped. Immediately, I knew he was in trouble, and I had to move quickly. I shouted to another father, "That kid is drowning!" The man was Tony Edison, a fellow I worked with briefly in the early 1980s and hadn't seen in years. We snatched the boat, dragged it to the water's edge, and launched it into the pond like we had been practising it all summer. I grabbed the paddles and began rowing toward the struggling boy. Tony sat up in front and guided me in the right direction. I knew we did not have much time—the kid was already exhausted from his swim over to the island. The wind kept pushing us off course as we slipped through the water.

The boy was not moving—he was just treading water, barely staying afloat. We yelled out to him that we were coming, trying to push him to fight, to stay above the surface. I braced my feet against the stern of the boat and put every muscle I had into rowing. I pushed hard into the wind and even heard the paddle crack from the strain. We were getting closer, but the poor boy was exhausted. I was turned back-on to him as I paddled, and I glanced over my shoulder to see how much farther. The boy went under and bobbed back up to the surface—he was fighting for his life.

Luckily, I was in top condition from playing many years of hockey and hiking across the lighthouse islands. I dug deeper for whatever strength I had. I was shooting mini whirlpools out from the backs of my paddles. My muscles ached and sweat poured off me, but I knew we were almost there. I put every last draft of energy I had into that last hundred feet of rowing. Finally, Tony shouted for me to stop. We had reached him—but before Tony could reach out to the boy, he shouted, "He sank! He's gone!" The boy had gone below the surface.

As luck would have it, in our mad rush, a few feet of our painter rope was left dangling out over the bow of our boat and into the water. The boy's body and head sank first, but with his small, outstretched hand, he managed to grab hold of this hanging rope just as he was sinking to the bottom. Suddenly, he burst back up to the surface, crying and spitting out water. Tony quickly grabbed hold of his arm. It was unbelievable. The scene played out like a movie. One second later and the poor soul would have been on the muddy bottom.

I was exhausted and shaking. We rested for a few minutes while comforting the young lad. In between his sobbing, he told us his name. We told him he was going to be fine and that he was in good hands—Tony was a highly trained paramedic at James Peyton Memorial Hospital in Gander, and I was a lightkeeper with the Canadian Coast Guard. We gently floated him back around to the stern, then we pulled him in over the back and into the safety of our boat. I placed a beach towel around him. The little boy was upset, exhausted, and scared. He knew how close he had come to drowning.

By now the wind had driven us across the pond and near to the rocky shoreline under Campsite 7. I took my time rowing back to the beach area to let my heart rate return to a somewhat normal after that nail-biting rescue. Several people were standing on the beach. They had watched the whole rescue mission. When we landed, the boy's younger brother was there to greet him and gave him a big hug. He told him he loved him. That was very touching to me—my son was around his same age. Tony and I dragged the park boat back in place, then talked for a few minutes. If I had not reacted when I had, there would have been a drowning in the park that day. I thanked Tony for his great assistance and said goodbye.

The whole thing happened so fast that I never really got many details. The young boy was eleven at the time, and I think he was a Budgell from Bishop's Falls. The dramatic event did not really hit me until hours later that evening. My kids and I went for a relaxing walk around this peaceful park just to wind down. We strolled up around the loop when, from a distance, I happened to see the boy and his younger brother laughing and playing with their mother at their campsite. It was so sweet, I thought, and it hit me just what could have happened earlier that day on the pond. His mother really did not know how close she came to losing her dear son. It was very emotional for me, and I cried!

Thursday, June 22, 2000, was a sunny afternoon. Alice was working, and I was home getting my son ready to go to Cody's birthday party down the road. Living in beautiful downtown Porterville, my home faces the ocean, and looking out across the majesty of the harbour is automatic, just like breathing. In my heart, it's God's country. This time when I looked out, I thought I saw something unusual out across the bay in the area we called the Banks. At the same time, my cousin Hubert and his son Marc drove up my driveway. Hubert said that there was an empty boat out on the Banks.

I put up my binoculars again to take a better look, and sure enough, it looked like my Uncle Harrison's boat out there. I could also see a bright orange life jacket that appeared to be hanging onto the stern of the boat. The more I looked, the more certain I was that it was my uncle's new fourteen-foot Atlantic fibreglass boat sitting out there in the middle of the bay. It also appeared that he was in the water but hanging on to his prized boat.

Uncle Harrison Porter was a well-respected man in this area. In his day, he was the community leader. He was my father's eldest brother and also his working partner for decades in their logging and farming business. When my grandfather Caleb passed away in August 1936, he left behind a large family, my father being only five years old. My Uncle Harrison, being the eldest boy, was the glue that kept the large family together. He was a tough old character—he had worked hard farming and logging all his life. He also loved being on the salt water in his speedboat and enjoyed the treats the ocean provided. During this period, the cod fishery was shut down and no cod fishing was allowed, but my dear old uncle was known to sneak up around shore to catch a fresh fish now and then. Just one for the pot! After all, he was almost eighty-four years old, and like many seniors, this was a part of his life growing up.

I had seen him cruise up through the harbour a few hours earlier that morning. He usually went up near the Red Cliff area and try for a fish. Apparently, somewhere around there, he had accidentally fallen overboard into the deep blue sea. Give him credit—Uncle Harrison was a smart man wearing his life jacket, and he was holding his painter rope when he fell over. He was not letting his new boat drive away—a boat he had recently purchased! He held onto that rope as he tried to re-enter the craft. One thing is certain—once you fall out of a boat, it is almost impossible to climb back in unless you have a swim ladder. He tried in vain, but being wet and cold, he could not get back aboard.

This was June, and the local harbour ice had disappeared a month or so earlier, so the salt water was still terribly cold. Uncle Harrison told me several months later that he tried swimming ashore with his boat, but towing his boat behind him was too difficult. He could not do it, but he decided he was not abandoning his boat. Instead, he placed his arm in over the counter and just hung on for dear life. Slowly, the tide started drifting him out the bay toward the Banks and near the Ships Run, which led into the port of Botwood. The water must have been brutally cold, but a lifetime of hard physical work had toughened him up. After a couple of hours, he had passed along outside of Jealous Island and had drifted out the bay about one and a half miles. He was now near a fishing ground called the Banks, and best of all, he was visible from the main road in Porterville. This is where Hubert and I first spotted the boat. Time for another rescue!

I left my son with Denise to drop him off at the birthday party, and I took my daughter next door to my parents' house. At the time, I was boatless, which was not good. I had sold my good old boat, the SS *Beagle*, so I had to go borrow one quickly. I asked Marc to come with me, and we went down the road looking for a speedboat. Neil Porter had his sixteen-foot boat at his wharf, already in the water, so we jumped aboard it. I knew every minute counted. Uncle Harrison had been in the cold salt water for some time by now. Hypothermia was a major concern at this stage of the rescue.

Neil had a Honda outboard motor on his boat, which I was not that familiar with, but after some tinkering, I got it started. That was a great sound! I put it in gear and tore off out toward the Banks. We got about halfway, when the motor died. We could see the empty boat in the distance. Half an hour had passed since we had first sighted Uncle Harrison's boat from my house. This is a long time when you are immersed into the frigid Atlantic Ocean. Marc took out the paddles and began rowing while I fussed with the motor again. Finally, it fired up, and off we cruised toward my dear uncle, full throttle.

As I approached the boat and slowed down, I could not see him—he was not hanging on to the back of the boat anymore. That was scary. Where was he? Had he sunk? I told Marc to keep an eye out and that this might not end well. I carefully idled up to the empty boat and gently motored around the side, and there he was, lying on his back, floating motionlessly. Always smart, he had tied his boat to the loop on his life jacket. He knew that if someone found his boat, they would also find him, dead or alive.

I carefully approached my uncle, not knowing what to expect. The poor man had been in the cold water for a long time. I shouted out to him but got no reaction—nothing. I was expecting some response. Minutes later, he slowly opened his eyes but never said a word. I floated him to the back of our boat, because there was no way to pull him in over the side. We spoke to him, but he didn't respond—he was just staring blankly up at the heavens. Somehow, we had to get my wet, cold, and heavy uncle out of the freezing salt water.

I tried to lift him up over the stern but only got him halfway in, and I had to let him slide back into the water again. This was going to be difficult—he was a big man and weighed down with his wet clothing. Marc and I tried again. This time we got a better grip on the back of his belt. I mustered up all the strength I had and pulled him up over the counter of the boat and inside with a thump. We almost pulled the dear man in two, and it was only then he finally grunted and mumbled a couple of words.

We laid him down on the floor of the boat, and I put my jacket over him—he was freezing. Then we bolted for shore as fast as we could. As we got closer to Neil's wharf, I could see several of his family members there to greet him. Uncle Harrison never spoke a word during the ride back. Shortly after we docked, with assistance, he slowly walked to a waiting truck with his family. He went home with his wife, Aunt Louise. His family wanted him to go see his doctor, but he refused—Uncle Harrison could also be stubborn at times. A short time later, though, he began vomiting, so the family took him to see his doctor, who admitted him into hospital for overnight observation. Dr. Hewitt said that his body core temperature was so low it was amazing he survived.

A couple of years later, Colin Hiscock, the Boat Safety Officer for the Canadian Coast Guard, told me he had heard about the rescue and had visited Uncle Harrison. He wanted to talk to him about the incident because it was a good-news story—an older boater wearing his life jacket, helped save his life. But apparently my uncle was not interested and did not want to talk about the incident. Remarkably, at eighty-four years old, my uncle recovered from this life-threatening ordeal in the frigid Atlantic. I am proud to say I was in the right place at the right time, and Uncle Harrison lived another ten good years with his wife after that eventful day when I plucked him out of the ocean.

Thursday, July 17, 2003: This one also takes place at Notre Dame Provincial Park. We were again camping in our fifth wheel trailer at Campsite 7 next to the lovely pond. It was another hot day, and we had spent most of our day swimming. By now it was close to suppertime, and we were relaxing at our campsite when a cooler full of fresh crab was dropped off to us. Our camping friends Dave and Kathy Mercer from Gander had a surplus of crab and kindly gave us some. The crab had to be cooked, so I started boiling them up on my Coleman stove. This fresh crab was a real treat. We had way more than we could eat, so I shared some with our neighbours. There was also a new trailer from Ontario setting up across the road. Doing what Newfoundlanders do, I took over a bowl of cooked crab to these strangers.

After a short chat, I was walking back to my trailer, when suddenly I met Alice running toward me. She told me she could hear somebody crying out, "Help, I'm drowning!" I shifted into rescue mode immediately and raced across our campsite, through a bunch of spruce trees, and down over the hill toward the pond. As I was running, I heard the scream for help. Goosebumps rushed over me. It was about 7:00 p.m., sunny, with not a breeze of wind. The pond looked like a mirror when I got to the water's edge. I looked out across the waters toward the famous island to see two young boys struggling to stay afloat. It looked like one kid was holding on to the boy in front of him. He was crying out for help and treading water for both and trying to keep his buddy above the surface. Occasionally, they would bob under the water, then resurface. I could tell he was not going to hang on much longer.

Fortunately, I had pulled my eighteen-foot kayak onto the rocks right under my campsite. I shouted out to the boys that I was coming. I jumped into my kayak and began paddling. This kayak could slice through the water like a knife. I shot out across the water as fast as the boat could move, watching as the kids went under, then resurfaced, spitting out water. Glancing to my left, I could see a dozen campers standing on the edges of their waterfront sites. There was nothing they could do but watch and pray. I had been told that in situations like this, the drowning kid panics and grabs hold of the stronger swimmer and usually takes them both to the bottom.

The boys only had seconds left before they sank under the surface for good. They were getting tired and sinking deeper as they kicked and splashed. I flew across the flat water at maximum speed and finally reached the two boys. I was moving so fast, I reached out my right arm and scooped up both of them in one swift move, dragging them across the water until I stopped. It didn't matter—they were out of danger now, and I was not going to loosen my grip. They were exhausted and scared, but I assured them everything was going to be okay.

I couldn't get them in my kayak, so I just held on and waited for the park wardens. During all the screaming and commotion, somebody had informed the park wardens that two boys were in trouble in the water. The wardens had raced to the beach area and had started to paddle out to them. Luckily, I got there first, because it took the two wardens another five or ten minutes to reach us. Coincidentally, the wardens used the same boat I had performed the other rescue in four years earlier. We transferred the two young boys into the wardens' boat, and they returned them safely to the beach area.

My rescue kayak and the popular island in the background at Notre Dame Provincial Park

Later that night, a park warden came to my campsite requesting an official statement from me. I learned that the two boys had swum to the island, and on the return trip, the younger boy became tired and began to sink. That was when his buddy grabbed him and began crying out for help. I never did get their names—one boy was from Glenwood, and the other was a friend visiting him from Ontario. It was another close call. The next day, several long-time campers at this park came to our campsite and told me they watched my kayak shoot across the pond like a torpedo that evening and were so pleased I was there to save the young lads. They thanked me and also told me, quite seriously, that if those boys had drowned that evening, they would never be able to camp in that lovely provincial park again.

It was another exhilarating experience for me to save another couple of lives. I guess I was meant to be there.

A "lifekeeper" was on watch!

Days-Off Adventures

Ever since I began working at Long Point Lighthouse, I had a strong desire to drive across the country by motorcycle. This dream of mine started shortly after I began driving motorcycles when I was fourteen years old. That was when I bought my very first motorcycle from my brother Dennis—a well-used 1968 blue Suzuki 150. It was a terrible bike—it did not run very well, it was hard to start, and it always fouled up its spark plugs. Also, it puffed out blue smoke just like my father's old smokehouse in which he used to smoke salmon. The oil injection never did work properly, either, but that old temperamental Suzuki planted the bug in me—the desire for the wide-open highways and the wind in my face!

Over the years, I have had many different motorcycles. The second motorcycle I purchased was a brand new 1973 Honda 175 from the Honda shop on McCurdy Drive in Gander. I was extremely happy to have a bike that ran properly. I paid $900 cash for it, all hard-earned money I had saved up from several summers working on the farm, be it planting seeds, weeding, harvesting potatoes, thinning out miles of turnips and carrots, or making hay. The next year, in the fall of 1973, I moved up to a nice used dependable 1972 Honda CB450. I bought this one from Gord Rowbottom with not a scratch on her. It was a reliable bike on which I put over 20,000 miles. I once left home and drove all the way down to Bay d'Espoir to visit my girlfriend. I rode down there by myself and on mostly gravel roads back then—no fear!

My rookie "bike tour" was back in the summer of 1975. It was a bike ride out to Kona Beach, South Brook, and Springdale area on my mighty CB450. I was accompanied by my buddy Carl Canning on his Honda CB350. That was a beautiful ride, an excellent experience—except for the night we drank tequila for the first time. We both fell asleep with a candle burning in the middle of the cool orange pup tent that we had borrowed from Carl's brother Wayne. We woke up the next morning with burnt grass for our floor. The candle had burned down and ignited the plastic floor, luckily, it had extinguished itself while we slept peacefully through the inferno. Carl's brother was not too impressed with the condition of his tent.

I sold that 450 and bought a sexy Suzuki GT 750, a three-cylinder, two-stroke with a digital gear position display—and fast! This bike was the first Japanese "water-cooled" motorcycle produced. I bought this Suzuki off my fellow bayman rider, the one and only Fred Freake, in May 1976. He had bought it about one week earlier, but he did not like it, so he sold it to me. He said it was not fast enough for him—it would only do 130 mph!

Every summer, the motorcycle bug would stir inside of me when the weather warmed up. In 1985, I bought a nice used 1981 Gold Wing 1100 from my buddy Den Fudge down on Fogo Island. The next year, Alice and I took our holidays and left home on our first official trip, on a real touring motorcycle, for ten days. We had no particular destination, just the open road ahead of us. This old Gold Wing 1100 was a game-changer—it rode beautifully, and it had great storage with excellent wind and rain protection. We did a slow ride up through beautiful Nova Scotia, taking in the Cabot Trail, and on to New Brunswick, ducking on and off the Trans-Canada Highway along the way. We visited Alice's brother Cam in Oromocto and my Aunt Audrey near Saint John.

One day while I was visiting a bookstore in Fredericton, I read in the latest *Rolling Stone* magazine that my favourite entertainer was playing in Hartford, Connecticut, which was only a good day's drive away. So, I immediately phoned the Hartford Civic Center to book two tickets, then we headed to the American border the next day. We crossed the US border and cruised on to the lovely city of Hartford to see the legendary Bob Dylan with Tom Petty and the Heartbreakers. What a show—both were in their prime! After the concert, we jumped aboard the Gold Wing and headed back north into Montreal for a night visit. Then we boogied eastward back to Newfoundland. I enjoyed this ride so much, a few days later I went straight to the Honda dealer in Grand Falls to see Des Kenny, the owner of Thru Way. There, I traded my used 1100 for a new blue 1200 Gold Wing Interstate. What a beauty of a bike—I still drive it to this day more than thirty-six years later!

During the long winter of 1986 and 1987 while I worked at Long Point Lighthouse, I was busy daydreaming and making plans for another major bike tour somewhere. I wanted to do it now and not wait until we settled down with children or retired. I bought a road atlas and spent hours and hours picking out various highways, interstate routes, and sights to see. That was about the extent of the research I could do considering these were pre-Internet days.

It was mid-May when my long-awaited and hard-earned holidays were finally approved. We had a big pre-tour birthday party at our house in Porterville with a few dozen friends. It was an excellent party and a great send-off for us. Over the next couple of days, we packed the saddlebags and the trunk full of the bare necessities. When travelling on a motorcycle, your cargo space is limited and you must pack wisely. We wore full leathers, including gloves, top to bottom. We packed two suits of good rubber clothes, one pair of jeans, swimsuits, two or three shirts, limited socks and underwear, my 35mm Nikon camera, two sleeping bags, and a one-burner stove. To top it off, I strapped my two-man pup tent onto my chrome rack on top of my trunk.

About an hour after lunchtime on a sunny Sunday, May 31, 1987, we said our goodbyes and pulled out of my parents' driveway in Porterville—westbound for California. My body was tingling just thinking about the adventure ahead of us. One of the first things I did was collect a film container of our clean, cool Atlantic Ocean and place it in the bottom of my trunk. We crossed the gulf on a Marine Atlantic ferry, then drove up through the Maritimes, stopping again at Cam's in Oromocto, New Brunswick. The next night, we shut down in Drummondville, Quebec, then drove straight to Whitby, Ontario. (From North Sydney to Whitby is exactly 2,000 km.) There we shut down at my cousin Carl Lidstone's for a few days. After some good rest and relaxation, plus a John Prine concert to boot, we headed out on the busy freeways again. We dropped in to see the scenic Niagara Falls, then crossed the Canadian border and entered Buffalo, New York. It was hammer down into an unknown world far, far away!

One of our first stops was the Honda motorcycle assembly plant in Marysville, Ohio. That's where all Hondas were built, and it employed over 4,000 workers. Finally, we shut down in Cincinnati, a 1,013-kilometre day. The next morning, we drove on to nearby Nashville, a lovely city. We spent a day checking out the country music scene and the history there. The Marshall Tucker Band was having a small, private concert and album release party near our hotel. Being big fans of their music, we walked straight into the hall to check out what was happening. At the second door check, we were politely told to leave—it was a private event. Hey, it was worth a try!

The next day, we headed westward to Memphis only 400 kilometres away. We checked out Beale Street, "Home of the Blues." It was a real touristy place, and it had a lot of security around. There I ate my first baked catfish for supper and then caught two old blues guys jammin' on the corner. By now it was getting late, time to get a hotel and shut down for the night. When we drove out of the Beale Street district, I got my directions mixed up—one of the few times ever—and drove off in the wrong direction. (A modern GPS sure would have helped me there.)

After driving several blocks, I noticed the buildings and houses were getting shabby-looking—no Holiday Inns or Deltas to be seen anywhere. The sun was starting to set when I stopped at a red light. While waiting patiently for the light to change, a creepy feeling came over me. I glanced to my left, to my right, and all around, and all I could see were questionable, hard-looking faces sizing up the two young, lost Newfoundlanders like a dessert platter. I knocked the bike into first gear, pulled a U-turn right there, and booted back as fast as I could out of that shady part of the city. Block after block we cruised until we hit the main drag again and checked into a nice hotel. Time for a cold beer, pizza, and relaxation. That was our first uncomfortable encounter on our trip. We had another one about a week later.

The next day, we were up bright and early, drove over to Elvis Presley Boulevard, and walked through the famous Graceland. We saw everything from his famous "jungle room," his two airliners, motorcycles, cars, gold records, suits, and even a snowmobile with wheels. It was beautiful to see, but it was also kind of eerie—in every room, building, and at every display, Elvis's music was playing in the background. Elvis and his family were even buried there in their own little graveyard out back. At the time, his Aunt Delta Presley Biggs was still living in the mansion in 1987. After hours touring through Graceland, it was time to head on down the road again and on to Little Rock, Arkansas.

My back and neck muscles were starting to hurt. I visited the local Honda shop there and had them install a driver's backrest and another set of foot pegs for me. That gave me a place to switch up my leg position ever so little, but it made a major improvement in my riding. I didn't have another problem with my back during the rest of our tour. Around this area, I wanted to get off the interstate again and see the beautiful Ozark Mountains that I had heard about. The countryside was like a time warp—people driving old 1950s and 1960s pickup trucks, and even old gas pumps at the garages. Some of the roads were like tunnels through the thick green forest.

From there we entered the flat and blisteringly hot wheat fields of Kansas. The temperatures there hit 102F. We actually burned our ankles where our pant legs and sneakers met. That was wickedly hot for us saltwater-blooded Newfoundlanders. In the state of Kansas, helmets were not mandatory, which I found odd. I drove helmet-free for a few miles but felt unsafe, so I strapped it back on again. In the heat, I would pull into a gas station every few hundred miles, gas up, walk to the garage area, and stick their water hose inside my shirt to soak myself. The locals would give me strange looks, but it would cool me off nicely for the next ten or fifteen minutes while driving.

We continued on to Colorado, the prettiest state we visited so far. The snow-capped mountains in June were breathtaking.

As we entered the city of Denver, the highway interstate went under one of the airport's runway strips! We shut down there and took a little break. The next day, we went whitewater rafting down the Arkansas River. The water was just like home—it was icy cold from the melting snow in the mountains. We did a thrilling half-day river raft ride for miles down through the canyons. It was the real deal—there were six of us paddling along with one guide. We would plow through a white rapid, and I and the guy opposite me were in charge of bailing the cold water out of the raft with two five-gallon buckets. It was hard work but a thrill of a ride.

We left there refreshed and decided to check out the Million Mile Highway. Days earlier, some bikers in Nashville told us to check out this route. This highway was rated as one of the top two most beautiful and most dangerous motorcycle roads in North America. It was a secondary narrow road, built in the 1920s, twisting through the stunning Rocky Mountains range. Only a couple of feet from the right shoulder were sheer cliffs that dropped off 500 to 1,000 feet—straight down. Mixed in were hairpin turns rated at ten mph speed limits. Besides the view, the most incredible part of this drive was the lack of guardrails on the outside edges, only old white wooden Crosses. They were scattered along the roadway—lonely memorials for snowplow operators who had unfortunately driven over these deadly cliffs. From time to time, if you dared look, you could see the odd old, abandoned prospecting camp frozen in time across the valleys. We drove through several dark tunnels, and then we finally crossed the Continental Divide, the point where all waters flowed either to the west or to the east. We were sitting 11,542 feet above sea level. The air was so thin, it felt like I was high. We stopped at a rest area, and when I dismounted off my bike, I stumbled. Even the carburetors on my bike strained to perform with the thin air mixture. We were an exceptionally long way from my workplace, Long Point Lighthouse, which sat only 300 feet above sea level.

From the Colorado Rockies we cruised out toward another mind-blowing sight—the mighty Grand Canyon of Arizona. The landscape there reminded me of the old black and white westerns that were on TV when I was a kid. This was Roy Rogers country—giddy-up! The Canyon was ten miles wide in places. We walked down a winding, narrow trail for about thirty minutes just to dip below the surface of the earth to get the feel of it. That short hike was far enough for us to see a few mountain goats and meet some park wardens assisting someone back up the steep trail with a bandaged head.

From this famous landmark we went on to check out the huge Hoover Dam. That was quite the piece of cement work. Then we rode on to world-famous Las Vegas, where we planned to experience it for real and "lose" some cash! We got a hotel, then walked the downtown Strip and took in some entertainment. We saw the Smothers Brothers show (Dick and Tommy). They performed at the legendary Desert Inn, which was Frank Sinatra's old hangout. They opened for the great Ray Stevens. A couple of Ray's hits were "The Streak" and "Everything is Beautiful."

Alice and Barry at the Colorado Rocky Mountains

The next day, it was time to head west again. We were excited to be getting closer to the ocean. We rose early and departed Vegas at 6:00 a.m. I wanted to get across the Mojave Desert before the intense heat hit—120F. I was advised by the locals to leave early because the desert heat could do freaky things to your bike's fuel lines and rubber tires. This bone-dry wasteland was not a place to break down on two wheels. Finally, after approximately 400 kilometres, we broke out at Long Beach, California. After weeks of driving west, we were thrilled to see the salt water again.

We walked down to take in the salty but smog-filled air on the beach area and to perform my little salt water transfer ceremony. I took out my film container of Atlantic Ocean and prepared to pour it into the Pacific Ocean. A minute before I carried this out, I asked a couple of local lads on the beach if they wanted to see the Atlantic Ocean. They gave me a strange look and slowly stepped away. Oh, well. After scooping up some Pacific, we returned to my bike, only to find a $23 parking ticket attached to my handlebar. Welcome to LA! I still owe that ticket, by the way.

I found a phone booth and called my parents back home for the first time since we had left Ontario. That was when I learned my beagle, Gypsy, was seriously ill. We then got a hotel at Santa Monica Beach for a few nights of rest. From there we checked out the sights of the City of Angels—the beautiful palm trees mixed with ugly smog, and the Porsches and Jaguars everywhere. Los Angeles did not impress us—I would rather Long Point, Twillingate, any day. After a couple of days there, we drove 631 kilometres north to Porterville, California.

This had been the main destination for this entire journey. It was a nice, clean city, population 24,000 (today 60,000). It was cool and strange to see signs like Porterville High School and Porterville Police Department. I discovered the residents were hard-working farmers just like back home. Here, they grew oranges, olives, and grapes and produced a little oil. Sadly, there were no Porters living here, so I had no cousins to look up—something I had a habit of doing across Canada. This Porterville was settled by a man from Mexico whose first name was Porter.

The day we arrived, there was a great car show along with special events. We got talking to some local residents, and the next thing, we were being introduced to the president of the Chamber of Commerce, the deputy mayor, and other dignitaries. The locals were blown away that we were actual Porters from Porterville, Newfoundland, Canada, and visiting on motorcycle. I had taken a few tourism booklets with me from the supplies I had at Long Point Lighthouse, and I distributed them throughout the US, including Porterville.

The next day, we visited the Honda shop there for another oil change and bike inspection. My Gold Wing had been performing well in the hot temperatures and over the many miles. The shopowner gave me two Porterville baseball caps and a sweet chrome licence plate holder. It was chrome with "Porterville" stamped into the metal—I still use the holder today. A day or so later, it was time to make tracks again. Due to my sick beagle, we decided to rush the trip a little, which was difficult to do when we were at the opposite end of North America.

We said goodbye to Porterville by midday and headed out as far as the town of Livermore that evening. This was the home of thousands of huge white wind turbines spinning for miles and miles. There they generated electricity, which was sold to the nearby districts. It was early that Sunday morning when we departed Livermore and headed to the old city of San Francisco, which was a few miles east.

We were cruising through the rolling green hills as I was preparing to merge onto the main freeway to make better time. While I glanced back to check for oncoming traffic, all I could see were a dozen or more big old Harley-Davidsons barrelling down toward me. No time to change plans—I had my speed up and was already committed to the merge. I slid out directly in front of these bikers and wondered what the heck was going to happen next. We were riding through the tops of these rolling hills peppered throughout with wind turbines. It was blowing a gale, and I was nervous about these hard-looking bikers only a few feet behind me.

Cruising at a good 120 kph, I dropped down a gear just in case I had to make a quick exit. I watched the noisy bikes in my mirror as they crept closer and closer to me. I had come in peace! One thing I did know, it was early in the morning, it was extremely windy, and I was confident and comfortable in my motorcycle's ability. It was performing exceptionally well and was cutting through the wind like a knife. After being at Long Point Lighthouse for three years, I had become accustomed to a bit of wind.

Those bikers were sitting on loud, oil-leaking Harleys with no wind protection and no helmets. Ever so slowly, they thundered up past, one by one, on either side of us on this double-lane highway. I could tell they were sizing us up—I could feel it in my skin. I was on full alert, checking in my mirrors every few seconds and watching the bikers roar past us. They were dressed in leather and dirty denim with faded tattoos and their long, dirty hair and beards blowing in the wind. Slowly but surely, the majority of the bikers rode out ahead of us, at which time I could smell stale booze coming from them. They were hardcore. It reminded me of the aroma from the old Blue Fin Lounge in Lewisporte the morning after a big dance. Finally, the last biker inched closer. I waited patiently for the guy and his biker mamma to pass me. I guess he was their leader—their captain, maybe. Anyhow, after several nervous minutes, he cruised up to the left side of me and stayed there with the wind whistling around us. I could see he was a big brute. A few minutes later, he stared over at us, ever so coolly gave us a big friendly thumbs-up, and then roared away. What a relief! I think the dude was holding back behind me so he could read my foreign licence plate. I assumed these bikers had been out on a run the day before, partied all night till sunrise, and were heading back to the city—probably tired and hungover and did not want to mess with a couple of brave Newfoundlanders. Whatever—it was quite the rush!

We made it to San Francisco safe and sound. While looking for a place to grab breakfast, we had to backtrack and drive down a small side street. There we saw two men living in a large, taped-up cardboard box. It was sad to see this in the real world. Alice was blown away by this sight. We did not spend much time in San Francisco. Soon, we rode over the famous Golden Gate Bridge and glanced across the bay to see Alcatraz surrounded in a cloud of fog. We rode on north through California's famous wine country and stopped at a winery to have a taste, which was refreshing. Then we drove into the giant Red Wood Forest and took the road called "Avenue of Giants." The trees there were monsters. You could drive your car through them and have your picture taken. I saw many large tractor-trailers loaded down with three trees—just three—large enough to fill their flatbed trailers.

The following day, we left Eureka, California, heading north toward Canada. We passed dozens of old Volkswagen vans cruising along the roads in this surfing country. We blew through Oregon, passing just west of Mount St. Helens and gazing at it in the distance approximately twenty-five kilometres away. Finally, after a long day, I turned the bike key off in the town of Everett. We had made it to the state of Washington, another 1,000-kilometre day under our butts. No problem—my Gold Wing had been running well day after day, mile after mile. It seemed like the harder I pushed my bike, the better she performed. The Gold Wing was certainly made for long-distance touring!

On Tuesday, June 23, we crossed back into Canada. What a great feeling to be back in our great nation! When you are in the United States of America, Canada practically does not exist. There is no Canadian news and no coloured money, only a different attitude and a different lifestyle. We went through customs with no problem, then took the ferry and headed west one last time. Out at Victoria, we visited Alice's brother Frank and his family. After weeks of being surrounded by strangers, it was great to see familiar faces again and to be with family.

We had a great visit there—a pretty city with lots of greenery and flowers everywhere. I put my bike in the local shop there to replace my rear tire. You need good rubber when you are driving big miles every day. By Thursday, we packed up and headed east for the first time since we had left home in May. We drove through the scenic Canadian Rockies with fresh Canadian wind in our faces. We stopped for a quick, refreshing swim in a cool mountain spring midway, and two days and another 1,549 kilometres later, we arrived at my old friend Carl Canning's in Edmonton. Carl was my tequila and bike camping buddy from 1975. The next day, Carl and Pauline jumped on their Honda motorcycle and rode along with us to Saskatoon. It was good to have company on the highway for a change.

Then, 597 kilometres later, we arrived at Tony Fudge's in Saskatoon. He and I had gone across Canada by CN train to Winnipeg, Manitoba, in 1976. The next day, we said goodbye to my home friends and rode on east to Winnipeg. We were on a mission to visit my sick dog in Ontario.

In Winnipeg, we stayed with Jim Sceviour, a hometown buddy I had known since I was four or five years old. While there, we also visited Alice's brother Dwight and Deb Porter, my friend from Thompson. In no time it was time to leave, and we hit the road again. There was a sick beagle who was sitting by herself in the animal hospital in Guelph. We did a major trek around the Great Lakes hitting 1,107 kilometres one day from Dryden to Sault Ste. Marie. Anyone who has driven through northern Ontario knows the landscape is similar to Newfoundland—with beautiful hills, trees, and lots of lakes.

The next day, 720 kilometres put us back to my buddy Carl's house in Whitby. We took a few days' rest here and made a couple of visits out to the University of Guelph / Ontario Veterinary College to visit Gypsy. She had a slipped disc and become paralyzed while we were away. I had flown her up to Guelph for major back surgery.

Then it was time to hammer down again and head east for the Rock. We had another pit stop in New Brunswick, where Cam Fudge joined us on his bike and accompanied us for the return drive home. By now we were getting anxious to return home and sleep in our own bed. Three of us crossed the Gulf of St. Lawrence on the ferry and then had lunch in Corner Brook with Alice's other two brothers, Wayne and Barry Fudge. Then we were on the home stretch. We made one last stop just west of Badger, where we met our friends Dave and Colleen Morrison, who were headed back to Ontario for their summer holidays. They were music teachers in Lewisporte, and they were returning home to Lindsay, Ontario, for two months.

Finally, on July 8, after thirty-nine long, exciting days and about 23,000 kilometres under our butts, we returned to beautiful downtown Porterville. We had driven through nine provinces and eighteen States. What a nice feeling to be home and to know we had completed this incredible once-in-a-lifetime journey! After we finally shut down, we slept for about two days. We were tired and exhausted, but we did not really feel it until we turned the key off on my Honda.

Friends told us later that when we left on that bike trip, they did not think they would ever see us alive again. It was quite an adventure, to say the least. Driving a motorcycle on any trip, you really get to smell, taste, and see so much more than you do while sitting in an air-conditioned car or motorhome. We saw many landmarks and unique sights and met so many wonderful fellow bikers and interesting people.

I had many memorable "days off adventures" while working at the lighthouses for the Canadian Coast Guard. After I transferred to the island lighthouses, I was blessed with much more time off compared to Long Point. The Bacalhao Island Lighthouse shift gave me roughly a month on and a month off the island, plus a month of holidays. This was during what I call our BC period—before children. Alice and I took full advantage of these years before we settled down to become wrapped up in parenthood!

We took several motorcycle trips throughout Atlantic Canada, Quebec, Ontario, and returning through the United States, always taking a different route on each adventure. In 1989, we drove right down into Manhattan, New York City. I had just finished my shift on Bacalhao Island on May 31 and returned home. I had my thirty-two days off plus my holidays. On June 23, Alice and I packed up the motorcycle and headed out toward the US border. I had just come off an island with a population of two and was headed to the island of Manhattan with a population of almost 1.5 million!

The ride toward the Big Apple was thrilling. We drove south along the coastline, staying off Interstate 95 when we could, taking in beautiful Portland and the Portland Head Lighthouse, which was first lit in 1791. About an hour outside of New York City, we pulled off at a truck stop before the freeway would take us deep into the city. Alice and I were nervous and debated whether we should continue this journey into unknown territory. Being on motorcycle, alone, was no place to screw up. I was double-checking the road map when I noticed a tour bus from the city pull in. I waited for all the passengers to get off, then I walked over, dressed in black leather, sweating bullets in the thirty-two-degree heat, and struck up a chat with the driver. I figured he knew the best route for me to take. He was a giant of a man, about six foot six, 350 pounds, and black. I explained where I was headed, and he rhymed off the best route in seconds. He certainly knew the roads.

Portland Head Lighthouse, Maine

The next thing we knew, we were driving over the Bronx highway with burned-out high-rise apartments to the sides of the freeway and a scattered scrapped car sitting right on the shoulder lane. If you broke down and left your car there, it was stripped of parts in no time. We drove under the East River through a stuffed tunnel with bumper-to-bumper traffic. It was hot and full of crazy drivers. Surviving that, we rode right down the middle of Broadway. What a great feeling! We quickly got a room at the Wellington Hotel and parked the bike. Quite a culture shock considering only a few days ago I was on Bacalhao Island. Now I was standing in Manhattan with a buzz of human activity everywhere I looked—above me, below me, and around me. For the next four days, we walked miles throughout the crazy but fun Big Apple. New York was an amazing place to see. Then we packed up the bike and returned to Newfoundland.

To this day, I still ride the same bike, now with over 90,000 kilometres on the odometer. I have crossed all ten provinces and twenty-five states in total, always dressed in black leather and sitting on two wheels with my best buddy, Alice, right next to me.

We also did several tours in car. In June 1991, we flew across the Atlantic Ocean to Heathrow Airport in London, England. Then we took the train to the coast, where we crossed the English Channel to Calais, France, in a huge hovercraft ferry. There we rented a little Renault car and hit the back roads of Europe. My first stop was a visit to the famous Beaumont-Hamel Newfoundland Memorial site. I made sure I wore my Newfoundland, Canada, T-shirt that day.

At the Beaumont-Hamel Newfoundland memorial site in France

It was strange that I had no connection with World War I but felt a calling to visit this historic site. From there, we got lost for four weeks soaking through the roads of historic France, Italy, Monaco, Switzerland, Germany, Luxembourg, Belgium, and the Netherlands. After taking in the amazing sights and history there, we crossed back over the English Channel. Then we spent an unnerving week driving through England and Wales, on the wrong side of the road, before returning home.

A few years later, Alice and I flew out to Whitehorse, Yukon, to visit her brother Keith. There we spent two weeks driving through that beautiful territory and into Skagway, Alaska.

Alice and I have toured thousands of miles around this island, across Canada, the United States, Europe, and the Caribbean. We have had many memorable experiences on my days-off adventures!

One word of wisdom—if you have a dream to travel, do it now, not later. Life is too short.

Canadian Coast Guard Helicopters, Techs, and Ships

Those shiny red helicopters with the wide diagonal white stripe flying overhead from time to time were the workhorses and pack mules for us lightkeepers around our coastline. They provided important transportation services to and from the lighthouses during shift changes. The keepers would phone into St. John's days in advance and request a helicopter for our taxi services. The pilots would often use the local government wharves in the small communities for their helipads because these landmarks were easy to locate and not busy in the winter months.

These whirlybirds would pick me up or drop me off at the Porterville wharf on a regular basis. I would get a phone call in the morning from the Marine Aids Office confirming the changeover was taking place, so I'd tie up my final cardboard boxes of supplies and get ready. Then it was a waiting game. Often the chopper had to fly out of St. John's and maybe carry out changeovers on two or three other lighthouses along its way. If the chopper was assigned to an icebreaker, the wait was usually much shorter. Luckily, the government wharf at Porterville was not far away—I could see it from my dining room window. Once, during a shift changeover, the pilot dropped me off right in my backyard very close to my house.

I thought for sure the wind from the blades was going to rip the shingles off my roof! It was convenient but a little too close for comfort.

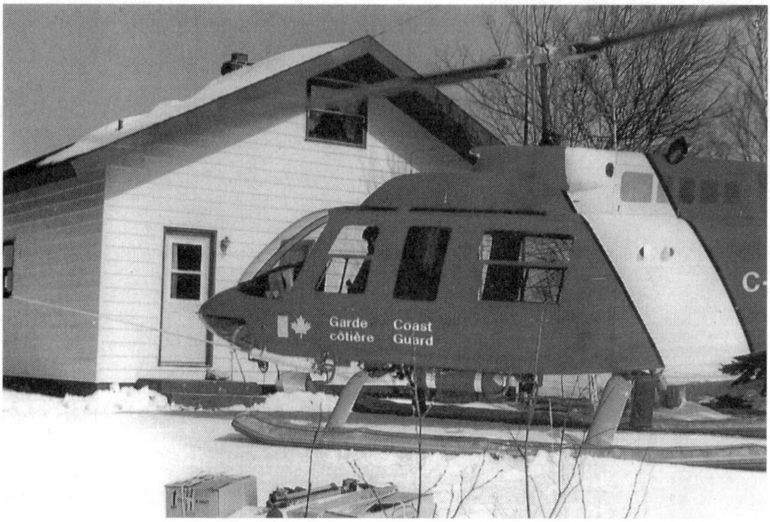

Canadian Coast Guard helicopter in my backyard

Often, there would be little communication, only a phone call early in the morning, that the chopper was flying. I'd have no idea how many stops were along the way, so I would have to wait for hours to hear that familiar chop, chop coming from a distance. Then it was a race to the wharf, where the pilot would gently touch down but would never shut off the motors. He would idle the motor down a little. Through the noise and the wind from the spinning blades overhead, I had to quickly stuff my monthly food and belongings aboard. It usually went into the rear storage compartment or the back seat, depending on which model of helicopter showed up. Every pickup or drop-off felt like a race, a time trial. I had to load as fast as I could, because the helicopter's time was valuable. It seemed as if it was always heading somewhere else for another job. I would jump into the front seat, fasten the complicated seat belts, and put on the green headset with the microphone because of the noise. The skilled pilot would power up the amazing machine and slowly lift off. It was always thrilling to fly. He would lift upwards, turn like a bumblebee, and make a straight run to either Surgeon's Cove Head Light or Bacalhao Island Lighthouse. I always enjoyed seeing the Porterville and Thwart Island areas with this bird's-eye view. There was so much more you could see—all the snowmobile trails, the bogs, ponds, and even wildlife. Over the years, I videotaped and took dozens of photos during these exciting changeover trips.

Certain pilots would enjoy cruising over the treetops, spy a moose or two a few hundred feet below, and do a quick, bone-chilling circle, half upside down, and go back for a better look. Back in the 1990s, when the moose population was at its peak around home, my trips back to Porterville often meant a flight beyond home, miles up toward Laurenceton and around Burnt Arm Pond. There we would take a little moose-sighting tour. There would be animals everywhere. You could even see the moose leads through the woods and snow. It would be common to see a couple dozen animals hanging out in this small area. It was always a treat to see these large wild beasts from overhead.

Barry Porter attaching strap to Lister motor

The Canadian Coast Guard pilots soon figured out I did not like flying that much. My first airplane flight was back in June 1974, when I flew to Labrador to go to work at the Iron Ore Company of Canada (IOC). I was young and scared to death. I threw up every time the old Eastern Provincial Airways plane landed—which meant in Deer Lake, Goose Bay, and Wabush. I did not enjoy flying back then, and I still do not enjoy it. I could handle a straight flight in good conditions, but throw in a couple of high-speed doughnuts mixed with a dive or two, and I break out into the hot sweats! I know the pilots got a great kick out of this.

Techs L-R: Unknown, Dave Periera, Lightkeeper Eric Dove, Gary Soper

I remember one time when Kenny picked me up at Surgeon's Cove Head to transport me back home. Our helipad was approximately 300 feet above sea level perched on the very edge of the rugged cliffs. He lifted the helicopter up about one full inch off the wooden pad, slowly drifted over to the southwest side, and then basically went into a free fall for another 299 feet. I was strapped into the front seat, half upside down, hanging on for dear life as we plunged to what I thought was certain death. As we fell, we were picking up speed, and the cold ocean was getting closer by the second. Then, ever so slowly, Kenny pulled the chopper back up from certain doom about half a mile out from the cliffs. I was soaked with sweat pouring off my body as I looked across at Kenny, who was grinning from ear to ear. The bugger! By the time I reached Porterville some twenty miles and a few more roller-coaster rides later, I had the entire side and front windows near me steamed up from the heat pouring off me. The inside of my zipped-up orange survival suit was a sauna, and I know I was white as a ghost. Thankfully, Kenny landed when he did—another twenty seconds of flying and I would have puked all over the rascal! I jumped out of the helicopter, and the cold air brought me back to life again. Seconds later, Kenny was off again, still grinning from ear to ear.

Lightkeeper Carl Greening arriving at Surgeon's Cove Head on the Bell Long Ranger 206

In the 1990s, the helicopters started to deliver all our annual station supplies from the Canadian Coast Guard ship, eliminating the need to use the slow and somewhat dangerous spar, boom, and winch system. This included everything from cases of paint, cleaning supplies, drums of motor oil and gasoline, toilet paper, and more. They flew in sling-loads of supplies from the ship that would be anchored below the cliffs. There was also the never-ending job of flying Canadian Coast Guard technicians to and from the lighthouses around the coast.

The large Huey 205 helicopter on Bacalhao Island's helipad

The larger Bell Huey 205 helicopter was usually used for extremely heavy loads or extra passengers. You could hear this flying beast approaching a good ten miles away. Their aircraft engineer, Melvin Crew, always accompanied this helicopter on all its flights to the light stations. Sometimes the helicopters would attach what they called a "long line" for dropping or moving fuel tanks or other items around the dwelling or near the light tower. These flying workhorses also flew in the newly rebuilt Lister motors when required.

At times these great pilots flew in some harsh conditions, but they always avoided the dark and would not fly in freezing rain. Freezing rain and helicopters really do not mix—it makes them heavy, causing serious problems.

One time on February 25, 1993, I was being flown out to Surgeon's Cove Head on a regular changeover shift, and the weather suddenly deteriorated and turned to freezing rain. The chopper managed to drop me off at the light, but due to the fear of icing up, the pilot was unable to pick up my co-worker in Campbellton to complete the shift. Instead, the pilot headed back to the safety of the Canadian Coast Guard icebreaker sitting near Thwart Island. It was another six days before the weather improved and Arch was flown out to complete the shift changeover.

Helicopter landing at Surgeon's Cove Head and a Canadian Coast Guard carpenter hanging on to his bags and tools

The helicopters provided an important and much-appreciated service to us isolated lightkeepers. These pilots were all first-class guys and highly skilled. They often dropped in for a cup of tea and a chat with us after landing. They were even known to drop off wild rabbits, or 3,000 feet of cabin water hose, or give an eight-months pregnant lightkeeper's wife a lift home. Thank you!

Helicopter landing on the *Ann Harvey*

Helicopter preparing to sling supplies off
the *Sir Humphrey Gilbert* near Surgeon's Cove Head

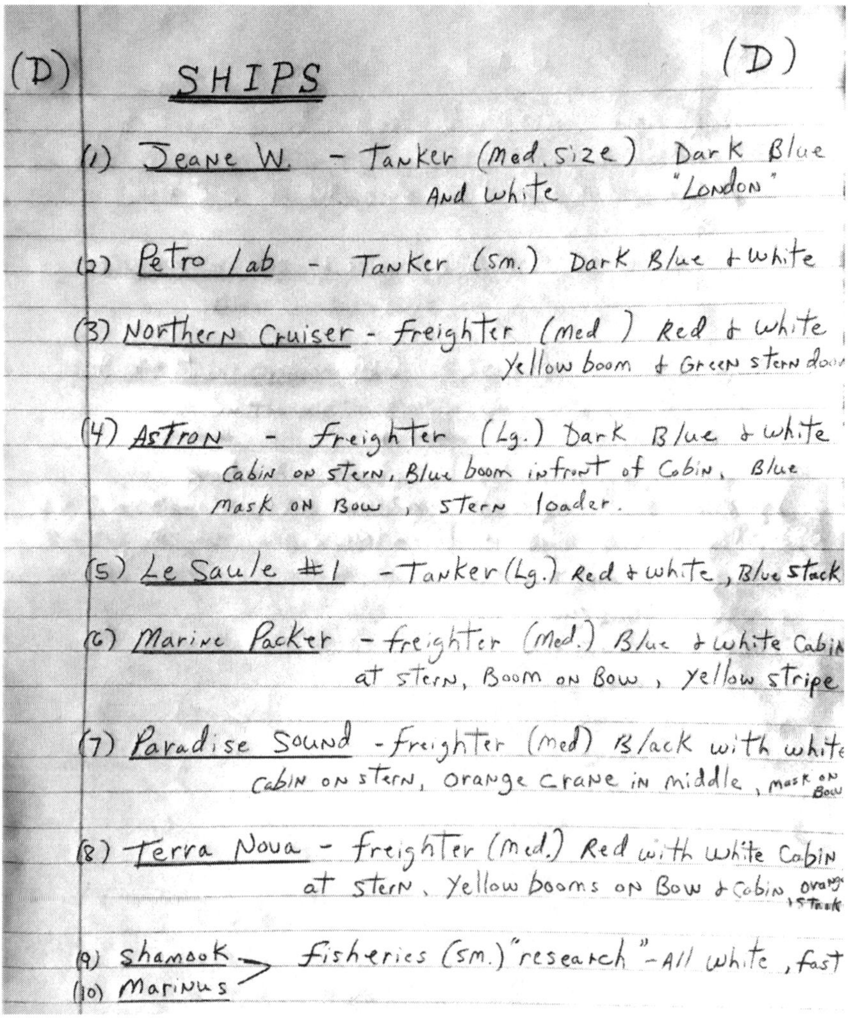

(D) SHIPS (D)

(1) Jeane W. - Tanker (Med. size) Dark Blue And white "London"

(2) Petro lab - Tanker (sm.) Dark Blue + white

(3) Northern Cruiser - freighter (Med) Red + white Yellow boom + Green stern door

(4) Astron - freighter (Lg.) Dark Blue + white Cabin on stern, Blue boom infront of Cabin, Blue mask on Bow, stern loader.

(5) Le Saule #1 - Tanker (Lg.) Red + white, Blue stack

(6) Marine Packer - freighter (Med.) Blue + white Cabin at stern, Boom on Bow, yellow stripe

(7) Paradise Sound - freighter (Med) Black with white cabin on stern, orange crane in middle, mask on Bow

(8) Terra Nova - freighter (Med.) Red with white Cabin at stern. Yellow booms on Bow + Cabin, orange stack

(9) Shamook
(10) Marinus
→ fisheries (sm.) "research" - All white, fast

My personal ship and cabin cruiser reference list

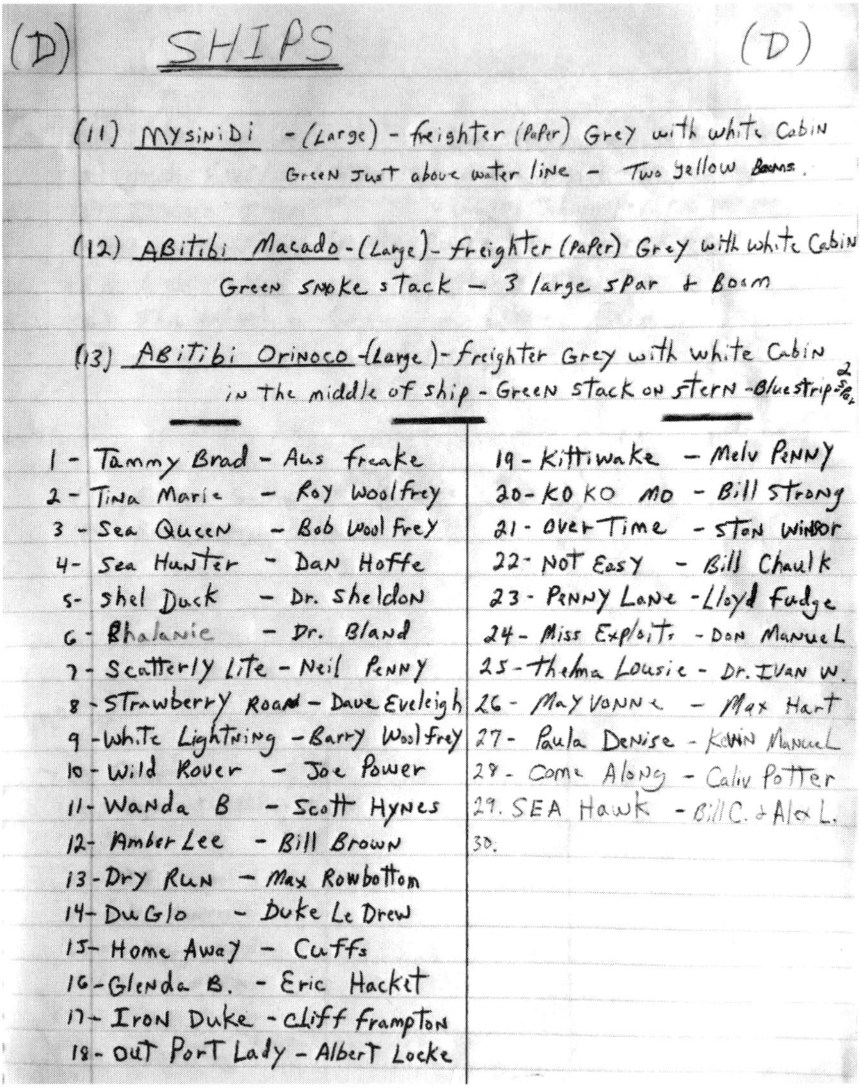

(D) SHIPS (D)

(11) MYSINIDI - (Large) - freighter (Paper) Grey with white Cabin Green Just above water line - Two yellow Booms.

(12) ABitibi Macado - (Large) - freighter (Paper) Grey with white Cabin Green smoke stack - 3 large spar + Boom

(13) ABitibi Orinoco - (Large) - freighter Grey with white Cabin in the middle of ship - Green stack on stern - Blue strip 2 stacks

1 - Tammy Brad - Aus Freake	19 - Kittiwake - Melv Penny
2 - Tina Marie - Roy Woolfrey	20 - KO KO MO - Bill Strong
3 - Sea Queen - Bob Wool Frey	21 - Over Time - Ston Winsor
4 - Sea Hunter - Dan Hoffe	22 - Not Easy - Bill Chaulk
5 - Shel Duck - Dr. Sheldon	23 - Penny Lane - Lloyd Fudge
6 - Bhalanie - Dr. Bland	24 - Miss Exploits - Don Manuel
7 - Scatterly Lite - Neil Penny	25 - Thelma Lousie - Dr. Ivan W.
8 - Strawberry Road - Dave Eveleigh	26 - May Vonne - Max Hart
9 - White Lightning - Barry Woolfrey	27 - Paula Denise - Kevin Manuel
10 - Wild Rover - Joe Power	28 - Come Along - Caliv Potter
11 - Wanda B - Scott Hynes	29. SEA Hawk - Bill C. + Alex L.
12 - Amber Lee - Bill Brown	30.
13 - Dry Run - Max Rowbottom	
14 - DuGlo - Duke Le Drew	
15 - Home Away - Cuffs	
16 - Glenda B. - Eric Hackit	
17 - Iron Duke - Cliff Frampton	
18 - Out Port Lady - Albert Locke	

My personal ship and cabin cruiser reference list

Tech Paul Squires at Long Point

During my lightkeeper career, the Canadian Coast Guard flight services had several helicopters based in St. John's and one in Stephenville. Some of the skilled pilots I flew with over the years were Gene Mathews, Casey Buckle, Bob Tulk, Gordie Simmons, and Kenny Steele.

Gordie Simmons died from drowning/hypothermia after crashing his Coast Guard helicopter into the icy Atlantic Ocean. This terrible accident occurred off the Burin Peninsula, near Marystown, on December 7, 2005. His passenger, technician Carl Neal, also died at the scene. Two years later, Kenny Steele died on October 3, 2007, in a tragic helicopter crash near Postville, Labrador.

The Canadian Coast Guard base on the southside in St. John's was the heart of the entire operation. This was where many Canadian Coast Guard ships and the repair shops were located—mechanical, carpentry, welding, engineering, Marine Aids Office, Ice Operations, St. John's Traffic, and Maritime Rescue Sub-Centre.

Over the years, dozens of technicians flew out by helicopter or travelled by hired boat to our lighthouses to carry out the necessary repairs. At Long Point, the techs stayed in Twillingate and drove to the light station. It could be a furnace repair job, a new drop pad to be built for the helicopter, a new steel catwalk welded onto the light tower, or a Lister diesel that needed to be repaired or replaced. Usually, the techs came in pairs and would set up and make themselves at home. They would bring their sleeping bags and their own food. They might drop in for a few hours' work or stay with us for two nights, or even seven nights, depending on the project at hand. I always looked forward to having a couple of other men around the station. A different face to talk to during the long shifts was a comforting change, especially during the long winter months. Depending on the job, we sometimes gave them a helping hand. After supper was cleaned up, it usually meant a few games of cards or a board game. With this came many laughs and countless stories. Having these technicians around always helped pass the days and the nights away. My experiences with all these CCG workers on the lighthouses were enjoyable and left great memories.

The Canadian Coast Guard ships were often patrolling or icebreaking or servicing the four lighthouses that I was stationed on. The main ships in my area during my work period were the *Sir John Franklin*, *Sir Wilfred Grenfell* (the old one and newer one), *Sir Humphrey Gilbert*, and *Ann Harvey*. Other ships seen less frequently were the *Jackman*, *J. E. Bernier*, *Leonard J. Cowley*, *Henry Lawson*, *Terry Fox*, *Bartlett*, *Hood*, and the *Louis S. St-Laurent*.

7 Puffin Island Lighthouse, 2003

Scenic Puffin Island Lighthouse was built in 1873 on an island near the harbour entrance of the historic town of Greenspond on the northwest side of Bonavista Bay. Puffin Island Light is approximately seventy feet above sea level with a normal range of ten nautical miles. The main light is white and flashes every five seconds from the wooden pyramid tower, which is 24.9 feet high. The dwelling, the light tower, and shed are white with a red horizontal band in the centre. The original light tower was built by contractor Smith and Han. It was built from granite stone and has a slate roof, similar to the lighthouse located at Rose Blanche on the west coast of Newfoundland, which was also built by Smith and Han. The original dwelling was torn down in 1951 and replaced with a wooden two-storey dwelling. The foghorn blasts for three seconds followed by silence for twenty-seven seconds.

This light station was the oldest one I had ever worked on, and it was on the smallest island. The island measured less than a quarter-mile in length and approximately 500 feet wide. It had a boathouse with a winch and a slipway on the eastern side of the island. The lighthouse is positioned approximately one mile from the community of Greenspond. This is one of the oldest outports in Newfoundland, having been settled in the 1690s. It was a busy commercial centre during the nineteenth and twentieth centuries and was known as the Capital of the North.

Some of the early lightkeepers were Robert Kelland Oakley (1872–1874, the first keeper), Fred William Oakley (1875–1897), Nathan Saunders (1898–1900), Frederick William Oakley (1901–1904), Walter Jennings (1905–1908), Joseph Butler (1909 to at least 1912), Edward Wheeler (at least 1927 to at least 1938), Alex Herron (1941–1963), Albert Wakeley, Abraham Burry, and Averill Wakely. The lightkeepers I knew there were Carson Sturge, Tom Bragg, and his brother Stu Bragg. Craig Burry was the newest lightkeeper stationed out on the island. A couple of other keepers who worked there were Joe Goodyear and Larry Keeping. Sadly, Larry drowned in a kayak accident not far from the lighthouse in 2001.

Puffin Island from the helicopter

It was on a Friday afternoon, May 9, 2003, when I received a phone call from Gerry Cantwell at the Marine Aids Office asking me if I could fill in for about two weeks at Puffin Island Lighthouse. They required a lightkeeper for part of a shift out on the island. At the time, I had been off work for a while finishing up my "care and nurturing leave." I had been home caring for my son and daughter. Having been put back on the Canadian Coast Guard payroll a few months earlier, I felt I could not turn down Gerry's request. I agreed and began picking up supplies for this new adventure on this unfamiliar island. Later, I found out that Gerry had phoned a few other lightkeepers before me, but they all refused to go to work at Puffin Island Lighthouse.

Over the years, I had heard several interesting stories about this lighthouse from their keepers at Canadian Coast Guard meetings or training courses—tales about the hundreds of ducks in the area, the fish, and of course their lighthouse bird dog that always lived on the island with its keepers. It was tradition to have a Labrador retriever on the island to help retrieve any ducks the keepers shot from the rocky shores. Now, I was finally getting the opportunity to work out on historic Puffin Island.

On a sunny Tuesday, May 13, I drove to Gander and took the drive down around the loop toward Greenspond. I have driven around the loop many times, but it was my first time visiting this small fishing community. It was a beautiful morning to return to my position of keeper of the light. Shortly after arriving in the community, the Canadian Coast Guard helicopter 360, piloted by Gordie Simmons, picked me up at a designated area near Greenspond. He flew me out to the island with all my supplies required for my stay. It looked beautiful from the air as I took a few photos with my camera. The pilot was a photographer, so he could appreciate me taking a few photos. He hovered in a couple of ideal locations allowing me to capture a few images of the lighthouse, the island, and the many shoals in the area. Gordie always flew with his trusty Pentax camera sitting in his lap, ready to capture that perfect image. Gordie and I always talked cameras and photography. He had taken thousands of photos all over this picturesque province from his comfortable front-row seat.

The helicopter was working around Puffin Island that day slinging lumber and sand to the island. Gordie was a nice man, quiet, and a professional pilot. I'd often seen him spend several minutes completing his paperwork and log-books every time he landed at the different lighthouses I worked on. Then he would always come in to the dwelling for a friendly chat and a cup of tea. I first flew with him back in the spring of 1984 and dozens of times since. Little did I know at the time this would be my last flight with this fine gentleman.

New solar panels on Puffin Island with longliner and iceberg

When I stepped onto the helipad on Puffin Island, Lightkeeper Craig Burry was there to welcome me with a big smile and a hearty handshake. Not far behind him was his beautiful black Labrador retriever, Scooby. I had landed smack dab in the middle of a major construction site. The Canadian Coast Guard was spending big bucks on Puffin Island Lighthouse. They were upgrading and modernizing the entire light station. By this time, most of the remote island lighthouses around Newfoundland had been automated and de-staffed. Only five remote lighthouses remained staffed by real living lightkeepers instead of a modern computer chip and solar panel!

Puffin Island was a remarkably busy island. There were three Canadian Coast Guard carpenters working and living with us daily. They were Bill Mercer, Bob Druken, and Frank Gosse, and local Randy Burry was also hired to help. There were building materials, a cement mixer, boxes of new equipment, and power tools everywhere I looked, plus a nice mini excavator on site. My first observation was of the new cement foundation work being done on the old dwelling house that day. It appeared that several projects were being carried out on the light tower, the engine room, and solar power building, and at all different stages of completion. There was a bank of new large solar panels mounted to the east of the dwelling, which were meant to replace the noisy Lister diesel generators. As I stood there observing it all, there was a helicopter overhead slinging in extra drinking water, lumber, and tools.

The dwelling house was brand new on the inside—the windows, Gyproc, bathroom, plumbing, kitchen, and satellite TV had been upgraded, and it looked beautiful. I took my bedroom upstairs and put on my new light blue uniform for the first time and settled in. I was on duty! After all these years, we lightkeepers were finally issued proper Canadian Coast Guard uniforms. In total, I was stationed on Puffin Island for a partial shift of sixteen days, but they were sixteen enjoyable days.

Time flew by on Puffin Island. With so much activity, there was always something to be done. The scenery around there was beautiful—we had huge icebergs floating around the island every day, mixed with speedboats or longliners cruising to or from the fishing grounds. On my second day on the island, I launched the government boat off the slipway and cruised into the nearby town of Greenspond to pick up a few extra supplies the carpenters needed. On my short journey in, I noticed the many rocky shoals around the island. It was very treacherous water all around this coastline. I entered the local store there, and of course everybody knew I was the new kid on the island, and they wanted to know the scoop on me. While ashore, I visited retired lightkeeper Skipper Tom Bragg. It was good to see him again. Tom always had a few funny stories to tell you. Then it was back aboard the eighteen-foot speedboat for my return to Puffin Island.

On Friday, the carpenters returned home to St. John's for a few days, so it was just Craig and me. The next day, I counted twenty-eight sculptured icebergs and over 200 saltwater ducks from the station. It sure was nice to see this extra activity on the blue waters around this rock. We carried out a little repair job across the island at the boathouse. It was so lovely there with a nice view of Greenspond and its harbour in the distance. We later returned with the small portable barbecue and had a peaceful supper there along with a great yarn and a laugh.

The next day, there wasn't much happening, and the carpenters hadn't returned yet, so I started up the mini excavator that was just sitting idle. I grew up driving Father's farm tractor and his old John Deere 1010, so I figured I'd start it up. I played with the controls a bit, then drove it over to a little patch of soil in the middle of the island. This was where the old lightkeepers used to grow a few vegetables, but it had grown over with tall grass. I tinkered with it for a few hours clearing off grass and exposing the topsoil. I guess it was the old farmer blood in me, and it was great fun.

Helicopter using the "long line" for slinging on Puffin Island

Over the weekend, I received a phone call from another lightkeeper informing me that my new position of Boat Safety Officer Assistant was cancelled. That was disappointing news for me.

By Thursday, May 22, the Canadian Coast Guard helicopter had returned and was slinging materials to the island again for the carpenters. On Friday, Randy and I took the boat and went ashore to assist them with the slings and nets for the helicopter work. This time, before I left, I had a quick visit with Stu Bragg, another retired lightkeeper. Then it was back to the island.

Saturday May 24, was a special day for me. It was my birthday, another one away from my loved ones. All hands planned to have a barbecue and a "cuffer" down at the boathouse later in the day. It was a beautiful sunny day with a few icebergs soaking around, so Craig and I walked over to the boathouse to set up for the barbecue. We placed a few buckets and boxes for seats and tables. We had glasses and plates, and I had brought out some rum to have on my special day. The only things

Barry Porter on Puffin Island, 2003

I forgot to bring were ice cubes for our drinks! With several icebergs around, you would think there would have been a few small bergy bits washing around the beach, but there was not a piece to be found. Craig and I set things up and lit the charcoal for my birthday feast. Later, just as the carpenters arrived after their walk across the island, we heard a thunderous explosion. It was just like a loud cannon had fired!

A large iceberg had been grounded just up around the rocky point in the next cove several hundred feet away. Well, I could not believe it—the iceberg had splintered into a million different pieces of pure white ice. With help from the tides, within twenty minutes the entire cove in front of our boathouse was packed full of 10,000-year-old crystal-clear iceberg ice. It was amazing—it had worked out perfectly for my one and only birthday barbecue on Puffin Island. Cheers!

Bob Druken and Lightkeeper Craig Burry with iceberg ice

Wednesday, May 28, was changeover day for me. It was a great experience to take part in life on Puffin Island and to keep light there. It was a gorgeous little island, and I enjoyed every day I was there to meet the work crew, to check out the island, and of course to work with my fellow lightkeeper, Craig, a fine young fellow indeed. I will describe him as what he said about me: "The finest fellow to ever put on a pair of rubber boots!" As I was leaving, Craig suggested I should apply for a transfer to his station. It was not a bad idea, but I was truly finished with working at remote island light stations. I had that T-shirt, thank you.

I threw my boxes aboard the boat and cruised into Greenspond, where my truck had been parked for the past sixteen days. One last thing I did while steaming in the speedboat was grab a large chunk of clean iceberg ice that was floating nearby. I could barely lift it but managed to pull it into the boat and threw it into the pan of my pickup truck. During my drive back home, I decided to drive east to Gambo and take the Trans-Canada Highway west back to home. It was basically the same amount of driving. While going through the town of

Gambo, I decided to drop in to see an old buddy, Bob Randell, whom I had not seen in a few years. Bob was familiar with the marine life—he was cook on the Woodwards ships. I had a coffee and a good chat with him and his partner, Yvonne. I left Bob a huge piece of the iceberg and then departed, Porterville-bound. This was my first time being away from my family in almost five years. I continued my two-hour drive back home, looking forward to seeing my sweet son, daughter, and wife.

8 Long Point Lighthouse 2003–2006

To my great surprise, after departing Long Point Lighthouse fifteen years before, I made my return to work again at my beloved old lighthouse on Labour Day, 2003. The lighthouse at Surgeon's Cove Head on Exploits Island had finally been shut down by the federal government automation program. Oddly, back in August 2001, my boss, Mike Clements, sat in my kitchen with my wife, Alice, and me and discussed the automation of the lighthouse. He promised me a new Canadian Coast Guard position of Boat Safety Officer Assistant. This sounded great for me. Well, that did not pan out. After that position was taken off the books, I was transferred back to Long Point Lighthouse.

Many significant changes had been made at Long Point since I left in 1988. One of the biggest was the lightkeepers were now working out of the small, one-bay garage instead of the original dwelling. A couple of years earlier, the government converted the old garage into an office space with a small kitchen and bathroom. The Canadian Coast Guard had also handed over ownership of the old dwelling to the nearby community of Crow Head for tourism purposes. The CCG still maintained the light tower with the main light and the foghorn.

Another big change was a new twenty-eight-day rotational shift with more lightkeepers working at the station. Due to the automation on Bacalhao Island and Surgeon's Cove Head, there was a surplus of lightkeepers in the system. There were six lightkeepers working at Long Point now. They were Hayward Canning, Jack May, Les Powell, Lloyd Lilly, Carl Greening, and me. It was crowded with three keepers working day shift, but that was the working schedule there now. The senior lightkeepers were near the end of their careers and only had a few years left before retirement, so they were just riding it out, counting down their days.

Work was pretty routine on Long Point. One day during my second month back, I discovered a serious problem. I was walking around the lighthouse grounds when I noticed a fault with one of the heavy guy wire anchors for the 270-foot VHF tower in the parking lot. This high tower had three huge anchors drilled into the bedrock and set in concrete. One of its three-inch-thick pins near the base had slid out of position. Somehow, it had shifted or vibrated out to the very edge. Another quarter-inch and the guy wires would have failed, and this mighty tower would have come crashing down.

I phoned the Marine Aids Office to report this issue. Soon, I received an urgent phone call from the Canadian Coast Guard Engineering Department. I explained how the large pin was close to slipping out of place, then I sent a primitive digital photo to them by email. Later that day, October 15, 2003, we received a phone call from our supervisor instructing us to immediately leave the office and the hill, until this anchor was repaired. If the tower came down, it could crush the lighthouse, foghorn building, or the office—a very serious situation. The entire road and hill were closed for three days. I returned home, and a work crew from St. John's came out and did the urgent repairs.

A lightkeeper was on watch.

A few weeks later, on November 6, I sighted two large icebergs ten miles northwest of the station. I promptly reported them to Comfort Cove Coast Guard Radio station because they were a hazard to shipping. These sightings were rare, but occasionally we would get the odd iceberg drifting down in the fall or winter.

Later, in July 2004, smack dab in the middle of the busy tourist season, Ryland's Construction from the west coast arrived on the hill to carry out a major facelift on the old light tower. Tourists were restricted from visiting the lighthouse or even walking around the hill. The job consisted of removing the dozens of layers of paint applied by the old lightkeepers for the past hundred years—weathered glossy red oil and lead-based paint on the large concrete tower and white on the curved dome top. The other part of their contract required the replacement of the unique triangular glass that surrounded the top of the tower. It was quite an undertaking considering the weather conditions we experienced there.

The men brought in their equipment and erected heavy tube scaffolding completely surrounding the twenty-nine-foot light tower and then covered the tower in tarps and ropes. Over the next couple of months, the workers soda-blasted the entire concrete tower and the dome section on the top. After the many layers of white paint were removed from the dome, we discovered it was a beautiful, shiny copper. The windy days made it challenging because all the old lead paint had to be contained and collected. Not one flake of this godforsaken toxic paint was permitted to touch the grassy hill. It was a crazy set-up—they had vacuum-hose systems and cables running everywhere. There was even a shower stall set up to wash off any "deadly dust" on the workers before leaving the tower work area. Slowly but surely, they completed the project. When Ryland's crew left the hill, the light tower looked pristine, totally refurbished and good for another 118 years.

On Saturday, February 5, 2005, I had one of the strangest and scariest shifts of my career as a lightkeeper. Earlier, on Wednesday, a large polar bear was sighted near Back Harbour and Crow Head only a few kilometres away. Polar bears are dangerous and smart animals. I remember being told polar bears had been known to hunt humans when they were hungry. Only a few years ago, I had the occasional scary dream of encountering a polar bear while skiing down across Bacalhao Island alone. It was something I did not want to experience—ever!

This polar bear had busted into a couple of sheds and taken food from a deep-freeze. Apparently, this bear was hungry, and that was a bad thing. On Thursday, the provincial Wildlife Officers were in the Crow Head and Long Point area in helicopter hunting for this dangerous animal, but they had no luck. The report was they sighted polar bear tracks down near Sleepy Cove, which was down under the hill next door to the lighthouse. He was getting closer! I was on shift this month and driving to and from the lighthouse every day. That Friday, before I left my home to drive to work, I took Father's trusty old 30-30 Winchester rifle with me. I liked this gun and had shot three or four nice moose with it in the past. It was hard to believe I might need a gun at work, but I was planning to work one of my few night shifts at Long Point—alone. I did not want to be on the menu for the bear's bed lunch. I would feel much more comfortable with my father's rifle sitting next to me in the office.

Sure enough, there were rumours of more bear tracks that day, which added to my work drama. At 1600 hours (4:00 p.m.), my co-worker and I finished our regular day shift. My buddy, Hayward, signed off and went back to his home in Back Harbour, but I stayed in the office and waited for my midnight shift to start. I locked the door and took a nap. When I awoke, the weather had turned milder with a northeast wind blowing in, causing foggy conditions and zero visibility. At midnight, I started my shift, and to record an accurate weather report, I had to leave the safety of my office and walk 100 feet up around the light tower.

Now, picture this—I was standing there by myself, in my sharp blue uniform, with banks of misty fog blowing around me. I was surrounded by snow on the ground, and I was scanning in all directions for a hungry snow-white polar bear with my 30-30 cocked and ready. It felt like something was watching me! The whole landscape was white, and my senses were on overload. This was the one and only time I had ever been in such a strange, spine-tingling predicament. I recorded the weather conditions, cautiously returned to my little office, and locked the door—safe and sound. Was Mr. Polar Bear watching me? I'll never know, but it certainly was an uncomfortable but thrilling experience.

Note: On April 3, 2012, Lightkeepers Craig Burry and Joe Goodyear narrowly escaped after being chased by a large, hungry polar bear on Puffin Island Lighthouse, approximately seventy miles east of Long Point!

On Thursday, February 24, 2005, I had the privilege to attend a special event in the Crow Head Community Centre. The Canadian Coast Guard officially passed ownership of the dwelling, the tunnel, and foghorn building to the town of Crow Head. There was representation there by the Canadian Coast Guard including Tony Fitzgerald (Property Manager with the federal Department of Fisheries and Oceans), an old work friend at the station from the 1980s, my co-workers Hayward and Leslie, Mayor John Hamlyn, and councillors. We had a lovely dinner, Tony presented Mayor Hamlyn with a bronze plaque that read, "Federal Heritage Building," and I passed over the keys of the dwelling to the mayor.

By 2006, I had been back working at Long Point for almost three years, and I was not enjoying my work situation as much. It felt odd working out of this tiny office where I could not even see the ocean or the marine traffic around us. Here, we had little contact with the tourists or the local visitors. We were overstaffed and were basically kept out of sight now, compared to when I worked there in the 1980s. I actually felt a bit embarrassed to be working there, which was sad. Another factor I found challenging was my long daily commute. My drive was a three-hour commute every day through fifteen different communities, plus an eight-hour shift, for twenty-eight days straight. I found the driving difficult, and I would get so tired I'd feel like a zombie by the last week of my shift. Then for the first few days off shift, I was beat and not much fun for my two kids and wife. And of course there was major wear and tear on my car driving over the rough roads and the high cost of fuel. I was burning a full tank of gasoline every two days.

I felt the Marine Aids Office was not helping things, either. I tried working a couple of night shifts on the odd Friday night to save at least one day's driving, but my supervisor in St. John's disapproved of this—maybe because we were overstaffed—and with the never-ending threat of automation looming, they did not care about my concerns. If I resigned, that would be one less body in their lightkeeper system.

I did not have my sea legs, so transferring to a Canadian Coast Guard ship was not in the cards. I had not forgotten about my near miss with the *Ocean Ranger* in 1982.

I needed at least another eight years working with the Canadian Coast Guard for any kind of pension, and I knew deep down I would never be able to continue this driving for that many years. I had carried out this commute for three long years ducking around potholes, snowstorms, school buses, moose, motorhome convoys, and the rest until I couldn't handle it any longer. So, after much serious thought and discussion with my wife, I made my decision. It was time for a change.

In late May of 2006, only days before I turned the big five-oh, and after almost twenty-three years of dedicated service, I resigned. I quietly exited from my federal lightkeeper position with the Canadian Coast Guard and returned to beautiful downtown Porterville. No more driving!

One evening, a couple of months later, I received an unexpected phone call from Mr. Ray Browne, the Regional Director of the Canadian Coast Guard. He had just found out that I had left the Coast Guard and was quite surprised. We had a nice talk about work and life in general. He thanked me for my service and wished me all the best. I was pleased that he had called me.

With that, my journey as a keeper of the light was over, and I moved on to continue with the always interesting journey through life!

Over and out.

ACKNOWLEDGEMENTS

I would like to thank my soulmate and wife, Alice, for tolerating my being buried into my laptop and notes scattered about for hours almost every day for the past sixteen months and for her suggestions and her skilled proofreading, spell checks, etc. I could not have written it without her support, love, and her smile.

I would also like to thank the many Canadian Coast Guard workers whom I reached out to recently for double-checking certain details in my stories: Gord Jones, Hayward Canning, Carl Greening, Ed Loveless, Len Woodford, Paul Squires, Jackie Lane, Craig Burry, and Chris Ropson.

Thank you also to Lydia Budgell, Charlie Falk, Carolyn R. Parsons, Bill Sceviour, Cliff Lilly, Charlie Kelsey, Wendy Rose of the Writers' Alliance of Newfoundland and Labrador, Ruby Hamlyn, and Paul Porter for his technical support. Also thanks to Larry Coady and Byron White for their early encouragement. Thanks as well to Graham Blair and to Jerry, Garry, and Margo Cranford and the team at Flanker Press.

Lastly and most importantly, I thank my parents, Max and Sheila, for raising me in a small town.

Note: Unless otherwise indicated, all photos in this book were taken by me. My final word of thanks goes to my son, Dylan, who is pictured on the cover in front of Ferryland Lighthouse.

Barry Porter worked as a lighthouse keeper on the northeast coast of Newfoundland with the Canadian Coast Guard for twenty-three years. He was born in the small farming community of Porterville. Barry attended a one-room school (no electricity or plumbing) with ten students from kindergarten to grade five. Later, he was bused to Lewisporte for school and attended vocational school there.

Over the years, he worked in several professions, as a welder, a photographer, a lightkeeper, and later the curator/manager of the By the Bay Museum in Lewisporte. He obtained a certificate in basic museum studies while working at the museum. Barry lived in Western Canada for two years and has travelled throughout North America and Europe but never lost his pride in his home province, his hometown, and their rich history. He volunteered on many local committees, including heritage and economic development, and served ten years on the board of the Lewisporte Memorial Public Library.

An avid outdoorsman, Barry enjoys boating, kayaking, snowmobiling, motorcycling, swimming, and quiet walks in the fresh air. Barry is a proud father of two children and resides in beautiful downtown Porterville with his wife, Alice, and his sweet beagle, Lucy.